Writing Groups Inside and Outside the Classroom

Writing Groups Inside and Outside the Classroom

ﬞ﮿ﮀ

Edited by

Beverly J. Moss
The Ohio State University

Nels P. Highberg
University of Hartford

Melissa Nicolas
Pennsylvania State University at Berks-Lehigh Valley

2004

LAWRENCE ERLBAUM ASSOCIATES, PUBLISHERS
Mahwah, New Jersey   London

IWCA
Press

This volume is a publication in the International Writing
Center Association (IWCA) Press Series, published by LEA, Inc.

Lawrence Erlbaum Associates, Inc., Publishers
10 Industrial Avenue
Mahwah, NJ 07430

Cover design by Kathryn Houghtaling Lacey

Library of Congress Cataloging-in-Publication Data

Writing groups inside and outside the classroom / edited by
Beverly J. Moss, Melissa Nicolas, Nels P. Highberg.
    p. cm.
  Includes bibliographical references and index.
ISBN 0-8058-4699-9 (alk. Paper)
ISBN 0-8058-4700-6 (pbk. : alk. Paper)
1. English language—Rhetoric—Study and teaching. 2. In-
terdisciplinary approach in education.   3. Creative writ-
ing—Study and teaching.   4. Report writing—Study and
teaching.   5. Writing centers.   I. Moss, Beverly J.   II.
Nicolas, Melissa.   III. Highberg, Nels Pearson.

PE1404.B9 2003
808'.042'071—dc21   2003046232
                                            CIP

Books published by Lawrence Erlbaum Associates are printed
on acid-free paper, and their bindings are chosen for strength
and durability.

Printed in the United States of America
10 9 8 7 6 5 4 3 2 1

Contents

Series Foreword
Byron L. Stay   ix

Contributors   xiii

1   Introduction: Writing Groups as Literacy Events   1
    Nels P. Highberg, Beverly J. Moss, and Melissa Nicolas

**Part I   Writing Groups Within the Curriculum:
Pedagogical Approaches and Concerns**

2   "I Don't Talk to Blacks," or Contextual   13
    Constraints on Peer Writing Groups
    in the Prison College Classroom
    Rebecca Jackson

3   Wrestling With the Angels: Writing Groups,   31
    Messy Texts, and Truly Collaborative Writing
    Thomas K. H. Piontek

4   Bringing the Writing Center Into the Classroom: 47
    A Case Study of Writing Groups
    Julie Aipperspach Anderson and Susan Wolff Murphy

5   Sponsoring Student Response in Writing   63
    Center Group Tutorials
    Magdalena Gilewicz

6   Shaping Writing Groups in the Sciences   79
    *Sharon Thomas, Leonora Smith,
    and Terri Trupiano Barry*

7   Reciprocal Expertise: Community Service   95
       and the Writing Group
           H. Brooke Hessler and Amy Rupiper Taggart

8   Coauthoring as Place: A Different Ethos   113
           Kami Day and Michele Eodice

       **Part II   Writing Groups in the Extracurriculum:
       Broadening the Focus**

9   "Species" of Rhetoric: Deliberative   133
       and Epideictic Models in Writing Group Settings
           Candace Spigelman

10   Questions of Time: Publishing and Group   151
       Identity in the *StreetWise* Writers Group
           *Paula Mathieu, Karen Westmoreland, Michael Ibrahem,
           William Plowman, and Curly Cohen*

11   Making Space for Collaboration: 169
       Physical Context and Role Taking in Two Singing
       and Songwriting Groups
           Rebecca Schoenike Nowacek and Kenna del Sol

12   The Thursday Night Writing Group: 187
       Crossing Institutional Lines
           *Linda Beckstead, Kate Brooke, Robert Brooke,
           Kathryn Christensen, Dale Jacobs, Heidi LM Jacobs,
           Carol MacDaniels, and Joan Ratliff*

13   A Group of Our Own: Women and Writing Groups: 207
       A Reconsideration
           *Terri Trupiano Barry, Julie Galvin Bevins, Maryann K.
           Crawford, Elizabeth Demers, Jami Blaauw Hara, M. Rini
           Hughes, and Mary Ann K. Sherby*

14   Community, Collaboration, and Conflict: 229
       The Community Writing Group as Contact Zone
           Evelyn Westbrook

Afterword   249
   Melissa Nicolas, Beverly J. Moss, and Nels P. Highberg

Author Index   255

Subject Index   259

Series Foreword

Byron L. Stay
Mount St. Mary's College (Maryland)

The past 20 years have seen a significant increase in the number of writing centers and in the development of writing center scholarship. From the birth of the National Writing Centers Association in 1980 to its transformation into the International Writing Centers Association more than 20 years later, the writing center community has become increasingly interconnected, as evidenced by its very active listserve, WCenter, and its national and international conferences. At the same time, the growth of writing centers internationally has continued to add not only to the number of writing centers across the continents but also to the diversity of writing center issues—political and pedagogical—that define their place within their institutions and within the field of composition studies.

Writing centers have also become increasingly instrumental to the missions of the institutions and the larger communities in which they reside. Writing centers do not exist merely in the trenches of composition programs; they are themselves the loci for research and faculty development. As such they exhibit complex and intimate ties to institutional goals and missions. They also frequently extend directly and indirectly into their communities. Writing centers have influence beyond their academic institutions.

Furthermore, writing center scholarship has moved increasingly beyond composition studies. Early writing center scholarship tended to offer explanations of writing center lore within the context of composition studies, to an audience of writing center practitioners. In fact, writing center scholarship has often moved, sometimes uncomfortably, between lore and overarching theory. However, more recent scholarship has broadened its scope to draw from a range of disciplines, including literacy studies, and to envision an audience beyond the writing center community.

Since its creation in 1995, IWCA Press has sought to forge closer connections between the needs of writing center professionals and the scholarship and reference materials required for the effective administration and maintenance of writing centers. The collaborative relationship between IWCA Press and Lawrence Erlbaum Associates will bring this process to a new level. Through this series, IWCA and Lawrence Erlbaum Associates will seek to identify areas of scholarship most critical for the writing center community and work to develop materials particularly well suited to carry out this mission. The collaboration will foster the development and publication of books relating to the pedagogical effectiveness of writing centers, their history, their international expansion, and the intertwining relationship between writing centers and the field of composition studies.

Writing Groups Inside and Outside the Classroom is the first book resulting from the collaboration between IWCA Press and Lawrence Erlbaum Associates. This book examines the collaborative processes of writing groups inside and outside the academy. Collaborative writing is obviously a process that lies at the heart of writing center theory and practice. In broadening their focus to include writing groups outside the academy, the editors enable us to look with fresh eyes at the nature of writing collaborations inside the academy. These essays provide a window to larger issues of literacy, or what the editors here refer to as "literacy events."

Ultimately, this book offers a vision of the writing center not simply as an institution of secondary and higher education but as an institution that is simultaneously shaped by literacy events outside its walls and as a proactive force in promoting community literacy. Many of the groups described here began with connections to writing centers. As a result, this book reminds us that the effects of writing centers reverberate into the community even when these effects may not be fully understood or acknowledged. *Writing Groups Inside and Outside the Classroom* crosses over to examine the literacy of the community and to bring this knowledge meaningfully back to its home in the writing center.

Acknowledgments

We wish to thank Jacqueline Jones Royster and Andrea A. Lunsford for their support and feedback early in the process. We would not have completed this project without the guidance of Byron Stay of the International Writing Centers Association Press. The anonymous reviews provided ideas that aided us in revision, and the contributors of individual essays provided patience and enthusiasm for this project from the beginning. Finally, we acknowledge the students at Ohio State who inspired this project, specifically the undergraduate peer consultants, students in the writing workshop, graduate student tutors, and our clients in the writing center.

—*Beverly J. Moss, Nels P. Highberg, and Melissa Nicolas*

Contributors

Julie Aipperspach Anderson teaches freshman composition, technical writing, and British literature at Baylor University in Waco, Texas. She recently published "Spectacular Spectators: Regendering the Male Gaze in Delariviere Manley's *The Royal Mischeif* and Joanna Baillie's *Orra*" in *Enculturation*. She is currently completing her dissertation at Texas A&M University on the performance of authorship in the prologues, epilogues, and other paratexts of plays by Delariviere Manley, Catherine Trotter, and Mary Pix. Her primary research interests include women writing for the early modern British theater, writing center studies, and service learning and the writing classroom.

Terri Trupiano Barry is a visiting assistant professor in the Department of American Thought and Language at Michigan State University. She completed her dissertation, "Rhetorics of Representation: Race, Gender, and Intermarriage in the Frontier Novels of Ann S. Stephens, 1838–1865," in 2001. She continues to investigate issues of gender and rhetoric as well as the intersections of rhetoric and science.

Julie Galvin Bevins taught composition and interdisciplinary studies courses at Davenport University in Grand Rapids, Michigan for several years, preceded by four years of collaborative work on portfolios and writing at the writing center at Michigan State University. Currently, she is a youth minister at St. Stephen Catholic Church in Grand Rapids, Michigan and loving every minute of it. She is also the recipient of the 1998 Dyer-Ives Poetry Award.

Linda Beckstead teaches journalism and English at Bellevue West High School in Bellevue, Nebraska. She helped redesign English classes for upper-level at-risk students and has presented workshops about using writing with at-risk students at local and national conferences. Linda has been involved with the Nebraska Writing Project for many years and continues to experiment with her own writing through the Thursday Night Writing Group.

Kate Brooke is a fine art printmaker who combines images with text, using relief and letterpress techniques over sumi washes and collage. She lives and works in Lincoln, Nebraska.

Robert Brooke is professor of English at the University of Nebraska-Lincoln, where he directs the Nebraska Writing Project and edits the *Studies in Writing and Rhetoric* monograph series. His research includes *Small Groups in Writing Workshops: Invitations to a Writer's Life* and articles on small group theory in *Dialogue, College Composition and Communication,* and *Writing on the Edge.* His current research interests focus on the place of writing in regional and rural community revitalization, as in the forthcoming book, *Place Conscious Education.*

Kathryn Christensen is a seventh-grade English teacher and the Literacy Leader for grades 7 and 8 for Lincoln Public Schools. She attended the Nebraska Writing Project while earning her master's degree from UNL which renewed her interest in writing and led her to the Thursday Night Writing Group. Although the demands of three children and a new job have caused her to be a writing group "drop out," she still composes and reminisces often of her time with friends from the Thursday Night Writing Group.

Curly Cohen is a member of the *StreetWise* writers group and contributor to *StreetWise* newspaper.

Maryann K. Crawford, Associate Professor of English, is the Director of Basic Writing and the Writing Center at Central Michigan University where she also teaches composition and linguistics. Her research, publications, and conference presentations focus on a variety of discourse and language and literacy areas, including genre issues, oral and written language use, composition pedagogy, and ESL writing. She is also Assistant Editor of *SHAW: The Annual of Bernard Shaw Studies,* and she is working on a biography of Lowell Thomas, the radio and newsreel personality.

Kami Day, PhD, is an associate professor of English at Johnson County Community College in Overland Park, Kansas. She and Michele Eodice completed a study of academic coauthors (*(First Person)²: A Study of Successful Co-authoring in the Academy,* Utah State University Press, 2001), and they continue their joint scholarship in the area of collaborative writing. Kami's scholarly interests also include writing across the curriculum, and she and a math instructor have developed a cross-disciplinary course for mathematics and composition. In addition, Kami is involved with the Center for Formation in the Community College, facilitating teacher enrichment activities based on the work of Parker Palmer.

Kenna del Sol received her J.D. from the University of Wisconsin Law School in 1974 and worked for fourteen years as a drafting attorney for the Wisconsin State Legislature before founding VoiceArts, an innovative vocal training program. She is also a published poet and songwriter.

Elizabeth Demers is finishing her PhD in colonial American history at Michigan State University. She is currently a senior editor at the Michigan State University Press.

Michele A. Eodice, PhD, is the director of the Writing Center at the University of Kansas in Lawrence, Kansas. She and Kami Day completed a study of academic coauthors [*(First Person)*^{2}: *A Study of Successful Co-authoring in the Academy*, Utah State University Press, 2001], and they continue their joint scholarship in the area of collaborative writing. Michele teaches courses in writing center theory and practice and in technical writing. In addition, she serves on the executive board of the Midwest Writing Centers Association and leads the Wheat State Writing Centers Consortium.

Magdalena Gilewicz received her master's degree in English philology at the University of Wroclaw in Poland and a PhD in English at the State University of New York at Stony Brook. Her teaching career spans Poland, Japan, and the United States. At present she is an associate professor of English at California State University, Fresno, where she teaches literature, trains tutors, and runs the University Writing Center.

Jami Blaauw Hara earned her MA in Teaching English at the Community College at Michigan State University. She now teaches and works at North Central Michigan College in Petoskey, Michigan.

H. Brooke Hessler teaches community-engagement writing at Texas Christian University. She is cofounder and president of Write to Succeed, a nonprofit corporation that supports and develops collaborative communication programs in local and virtual communities. Currently, she is adapting the cross-age Writing Partners approach described in this book to establish an online, reciprocal mentoring program for technical and professional communicators.

M. Rini Hughes is a doctoral candidate at Michigan State University, completing her PhD in American studies. Her dissertation discusses the historical processes involved in the transmission of ideology over time, focusing on the novel *Little Women* and its later film adaptations. She is presently an adjunct instructor at the University of Southern Mississippi where she teaches English composition.

Michael Ibrahem is a member of the *StreetWise* writers group and contributor to *StreetWise* newspaper.

Rebecca Jackson is Assistant Professor of English at Texas State University where she teaches undergraduate and graduate courses in rhetoric, composition, and technical communication. Her work has appeared in *Rhetoric Review*, and in several edited collections including *Preparing College Teachers of Writing, Strategies for Teaching First-Year Writing* and *The Writing Program Administrator's Resource*. She is currently co-editing, with Valerie Balester, a collection of essays in writing center studies tentatively titled *Up Close and Personal: The Possibilities of Narrative Inquiry in Writing Centers*.

Dale Jacobs, BA, MA (Alberta), PhD (Nebraska), is an assistant professor of composition and rhetoric at the University of Windsor. He is the editor of *The Myles Horton Reader* (2003) and coeditor (with Laura Micciche) of *A Way to Move: Rhetorics of Emotion in Composition Studies* (2003). His articles have appeared in journals such as *Composition Studies, National Writing Project Quarterly, North Carolina English Teacher*, and *The Writing Lab Newsletter*.

Heidi LM Jacobs teaches Literature and women's studies at the University of Windsor. She has published articles on nineteenth-century American women novelists and is coeditor of *American Women Prose Writers, 1870–1920* (2000). She is currently working on a book on emotion and sentimentalism in nineteenth-century American literature and on a novel about working in the world's largest shopping mall.

Karen Westmoreland Luce has a BA in English education from Michigan State University and an MA in writing from DePaul University. Currently, she is an instructional designer for a leading Web-based e-learning corporation. She is published writer and poet and continues to work with writing groups in nonacademic settings. Karen is grateful for the privilege of working and writing with the *StreetWise* Writers Group.

Carol MacDaniels was one of the original members of the Thursday Night Writing Group. She taught English education at the University of Nebraska-Lincoln and writing composition and communications at Peru State College. She was coeditor of the *Guide to Nebraska Authors*, and spent many years working with the Nebraska and National Writing Projects. Carol died from cancer in 2001.

Paula Mathieu is an assistant professor of English at Boston College. With Claude Mark Hurlbert and David Downing, she is editor of *Beyond English,*

Inc.: Curricular Reform for a Global Economy. She has worked with street newspapers and their writing groups in the United States and abroad.

Susan Wolff Murphy is assistant professor at Texas A&M—Corpus Christi, teaching writing and serving as the Faculty Partner in writing for the Writing Center. She is most interested in looking at the issues of oral language use and the practice and teaching of writing by drawing on the perspectives of discourse analysis, composition, writing center theory, sociolinguistics, and literacy studies. Currently, she is collaborating on a research project to investigate literacy practices and writing expectations of South Texas Hispanic students.

Rebecca Schoenike Nowacek is an assistant professor of composition and rhetoric at Marquette University. She has also worked as the assistant director of the Writing Across the Curriculum program at the University of Wisconsin, Madison. Her current research focuses on the place of writing in the interdisciplinary classroom.

Thomas K. H. Piontek is assistant professor of English at The Ohio State University. Working in twentieth-century American literature, gay and lesbian studies, queer theory, and cultural studies, he is the author of numerous articles and reviews on contemporary American culture, representations of AIDS, gay literature, and pedagogy. He is also the author of the book *Queering Gay and Lesbian Studies: Gender, Sexual Practice, and the Problems of Identity*.

William Plowman is a member of the *StreetWise* writers group and contributor to *StreetWise* newspaper.

Joan Ratliff has written handicraft instructions and advertising copy, edited computer manuals, and designed clinical-research databases. She has been writing creatively since she was five years old and was first published at the age of nine in an Omaha Public Schools anthology. Most recently her essays and cartoons have appeared in the women's spiritual journal *The Red Queen*, and she continues to write fiction in a wide variety of genres.

Mary Ann K. Sherby is a visiting assistant professor in the Department of American Thought and Language at Michigan State University. She completed her PhD in English with an emphasis in composition theory and reading theory in the fall of 2000 and continues to participate in the writing group. She lives in East Lansing, Michigan, with her husband and their two cats.

Leonora Smith's scholarship on writing is rooted in her own practice as a poet and fiction writer and in her daily work with her own and others' texts in progress. A book of poetry, *Spatial Relations*, is her most recent major publication. She teaches in the Department of American Thought and Language at Michigan State University, where she often works with faculty in the disciplines who seek innovative ways to use writing to develop students' disciplinary competence.

Candace Spigelman is an associate professor of English at Penn State University, Berks-Lehigh Valley College. Her published articles have focused on writing groups, authorship and ownership, personal essays, critical pedagogy, and student values. In *Across Property Lines: Textual Ownership in Writing Groups*, she examines intellectual property issues in the context of working fiction writers' and student writers' groups.

Amy Rupiper Taggart is assistant professor of English at North Dakota State University, teaching courses in academic and professional writing and community engagement. She is a cofounder and an active board member of Write to Succeed, Inc., the nonprofit company that developed the Writing Partners program discussed in the collection, and she recently began a similar Writing Partners project in Fargo, ND. Rupiper Taggart coedited the *Guide to Composition Pedagogies* with Gary Tate and Kurt Schick.

Sharon Thomas is an associate professor of the Department of Rhetoric, Writing, and American Cultures at Michigan State University. Five years ago, she and a colleague from Zoology began developing professional writing groups for graduate students in the sciences. Originally funded with monies from a Fund for the Improvement of Post Secondary Education (FIPSE) grant, that program now continues under funding from Michigan State University.

Evelyn Westbrook began her ethnography of the South Carolina Writers Workshop during her graduate studies at the University of South Carolina. Currently a doctoral student in rhetoric at the University of Texas, Evelyn continues to be interested in the role of conflict in writing groups and classrooms.

Editors

Beverly J. Moss is an associate professor of English at The Ohio State University, director of the Center for the Study and Teaching of Writing, author of *A Community Text Arises* (Hampton Press) and editor of *Literacy Across Communities* (Hampton Press). Her research interests include literacy in nonacademic communities, composition theory and pedagogy, and school-university partnerships.

Nels P. Highberg is an assistant professor of Rhetoric, Language, and Culture at the University of Hartford. He holds MAs in women's studies and comparative studies from The Ohio State University and a PhD in language, literacy, and rhetoric from the Department of English at the University of Illinois at Chicago. With Kay Halasek, he coedited *Landmark Essays in Basic Writing* (Hermagoras Press, 2001). His research/teaching interests include composition, representations of gender and sexuality, and medical humanities.

Melissa Nicolas is an assistant professor of English at Pennsylvania State University Berks-Lehigh Valley. Melissa has worked in writing centers for about ten years as a tutor, Peer Consulting Director, and as assistant coordinator of the Ohio State writing center. Currently she is directing the Writing Fellows program at PSU Lehigh Valley. Her research/teaching interests include writing center theory and practice, the history of rhetoric, women's rhetorical practices, and feminist theory.

CHAPTER ONE

ୟୄ

Introduction: Writing Groups as Literacy Events

Nels P. Highberg
University of Hartford

Beverly J. Moss
The Ohio State University

Melissa Nicolas
Pennsylvania State University at Berks-Lehigh Valley

I think I can speak for the Harlem Writers Guild. We're glad to have you ....
Well, in this group we remind each other that talent is not enough. You've got
to work. Write each sentence over and over again, until it seems you've used
every combination possible, then write it again .... So, Maya, you lived
through your baptism. Now, you're a member of the flock.

—Maya Angelou, *Heart of a Woman*

In the previous excerpt, author, activist, and entertainer Maya Angelou
recounts comments made to her the first time she read her work as a
member of the Harlem Writers Guild, a writing group to which she belonged with Paule Marshall, John Killens, John Henrik Clarke, and other
renowned African American writers, a group that had a tremendous impact on her growth as a writer. This writing group gave Angelou and its
other members support and encouragement while at the same time acting
as critic—sometimes harshly—pushing its members to work harder and
do better. More important, this writing group was ever mindful of the context in which they found themselves—a group of African Americans, writing in the turbulent sixties and trying to get published during a time when
few African Americans were being published. They were poets, fiction
writers, historians, playwrights, essayists. They were like-minded in many

1

ways, completely different in others. Yet they were a flock, a writing group, who depended on each other. As the excerpt illustrates, the group welcomed, judged, and motivated. Most important, they took an intense interest in helping members grow and succeed as writers.

Although the Harlem Writers Guild is unique in both context and makeup—no two writing groups are alike—some aspects of writing group participation remain relatively constant across groups and for each member. Worth noting is that every writing group, while engaging in meaningful and meaning-making talk about texts, operates in a particular context, and that context shapes the group, making certain demands on it. For some, those demands may become obstacles to work through or bridges that group members use to move forward, and, from time to time, they are both. Each group must negotiate a group identity and establish group rules, implicitly or explicitly. Every writing group is a socially constructed entity with language at its core, and through the process of interacting, each group influences the writing of its members. These constants as well as the uniqueness of each group are important sites of scholarly inquiry that, when investigated, can provide insight, for teachers, writing center staff, and group members, into making writing groups maximally effective in whatever context they operate.

Though many teachers think of writing groups as recent pedagogical inventions existing primarily in and around the academy, Anne Ruggles Gere, in *Writing Groups: History, Theory, and Implications*, reminds us that writing groups originated and existed primarily outside the academy in home communities and have been a staple in our society for centuries. Interestingly, they continue to grow in prominence across disciplines and occupations as well as across communities. This growth has led to such important work as Candace Spigelman's *Across Property Lines: Textual Ownership in Writing Groups*, which highlights the need to look inside writing groups, wherever they exist, to learn more about what makes them succeed, what makes them fail, and what makes them so appealing to writing teachers and community groups.

Writing Groups as Literacy Events: Collaboration, Power, and Community

For us, writing groups function first as literacy events. Shirley Brice Heath defines literacy events as "occasions in which the talk revolves around a piece of writing" (386). Such talk can center on texts that have already been written—an act of interpretation—or on texts in the process of being written—an act of production. Such talk of both kinds almost always centers on how to improve texts—an act of revision. Obviously, writing groups sit primarily (but not exclusively) on the productive side of literacy events, and thinking about writing groups in this context highlights the centrality of oral speech in the development of texts. Literacy events, though, are rather amorphous. They take many forms and embody numerous functions. Understanding writing groups as literacy events, then, requires, as we state previously, that they be seen contextually. And as such we can begin to comprehend more fully the different types of collaboration that take place in writing groups across settings and communities and the nature of those collaborations.

In academic settings, particularly classrooms, writing groups—commonly conceptualized as peer response groups—have become the most popular example of collaborative learning for writing teachers. Proponents of collaborative learning often assert that all writing can be seen as collaborative, that even individual writers never compose in a vacuum; their writing is influenced by membership in multiple interpretive communities; these individual writers seek the occasional input from others or, at the very least, shape their text with outside readers always in mind—all central tenets in the theories of social construction that continue to shape composition studies. Based on these assumptions, any text results from numerous, and sometimes competing, influences. Likewise, writing groups also embody numerous and, sometimes, competing influences.

Ideally, writing groups enable writers to make decisions about their personal texts with the supportive influence of readers/writers who are like-minded in their views of what it means to belong to and participate in a community of writers but who represent a diversity of perspectives, experiences, and opinions as readers and writers. In the classroom, teachers see writing groups as structures that empower students to become more thoughtful, engaged, and critical writers and readers. Outside of the classroom, writers believe that their groups will empower them to create a text that conveys their intended message as clearly and completely as possible. In both settings, members of writing groups not only try to empower each other, but they also constantly negotiate the power dynamics that inevitably exist within the groups.

Observing writers who gather in groups reveals the multifarious power relationships that shape group activity. Power is often envisioned in the obvious forms of the teacher who tells group members what exact questions to answer for each writer or of the dominating member who starts each critique with his or her extensive, detailed positions. But power is more complex, as the work of Michel Foucault makes clear. Although power can control, it can also create positive effects. Foucault writes:

> We must cease once and for all to describe the effects of power in negative terms: it "excludes," it "represses," it "censors," it "abstracts," it "masks," it "conceals." In fact, power produces; it produces reality; it produces domains of objects and rituals of truth. (194)

Writing group interactions cover the entire range of positive and negative experiences that ultimately produce texts, and the power relations of
any group cannot be ignored because they directly shape such texts.

Lisa Ede and Andrea Lunsford, in *Singular Texts, Plural Authors*, created a framework for discerning the place of power in collaborative situations. "Hierarchical" groups are "carefully, and often rigidly, structured,
driven by highly specific goals, and carried out by people playing clearly
defined and delimited roles" (133). In the writing situations studied by
Ede and Lunsford, hierarchical modes of group interaction exist as the
predominant form. Opposing such dominant models are dialogic groups,
which are "loosely structured and the roles within [them] are fluid: one
person may occupy multiple and shifting roles as a project progresses. In
this mode, the process of articulating goals is often as important as the
goals themselves and sometimes even more important" (133). Conflict becomes a vital part of these groups because "those participating in dialogic
collaboration generally value the creative tension inherent in multivoiced
and multivalent ventures" (133). Though Ede and Lunsford focus primarily on groups that set out to produce a single text, their concepts also apply to writing groups where individual writers produce individual texts.
Thinking about the hierarchical or dialogic nature of writing groups can
show, for example, how teachers or writing group facilitators ultimately
shape the functions of particular groups. We must, as teachers and facilitators, interrogate the relationship between our theories of group process
and our actual practice of such theories.

How we, as practitioners, conceptualize writing groups is often influenced by our notions of community. This is especially true when applied to
groups outside of the academy. Indeed, many of these groups are called
community writing groups. As always, the term *community* cannot be used
uncritically. It is a dynamic rather than static social construction and, as
such, is constantly in a state of change and constantly contested. M. Jimmie
Killingsworth offers a useful model for complicating the concept of community, distinguishing between global and local communities. Global communities "are defined by like-mindedness, political and intellectual
affiliation, and other such 'special interests' and are maintained by widely
dispersed discourse practices made possible by modern publishing and
other communication technologies" (112). Killingsworth's global community relates directly to Benedict Anderson's *Imagined Community*, where
"members of even the smallest nation will never know most of their fel-
low-members, meet them, or even hear of them, yet in the minds of each
lives the image of their communion" (6). Technological breakthroughs enable increasingly larger groups of people to feel connected because they
speak the same language, think of ideas in the same general ways, and understand where the other is "coming from." However, such mass groups

rarely meet face-to-face, and they work together in rather limited ways. They exist in the abstract—"we're all Americans"—or in cyberspace.

For Killingsworth, local communities are seen "simply as the place where writers ordinarily work" (111). Thus, writers are "involved simultaneously in both local and global discourse communities and will feel challenged to favor one over the other" (115). Writing groups are key sites where local communities evolve, and studying them enables one to explore the pressures of negotiating the relationship between local and global discourses. In other words, writers often write with numerous (and conflicting) audiences and goals in mind. Their participation in writing groups reveals the workings of these conflicts and relationships. These conflicts and relationships may center around the disciplinary demands of a local community or social divisions signaled by differences (and similarities) such as race, gender, sexual identity, and class.

Where We Began

As editors, though we embody diverse and multiple perspectives ourselves, we have a shared starting point in our scholarly conversation on writing groups. Our conversation began in a particular place. We are writing teachers, writing center veterans, and writers. Each of us has been (or is currently) a member of a writing group, and we've also used peer response groups in our classes. So we bring those experiences to this project. Its conception, however, can be traced to the two rooms where the three of us first came together, two small rooms filled to the brim with books, tables, couches, computers, paper, coffeemakers and teapots. It began in a writing center.

At The Ohio State University, students enrolled in the second-level, basic writing course meet in writing groups facilitated by undergraduate peer consultants once a week for eight weeks of the ten-week quarter. The peer writing consultants are trained in a quarter-long course taught by faculty in composition studies, and they are supervised by a peer writing consulting director who is housed in the writing center and the writing workshop (the university's location of the basic writing program). Beverly directed the writing center for four years and taught the peer consultant training course several times, and Melissa served as the peer consulting director for two years. Though Nels was a graduate student tutor and Writing Across the Curriculum consultant in the University Writing Center, he participated in the undergraduate peer writing consulting program during a quarter when we needed an extra consultant. He brought to this project his experience facilitating an undergraduate writing group. When Beverly and Melissa worked together as teacher and peer consulting director, they discovered a mutual concern: most tutor training books and writing center scholarship focus on one-on-one tutoring. At the National

Writing Centers Association conference in 1998, Beverly and Melissa noted the need for more scholarship on the connections between writing groups and writing centers, lamenting the lack of texts geared to group tutoring. Tutoring through the writing group model continues to be sorely neglected in the literature, leaving whoever teaches the peer tutor training course—as well as the undergraduate tutors themselves—to adapt assigned readings to the circumstances in which they find themselves. These circumstances first led the three of us to explore a project that focused on writing groups in the tutorial setting.

However, when we began to discuss such a project, it quickly became clear that this book could be more useful to teachers, tutors, and students if the book focused more broadly on writing groups inside and outside the academy. After all, writing groups are rarely neat, orderly, clearly defined entities. For example, while our students are in university-sponsored writing groups, they meet outside the classroom, sometimes on campus but more often off campus at coffee shops, fast food restaurants, or other student hangouts. The groups always meet without a teacher present and for the most part make decisions as a group about how they proceed, fulfilling Peter Elbow's *Writing Without Teachers* model. Although these groups are classroom mandated, they also operate somewhat autonomously, like nonschool-sponsored groups. Due, in part, to this autonomy, these groups share some characteristics with voluntary writing groups while simultaneously continuing to be classroom-mandated peer response groups. In many ways, the precarious nature and place of these particular involuntary writing groups extend classroom boundaries, making the boundaries more fluid, broadening the sites where writers interact.

Our experiences working with these undergraduate writing groups (in our various capacities) led to our recognizing the importance of these extended boundaries and led us to broaden the scope of how we understand writing groups. This book, then, investigates the variety of writing groups inside and outside academic settings. In broadening the focus of this book to include writing groups outside the academy, we found that many of the essays that focus on "outside" groups have much to say about and to writing center practitioners and classroom teachers; vice versa, many of the essays that focus on academic writing groups speak to concerns about how writing groups function in all settings. *Writing Groups Inside and Outside the Classroom* provides readers with the opportunity to see the connections as well as the differences between voluntary writing groups and school-mandated writing groups. Obviously, a central assumption of this collection is that students and teachers of writing have much to learn from writing groups in a variety of settings and configurations. Those in Ohio State's undergraduate peer-consultant training course as well as tutors and trainers in other writing center situations will be well served as they take a more comprehensive look at writing groups by crossing boundaries and breaking down the walls between the academy and the community outside those walls.

Writing Groups Inside and Outside the Classroom extends the scholarly conversation by emphasizing the value of studying writing groups in their particular contexts. Our goal in *Writing Groups Inside and Outside the Classroom* is to provide readers with a multivoiced, multilayered look at writing groups. In short, we want to present a complex, multidimensional portrait of writing groups. To this end, we selected essays for this collection that fall into many categories: classroom-based and community-based writing groups, academic and nonacademic writing groups, student and nonstudent writing groups, women's writing groups and mixed-gender groups, predominantly middle-class groups and predominantly homeless groups, among others.

To understand the contextual workings of writing groups requires the use of extensive methods of study and styles of presentation. What makes the essays in this collection particularly exciting is not just the breadth of groups examined but the various perspectives of the scholars themselves. The role of the researcher within the group changes throughout the collection. Some essays are written by individuals who either are or were members of specific writing groups, a few are written by scholars who employ elements of ethnographic study to comment on their observations of writing groups, and still others are written collaboratively by several group members about their own group, allowing them to comment on what it means to participate actively in their group. In other words, these authors are both outside observers and participant-observers, single authors and coauthors, and the diverse perspectives that result from these different positions become one of the most valuable facets of the collection.

Our Organizing Principle

Writing Groups Inside and Outside the Classroom owes its organizing principle to Anne Ruggles Gere who reminded us of the importance of writing groups that exist both inside the academy and in the "extracurriculum"—outside the academy (Gere, "Kitchen Tables," 79–80). Therefore, this collection of essays is organized into two parts: Part I, "Writing Groups within the Curriculum: Pedagogical Approaches and Concerns," and Part II, "Writing Groups in the Extracurriculum: Broadening the Focus." "Writing Groups within the Curriculum" explores how writing groups are used in academic settings—namely classrooms and writing centers. Rebecca Jackson and Thomas Piontek concern themselves with the challenges and keys to effective peer response groups within writing classes, but the classrooms and issues they portray disrupt traditional notions of what constitutes classroom practice. Jackson, in "I Don't Talk to Blacks," takes readers inside a prison classroom where the implicit rules of the prison community clash with the explicit teacher rules of successful writing groups in "regular" classrooms. Piontek illustrates how what one does in class—what the class reads, what and how they discuss readings and other issues, and what kinds of assignments are made—has an impact on the success of class-mandated writing groups.

From the examination of the classroom we shift to another "typical" academic space: the writing center. Julie Aipperspach Anderson and Susan Murphy and Magdalena Gilewicz focus on how writing groups enhance writing centers. Anderson and Murphy, in fact, blur the boundaries between the writing center and the composition class by examining how writing center tutors shape peer response groups in the classroom. Boundaries are further blurred by Sharon Thomas, Leonora Smith, and Terri Trupiano Barry, who, as writing center staffers, introduced writing groups to graduate students and faculty in the sciences. They ask readers to investigate the relationship between disciplinarity and writing groups, concerning themselves with the following key questions: When and how do disciplinary demands shape the work of writing groups? How do writing groups help its members come to understand disciplinary demands and the literacy requirements of a discipline? What role do writing groups play in helping its members produce literate texts as defined by specific disciplinary communities? Brooke Hessler and Amy Taggert connect the student writing groups in their classes with nonprofit community organizations by turning their school-mandated writing groups into community service writing groups.

The final essay in Part I, Kami Day and Michele Eodice's "Co-Authoring as Place" serves as a transition between Parts I and II. Day and Eodice report on research they've conducted on several academic faculty writing groups who write collaboratively. They look specifically at the ethos of these collaborative writing groups. This essay is placed in Part I because the writing groups that Day and Eodice study are academic, yet these groups are voluntary writing groups like the ones featured in Part II.

Essays included in "Writing Groups in the Extracurriculum" focus on the nature of specific writing groups beyond the academy. These shifts in location highlight issues of power, which commonly appears in these essays under the guise of tension, where authors attempt to discern how tensions within a group impact the texts under production. Like power, these tensions—at times positive and at times negative—are important issues to be negotiated within the groups. Candace Spigelman begins this section by using classical rhetoric to examine a creative writing group. She provides readers with a framework for studying the language of writing group members that demonstrates how a traditional academic lens can reveal new ways of seeing how writing groups function.

The next essays, all written collaboratively by writing group participants, provide an insider's view of power as it directly appears in writing group practice. Paula Mathieu et. al. demonstrate in "Questions of Time," their essay on Chicago's *StreetWise* writing group, how a group of writers who occupy various positions in what can be seen as the global and "powerless" community of the homeless empower themselves as writers through their group. Though Rebecca Schoenike Nowacek and Kenna Del Sol's "Making Space for Collaboration" and Linda Beckstead et. al's "Thursday Night Writing Group" highlight some of the tensions and power issues that specific groups face, these two essays also remind us that the literate texts studied by writing groups are as amorphous as the writing groups who respond to them and as the literacy events that these writing groups embody. Specifically, Nowacek and Del Sol introduce us to songwriting and singing groups where "text" is a song and often is presented in an oral performance. The "Thursday Night Writing Group" (Beckstead et. al) counts among its members a visual artist whose texts are rarely typed words on a page as well as more traditional writers. Yet this visual artist presents "texts" to her writing group to which they respond. These groups push the boundaries of how we come to understand "text." Nowacek and Del Sol, in addition, explore the importance of place and space in writing groups.

The penultimate essay in this collection, Trupiano Barry et. al's, "A Group of Our Own," places gender in a prominent position in the discussion of writing groups. Written collaboratively by women, they focus on how their respective writing groups have helped them grow professionally and personally. They describe their group as a safe place where they can blend the public and private in ways that they may not be able to were they a mixed-gender group. Evelyn Westbrook's essay provides a nice contrast to Trupiano Barry et. al. by examining a community writing group that is mixed in both gender and race. She sees the group as a contact zone where issues of power are constantly shifting and being renegotiated. We conclude this section with her essay because she provides insight into issues that exist in any writing group, whether those issues rise above or rest below the consciousness of group members. Finally, the collection concludes with an afterword that highlights the questions that emerge from our reading of these essays while suggesting avenues for further research. One thing we have learned in editing this collection is that there is a lot of work left to do.

Taken together, the essays in *Writing Groups Inside and Outside the Classroom* concern themselves with several questions. What impact does gender, race, and socioeconomic class have on power dynamics within writing groups? How does the local community of a writing group impact group members' participation in other local and global communities? When is a writing group a community, and are all writing groups communities? What actions contribute to a strong community of writers and what actions contribute to the breakdown of community? When and for whom are writing groups ineffective? Ultimately, what is it about belonging to a community of writers that makes writing groups appealing to so many within and beyond the academy?

We do not assert that the essays in this collection provide definitive answers to these questions. In fact, the authors of these essays can only answer some of these questions and only as they relate to their local writing groups. We must remain cautious about the pronouncements that can be made about the general nature of writing groups because, as supporters of writing groups, we must remain aware that groups always take different forms. We assume that writing groups can work, but we know not to accept them blindly.

Works Cited

Anderson, Benedict. *Imagined Communities: Reflections on the Origin and Spread of Nationalism*. New York: Verso, 1991.

Angelou, Maya. *Heart of a Woman*. New York: Random House, 1981.

Ede, Lisa, and Andrea Lunsford. *Singular Texts/Plural Authors: Perspectives on Collaborative Writing*. Carbondale: Southern Illinois UP, 1990.

Elbow, Peter. *Writing without teachers*. New York: Oxford UP, 1973.

Foucault, Michel. *Discipline and Punish: The Birth of the Prison*. Trans. Alan Sheridan. New York: Vintage, 1977.

Gere, Anne Ruggles. "Kitchen Tables and Rented Rooms: The Extracurriculum of Composition." *College Composition and Communication* 45 (1994): 75–91.

—————. *Writing Groups: History, Theory, and Implicatons*. Carbondale: Southern Illinois UP, 1987.

Heath, Shirley Brice. *Ways with Words: Language, Life, and Work in Communities and Classrooms*. New York: Cambridge UP, 1983.

Killingsworth, M. Jimmie. "Discourse Communities—Local and Global." *Rhetoric Review* 11 (1992): 110–22.

Spigelman, Candace. *Across Property Lines: Textual Ownership in Writing Groups*. Carbondale: Southern Illinois UP, 2000.

I

Writing Groups Within The Curriculum: Pedagogical Approaches and Concerns

CHAPTER TWO

ನಲ

"I Don't Talk to Blacks," or Contextual Constraints on Peer Writing Groups in the Prison College Classroom

Rebecca L. Jackson
Texas State University

I would like to point out that [Bruffee's] model of conversation, generous as it seems, can scarcely do justice to the actual constraints on discourse in many classrooms, constraints of a uniquely institutional sort.

—Kurt Spellmeyer

Students' stories often confound, correct, explode, or refine writing theorists' constructs, researchers' findings, and teachers' assumptions.

—Wendy Bishop

This is a story about my students' experiences with collaboration in a prison college classroom—about their struggles with writing groups as I, their teacher, had defined them, and their attempts to rewrite collaboration in ways that acknowledged and accommodated the multiple and conflicting contexts within which this practice was situated. It is also a story about my need to understand their struggles, both at the time they occurred—unexpected, unfolding before my eyes—and in the years that have followed. The story begins in the spring of 1995, when one of my composition students—an inmate taking college classes within the walls of a prison—refused to participate in required writing groups. His reason was disturbingly simple: "I have a problem here. I don't associate with blacks. Don't sit near 'em. Don't talk to 'em. Never have. Never will." So much for the "happy talk" of collaboration (Tobin 17). I had one student who refused to engage in collaborative activities at all, a writing group left to negotiate this dissenting student's absence, and several other groups struggling with

13

the idea of a writing group as a space for discussing ideas, giving and receiving response, negotiating and making meaning. "Why such reactions?" I wondered. "Why such overwhelming resistance to a pedagogy that, from my perspective, offered these men at least some degree of autonomy and control in a place where they had neither?"

As the semester progressed, as I observed, listened, talked with students, and reflected, I came to understand what many of these students had been trying to tell me all along—that their conflicts with and responses to collaboration were as much the product of tensions and antagonisms endemic to the layered institutional and ideological contexts in which they found themselves as of individual agency: as their instructor, I valued and practiced a collaborative, critical pedagogy, yet I was employed by an educational institution that used student "exit exams" to enforce a functional, skills-based model of literacy. Even more significant, both students and teachers worked in educational classrooms hidden behind the walls of a penal institution that discouraged trust, encouraged division, and forbade collaboration. These codes didn't need to be articulated verbally, although they sometimes were. They were clearly visible in the open-concept classroom, designed as such for security; the clusters of segregated students—African Americans with African Americans, Anglos with Anglos, Hispanics with Hispanics—the divisions signaled by the inmates' standard issue whites, the guards' starched uniforms, and the teachers' and outsiders' street clothes; the image of inmates studying college textbooks versus inmates walking the yard; and the overwhelming presence of fences, gates, and locks.

Recent work in composition acknowledges what this experience so clearly hints at: collaboration is a complex and messy business, a process embedded within and shaped by a network of historical, institutional, and ideological contexts, each mandating that students adopt particular roles and identities, each privileging particular literate practices (Bakhtin; Brooke, *Writing*; Flower; Harris; Leverenz; Perelman). As Laurel Johnson Black puts it, our students' collaborative behaviors are influenced by a "din of voices," voices arising from the immediate situation, from the communities to which students belong and are a part of, and from "histories of language that spin diverse narratives and offer [students] multiple roles" (29). Students must negotiate some kind of response to these multiple, conflicting contexts, a stance that mitigates or resolves tensions arising from various ideological forces and allows them to assert their investment in particular identities, their allegiance to particular groups. In turn, students' responses to collaboration and within collaboration make these contexts, roles, and identities visible; they dramatize students' negotiation of uneven, often difficult contextual terrain.

In this essay, I seek to illuminate the complex web of relationships, constraints, and forces that impinged on and shaped my students' collaborative interactions. Drawing on a mix of data from teaching notes, student writing group logs, and informal conversations with students, I describe and interpret responses to writing group culture in a first-year composition course taken by male inmates in a maximum-security penitentiary, responses ranging from overt refusal to participate in writing groups altogether, to what I've come to call masked rejection and negotiated participation. I argue that such moves are strategic; they are ways of negotiating the layered, often contradictory contexts within which students found themselves. Materially and ideologically, prisons oppose collaboration. Convict codes about minding one's own business clearly spring from these conditions, acting as yet another sanction against the kinds of interaction writing groups privilege. Traditional school culture exacerbates conditions of isolation even more, creating the larger culture of silence and division with which writing group members are forced to contend. Put simply, physical isolation and constraint join forces with discursive counterparts in traditional school culture, convict culture, course curriculum, and students' personal histories to undermine the value writing group culture places on conversation and interaction.

I begin by briefly describing the curricular context within which student writing groups were situated. I then describe categories of student response to and within writing groups—refusal, masked participation, and negotiated participation—and explore the contextual tensions that likely contributed to such startlingly unfamiliar, perplexing reactions. I end the essay by examining some of the implications of this experience for theories of collaboration and collaborative practice in free-world[1] classrooms.

Education Behind Bars: The Prison, the Classroom, the Course

If you didn't know what you were looking for you might easily miss the Ford Unit[2]—a massive brick structure complete with carefully tended grounds and flower plots—despite its central location downtown and the numerous "clues" that mark the city itself as a place that depends for its life on the idea of incarceration. Entering the prison for the first time, you realize you've stepped into a different world, a world with language and behavioral codes unlike those you've ever encountered. In this environment, guards ("bosses") sit in "towers," while inmates loiter in "yards" or move back and forth from the "house" to the "chow hall," from the "pill line" to school. Rit-

---

[1] I use the term *free-world classrooms* to distinguish educational spaces situated outside the confines of penal institutions—classrooms in colleges and universities attended by nonincarcerated individuals—from classrooms housed within prisons.

[2] All names and place names are pseudonyms.

ual "count times" ensure that inmates are accounted for, that no one has escaped. Activities resume when "count" has cleared; "lockdown" is imminent when count is off.

Visitors to this community, including personnel, staff, and faculty representing any number of institutions on the outside, must sign in at the front control center, allow the guard on duty to look through the contents of any briefcase or bag brought into the prison, and wait for clearance. Once cleared, faculty step through the first of several electronic pass-through gates and proceed to the education building (housing both library and classrooms), one of the nicer prison educational facilities in this area. To get to the building, inmates, guards, and instructors must walk through the yard, a noisy outdoor area where inmates congregate under trees, sit on benches, or play basketball. Former students are likely to watch for you so that they can say hello and ask how you're doing. Sometimes they'll stop to chat, asking you what courses you'll be teaching the following semester or telling you about their educational progress. Momentarily, at least, it's easy to forget that the thriving rose bushes fronting the yard are tended by inmate gardeners, that the basketball court is circumscribed by massive quantities of brick and wire, that the classrooms you teach in are monitored by guards.

Once inside the educational building, faculty retrieve their rosters and class materials (ten sheets of notebook paper per inmate and pencils for those who need them) and head toward their assigned classrooms. Inmates must first check in with the guard on duty, give the guard their prison identification number (names are rarely used), and specify their business. This mechanism is especially significant in the carceral environment for it works to support and extend surveillance and observation, the "rituals of power" upon which the prison's control over inmates is firmly grounded (Foucault). At this particular checkpoint, power is exercised through the ideological workings of language manifest in regulations dictating who may speak, when they may speak, where they may speak, and what they may speak.[3]

---

[3]In the carceral environment, guards often use language to demand language, to enforce subservience to the mechanics of observation. What I consider most provocative about these exchanges, however, is inmates' strategic use of silence as a way to defer and resist the authority the guard represents. Inmates can capitulate to the powers that be, speak their language—"yes sir"—and lose any identity they have constructed for themselves beyond their crime; they can oppose the powers that be, speak defiantly—"fuck off"—and be punished, or they can resist the powers that be, refuse to speak at all, and retain an alternate identity without, at the same time, losing what little freedom they have. As I interpret the situation, inmates maintain or recover some degree of agency by negotiating discursive boundaries—constructing meaning that mediates institutional constraints and individual motives, especially when these are at odds. Put simply, negotiation denotes discursive bargaining, an attempt, as Linda Flower puts it, "to find a path that honors multiple goals and voices or arbitrates opposing demands" (70).

College classes take place in one of six partitioned classroom spaces in a layout known as open-concept. In free-world schools, of course, open-concept classrooms were designed to promote freedom of movement and the idea of interdisciplinarity; open classrooms also undermined, in theory at least, systems of grade classification and hierarchies of achievement by enabling several grade levels to coexist within the same space. In the prison, open-concept classrooms are equally ideological, although here they work as security measures designed to control and prohibit inmate insurrection. The classrooms themselves are divided by short, three-tier bookcases filled with the readers and workbooks students enrolled in day school need to complete academic work at levels ranging from first to twelfth grades, including special education. All classrooms contain blackboards and overhead projectors and televisions equipped with VCRs are almost always available. In some rooms, short rectangular tables are configured to form a circle conducive to group interaction; in other rooms, tables are arranged traditionally in rows.

English 101 is a first-year writing course designed to further develop students' writing abilities and acquaint them with the role of research in writing. Students are required to write eight essays, each modeling a different mode of development, from descriptive-narrative and process papers, to cause-effect, comparison-contrast, division-classification, persuasive, and argumentative essays. In addition, all students are required to write and pass an exit essay administered on the last day of class to enroll in English 102, the next course in the first-year writing sequence.[4]

Asking students to engage in collaboration—a central feature of all writing courses I teach—was my way of reshaping a course I considered formulaic and outdated. It was also an overtly political act, a way of helping students in this environment acquire at least some degree of agency, authority, and control in a system founded on denial of these very attributes. In theory at least writing groups moved students in this direction by altering classroom dynamics and by fostering critical awareness of the ways in which the literate practices of those communities to which we belonged (willingly or unwillingly), or aspired to belong, shaped us as members of those com-

---

[4]Written by the department chair and administered on the last day of class, the exit essay asks students to write a three- to five-hundred word essay in response to one of three or four writing prompts, each specifying a particular mode of development. Students are given the full class time to write their essays, roughly 3 ½ hours, at which time the instructor collects the papers and delivers them to the main office. Procedure then specifies that the exams be given to another member of the English faculty for holistic scoring. Graders rank the essays from 1–5, scores 1 and 2 signifying a failing essay; score 3 a borderline essay; and scores 4 and 5, a passing essay. If the grader gives the essay a score of three, the grader then passes the paper on to another grader for additional evaluation. If the student passes the exit essay, he is then allowed to receive the grade he earned in English 101, the system deferring to the instructor. If the student fails the essay, however, he receives a failing grade for English 101.

munities and as speakers and writers within them. On the first night of class, I introduced students to the idea of writing groups, emphasizing that I considered them an integral part of the course—enough to make writing group participation 10% of their total grade—and discussing general guidelines for establishing and maintaining effective groups.[5] During the first classroom break, I sketched out tentative writing group assignments reflecting the racial diversity of the class itself, roughly one third Anglo, one third Hispanic, and one third African American. When students returned from break, I announced writing group assignments and asked that students meet with the other members of their writing group to get acquainted and establish ground rules or guidelines for weekly meetings.

Refusing to Participate: Individual Agency or Institutional Force?

What do you do when a student openly refuses to participate in required writing groups? When the reason this student offers is shocking and offensive—he doesn't "associate with or talk to blacks"? And when all of this happens on the first evening of class? This is precisely the situation I encountered on the first night I met with students in English 101. I was stunned, incredulous. I don't remember what I said exactly, but I do remember a gradual evolution of feeling, from shock accompanied by a loss of words to anger that took form in the traditional, "I'm the boss" style of teacher talk. I explained that I wouldn't restructure writing groups to accommodate his prejudice. He would have to make a choice. Either he find some way to work productively in the writing group to which he'd been assigned or he would work alone.

He chose to work alone, later explaining his actions solely in terms of individual preference and conflicting epistemologies rather than as products of myriad institutional and ideological forces, personal preference and learning style merely one part of a larger body of influence. Both of these ideas emerge in Gene's[6] final essay for the course:

> Do you ever get tired of a double standard or "it's my way or nothing attitude" of individuals who are supposed to be leaders or teachers of society? I do!

> Take for instance a couple of individuals who want to advance themselves by continuing their education through college. These students are average and try

---

[5]The document I distribute and discuss, "Using Writing Groups," focuses on variables necessary for effective group functioning, including the importance of getting acquainted with fellow group members, establishing group procedures, sharing ideas and receiving response in productive ways, exploring difference, and understanding group task and maintenance roles.
[6]All names are pseudonyms.

to learn by studying and working hard. They have beliefs of their own and tend to be loners who prefer to work as the individuals they are and not as a group.

But first they are forced into a group of students into which they have no desire to be. Then it's said that this is a percentage of the course grade. You lose your points if you don't.

Then you are told that "sometimes problems arise that you cannot anticipate—If you are not able to work well in your group you might prefer to talk privately with your instructor. Often the problem can be simply and efficiently resolved."

It was a problem and yes it could have been simply and efficiently resolved. But it wasn't and in turn it has only hurt the individuals concerned by causing an inner withdrawal and of not doing one's best. When enrolling into the class I enrolled as an individual of one, not two or three. I continue to be one, a loner, who tends to lead his own life as I was born, which is one. Not a group. By so doing this I am docked a mere 10% to be myself by myself so be it. Guess I will always be short that 10%.

Viewed together, Gene's refusal to participate in writing groups and the argument he advances in this last paper tell us a great deal about how he understands himself and how he wishes others to understand him in this particular context. In paragraph two, for example, Gene appeals to quintessential American values—individualism, competition, the work ethic—to justify his position against collaboration in the college classroom; he's just an "average" guy hoping to achieve the dream of "advancement" through individual initiative and lots of hard work ("studying and working hard"). This last idea is captured powerfully in Gene's description of himself as a self-chosen "loner who prefers to work as the individual [he is] and not as a group." Most of us probably also detect in Gene's self-image the clear echoes of traditional school culture, in particular the value it places on individual work, competition, hierarchy, and teacher authority, components that contribute to the "banking concept of education" (Freire). Students who arrive in the writing classroom with this kind of educational legacy expect that teachers will tell them what to write and will then evaluate the extent to which they've actually written what they've been told to write. Learning is linear—the teacher gives, the student receives; the teacher demands, the student produces—with success measured along a continuum, from most able to show or display what has been received to least able. When these role expectations are challenged or upset, as they always are to some degree in the collaborative classroom, students must find a way to manage the situation. For Gene, finding a comfortable place in the collaborative classroom is a difficult, finally impossible, task.

The emphasis Gene places on himself as a loner and not as a member of a group—manifest in his comments that "When I enrolled in the class I enrolled as an individual of one, not two or three" and "I continue to be one, a loner who tends to lead his own life as I was born which is one. Not a group."—works as a critique of collaboration as well, especially its tendency to deny or ignore individual personality and learning styles (Stewart) as well as individual cognition (Flower). Gene suggests that he chooses opposition to collaboration—he acts on "beliefs of [his] own"—because writing group culture conflicts with his own identity as a loner and as a particular kind of student and learner.

What we also begin to see is Gene's very clear recognition that institutionally mandated collaboration, however noble the instructor's intentions, always involves what Linda Flower calls the "paradox of power" (215). As teachers of writing, we ask students to participate in writing groups because we want students to share authority in the classroom, to take responsibility for their own learning, to become active creators of knowledge rather than passive recipients, to develop critical consciousness. Still, institutionally imposed collaboration is just that—institutionally imposed, mandated. As Flower points out, what we've done is reconfigure a natural social event, conversing with friends, fashioning it into an "unnatural" (not spontaneous or freely chosen) academic event arising from research in composition and our own ideological agendas. In this respect, collaboration is a "clear instance of both power relations in school and the structures, such as assigned activities, which maintain them" (215). When we mandate collaboration, we are engaged in the paradoxical act of using educational power structures to help students empower themselves. Students who resist our attempts at this kind of "noble coercion" are less likely refusing to learn than "refus[ing] to participate in an educational program that needs to be questioned" (Clark and Ede 279). Resistance, Clark and Ede contend, is a sign that students "know something that their teachers, however politically aware, do not and cannot know" (279).

Certainly Gene's interpretation of his own responses and behaviors is legitimate; it is, however, limited in the same that all stories told from single perspective are limited or incomplete, my own interpretation included. As I see it, Gene's narrative is an important yet very small chapter in the much larger story of collaboration in this setting. When we view Gene's responses within the broader contextual framework of convict and correctional cultures, we find a network of contextual forces in place, some competing with the influences Gene has already identified, some reinforcing these influences.

Of these, the prison structure itself is perhaps the most obvious. As the physical embodiment of socially constructed ideas of criminality and deviance, the carceral facility invites and reinforces the kind of opposition to writing groups Gene displays, influencing students to embrace the very systems of power they also despise and, ironically, seek freedom from. Put simply, prison design and procedure discourage both the actual practice and idea of inmate networking outside the classroom. As Foucault reminds us, prison architecture is founded on principles of physical and mental isolation, by limitations placed on literal and psychological community. On the literal, bodily level, criminals are first excised from the society whose constructions of decency they have violated—"from everything that motivated the offense, from the complicities that facilitated it" (236). Once incarcerated, inmates are further divided from one another, segmented into specific and separate cell blocks or living quarters based on such criteria as available space, disciplinary records, and gang affiliations. The cells themselves, bounded on three sides by solid brick walls, extend physical isolation by preventing contact with all other inmates on a particular cell block with the exception of cellmates. Isolation becomes a means of complete control, solitude being the "primary condition of total submission" (Foucault 237).

Eventually, literal isolation gives rise to a kind of isolationist behavior that replicates physical boundaries: inmates given the freedom to mingle together during select times of the day, to collaborate and interact as in the writing classroom, isolate themselves from one another like so much brick and concrete. The fact of bodily separation encourages a reciprocal idea of physical and mental isolation, a predisposition to mimic those behaviors that conditions of physical confinement demand, even when these conditions are absent. In Gene's case, I see this phenomenon joining forces with his personal history and sense of identity—each emphasizes the primacy of the individual over the group—to shape his particular response to writing groups.

The convict culture's unspoken mandate to stick with your own exacerbates institutionally imposed physical segregation suggesting a clear logic to inmate rejection of writing groups. As several students explained to me throughout the semester, territoriality, division and inmate cliques, are a powerful feature of life behind bars. In a writing group log written early in the semester, James articulates this position clearly. Throughout the entry, James refers to me in third person, perhaps to soften critique of what he rightly suggests is my ignorance about the power of contextual influence: "I haven't quite figured out what criteria Ms. Jackson used in her selection process. This being a prison environment, I certainly would think race would or should have been a factor in dividing the class. In this setting certainly whites and blacks and hispanics all are more open with people of their own race."

Danny conveys similar ideas in his first writing group log of the semester, blunting stating, "I don't like being put with a group of people I don't like. I was at a table with three guys that I like and communicated with well." In his concluding remarks, Danny reinforces the primacy of inmate subgroups: "I'll still do what is required of me," he comments, "but I won't put forth as much of an effort as if I was with my friends that were at my table." Another student admits that he's "disappointed with the way the groups were split," a position he arrives at for reasons, he tells me later, very similar to those Danny expresses—to the degree that he had deliberately chosen to sit with men he liked, he had also chosen to sit away from men he didn't.

Even when students did find themselves in groups with others they liked and respected, they were often constrained by convict culture's stricture against self-disclosure, the need to maintain a kind of machismo-like distance from other men who themselves were expected to mind their own business. Gary writes that he's "talked with some of the other men in other groups" and discovered that "they're not really happy about this grouping together." In a casual conversation I have with him and other members of his group during break one evening, Gary attributes this discomfort to conflicting codes. Sharing writing doesn't just demand talk; it demands a certain kind of talk—the talk of solicitation, the talk of genuine response, the talk of support. This kind of talk is very different from the kinds of talk inmates approve of—the talk of handball tournaments, the talk of weight lifting, the talk of food quality, for example. When codes clash, as they clearly do when the collaborative classroom meets prison and male convict, individuals scramble to quell the dissonance, to get back to a state of mental equilibrium or comfort. Of course, what "mental equilibrium" is and how one "gets back" to it acceptably varies from person to person and context to context. My point here is that convict culture is an important component in the contextual matrix out of which the behavior related to achieving mental equilibrium arises.

Without an infrastructure supportive of collaboration, writing group activity in the prison classroom may even be dangerous. In a subtle yet telling reaction to writing group assignments, another student in the class focuses on their potential to exacerbate the latent hostilities always present in the prison environment, noting that "the guys I'm in the group with seem to be alright as people but we will see what happens when they are all of a sudden telling me what's wrong with my writing; then we'll see how 'cozy' this relationship really is." In fact, the only other student in the class who openly refused to engage in collaboration, although only on one particular occasion, did so because he feared retribution: "My writing was too personal for me to share with the group. I felt that I would harm myself more so I worked on it alone." This student's response supports Goffman's observation that "inmates live with chronic anxiety about breaking the rules and the consequences of breaking them" and that they will "forego certain levels of sociability with [others] to avoid possible incidents" (*Asylums* 42).

Fear of potential conflict figures prominently in these students' responses, and for good reason. Thomas points out that the conventions of prison life "differ dramatically from those found among on-campus students, and the potential for disputes and the means for resolving them are somewhat more severe and direct. The social order of prisons does not stop outside the classroom door" (32). Writing group culture's emphasis on trust and self-disclosure asks student inmates to disregard self-preservation, to flout age-old convict codes to mind your own business, do your own time, live and let live, codes that have every bit as much to do with personal safety as privacy.

So what does this discussion tell us about Gene's or any inmate-student's refusal to participate in assigned writing groups? First, and most important I think, descriptions reveal that Gene is not gratuitously obstinate, although this conclusion may, initially at least, appear forgone. What we find instead is a logic to Gene's rejection, a rational way of dealing with the constellation of competing contexts (discourse communities) he finds himself in and a part of, each one demanding that he be a specific kind of person, possess a particular version of identity. See Fig. 2.1.

This is, of course, the way we all construct meaning—by managing the varied "voices" that confront us in any given situation, by deciding, consciously or unconsciously, which voices to privilege, which to ignore, which to modify, which to join. What distinguishes Gene's meaning-making process from my own, however, is that it occurs within the totalizing space of

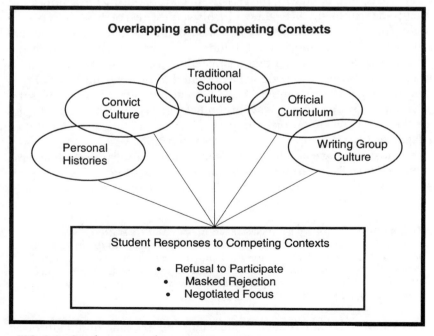

FIG. 2.1. Overlapping and competing contexts.

the penal institution, a place where prison house structure and the prison house of language become conjoined. Given such formidable obstacles, it's easy to understand why Gene rejects writing group culture altogether.

Masked Rejection: The Case of Conflicting Texts

Not all students who rejected writing group culture—that is, refused to participate actively in the writing group they'd been assigned—were as explicit or as open about their decision as Gene was. In this section I explore what I call masked rejection of writing groups, the attempt to obscure group disintegration or lack of productivity through visual and textual means, by dramatizing interaction, to use Goffman's performance metaphor, rather than actually engaging in it (*Presentation*). Students who engaged in masked rejection maintained the illusion of collaboration through physical arrangement, narrative accounts of writing group meetings, or both.

Groups wanting to look as if they were collaborating arranged their tables in octagonal "circles" and positioned their bodies inward, toward the group, rather than outward, away from it. Physical arrangement revealed the kind of negotiation they'd made between the classroom culture they inhabited from 6:00 p.m.–9:30 p.m. every Monday evening and the convict culture that overlapped with the classroom culture during these hours and structured the inmates' lives almost exclusively the rest of the time. A plausible interpretation of this activity is that students wanted to convince me, their instructor, that they were fulfilling class requirements, while at the same time avoiding behavior that conflicted with the convict code of minding your own business, a code itself designed to prevent the kinds of tensions that might lead to physical harm or death. In other words, it was the individual or group attempt to avoid conflict within groups that actually signaled conflict about groups, in particular the emphasis collaborative pedagogies place on substantive, intergroup conflict.

The most striking examples of masked rejection appear in student writing group journals as narratives of writing group meetings rather than evaluations. Manuel's entry typifies the writing group log as narrative form of student response:

> We got our papers on division/classification back and we started revising our papers. We gave each other feedback as to what we could do to improve our papers and we started giving opinions and suggestions for each other's papers so that we could improve our editing and writing skills. We read each other's papers and gave our thoughts as to how we felt [things] needed to be done and so then we started writing our papers.

I see two things happening here: like most people who find themselves in a new discourse community, Manuel tries on the language that constitutes this new place; he plays with the language to see how it works, how it fits, how it can be used. In adopting the rhetoric of collaboration, especially in a document that narrativizes rather than evaluates his experience, Manuel is also able to avoid the risk that judgment—being a snitch—entails in this context. In a similar discussion about conflict avoidance in a free-world writing classroom, Gergits and Schramer state that our students' preference for narrative over assessment, fiction rather than evaluation, should come to us as no surprise. Stories that focus on chronology and task offer students a way to "personalize their observations and to distance themselves from an evaluative task they perceive as difficult" (194).

If students in free-world classes feel this kind of anxiety, one can imagine the kinds of tensions inmate-students face, tensions that help us make sense of the ostensibly unexplainable, confusing, sometimes hostile ways students in this setting respond to collaboration. Narrative is particularly nonthreatening when reduced to a kind of formula fiction, stock characters performing stock actions in rigid chronological framework. James's writing group log conveys this idea remarkably well. James constructs the second paragraph of his writing group entry along a narrative framework, complete with fill-in-the-blank spaces for pieces of information he doesn't yet have:

> Group #__ met and discussed certain ground rules. We decided the following: we will spend approximately __ minutes on each paper, only constructive criticism will be permitted, profanity will be kept under control, and we shall strive to maintain a good demeanor during our time together.

James has only to complete the form and he has a ready-made writing group entry that appeases both teacher and fellow convict, a story of collaboration that succeeds in two very different worlds.

However, to argue that these students are engaged in a deliberate attempt to deceive the teacher is to miss the point of pragmatic self-presentation, Goffman's theory of negotiated agency. According to Goffman, the self emerges in moments of decision and negotiation, in strategic response to individuals' own personal motives and histories and to the social arrangements they find themselves in—the constraints such social arrangements impose and the opportunities they offer. Thus, while displays of self may involve deception at times, self-presentation is most often about the human need "to communicate, to get things done, to help others and to protect themselves" (Schwalbe 341). Schwalbe's claim that strategic impression management "is less a choice to be deceptive than it is a choice to survive" (342) helps to explain the seemingly aberrant behaviors of otherwise motivated students as negotiated, strategic responses to contextual realities. "Misbehavior," Brooke reminds us, is often a sign of "constructive, individual stance-taking" ("Underlife" 144).

Narrative accounts of writing group interaction allow students to "get things done"—complete course requirements—while "protecting them" from actual group wrangling, the kind of interaction on which effective collaboration is based but which deviates from the traditional models of "familial cooperation" students know best (Gergits and Schramer 193). As Gergits and Schramer point out, students' reluctance to allow or admit conflict "mirrors the desire on the part of family members to maintain social amity often at the expense of constructive criticism" (193). In the prison, familial sanctions against conflict converge with the value traditional school culture places on teacher authority and student performance and with the inmates' own understanding that the price exacted for conflict in prison is much greater than that paid for conflict on the outside. The result is the writing group memo as chronological narrative, a text designed to appease the multiple voices out of which it arises.

Negotiating a Compromise: When Writing Groups Do Grammar Instruction

In the previous two sections, I examined the conflicts inmate-students experienced with writing group culture in general—its emphasis on trust, self-disclosure, conversation, conflict, responsibility—and demonstrated how the constellation of intersecting contexts that students were a part of may have contributed to these tensions. These students responded to contact zone politics by rejecting writing group culture to varying degrees and in various forms, from open refusal to a kind of masked noncompliance. In the present section I examine a very different pattern of student response, what I call negotiated participation, to a very different set of conflicts. Students in this category struggled less with the idea of writing groups than with the situated use of collaboration in this setting, with the uneasy relationship they perceived between my goals for first-year composition and the objectives implicit in official, departmentally mandated curricula, namely the requirement that all students take and pass an exit exam before moving on to the next course. Motivated by situational exigency, these students refashioned writing groups altogether, using them as a forum for evaluating the grammatical errors they'd made in their rough drafts, rather than a place to gather and test ideas, get audience responses or solicit suggestions—the writing group focus I considered most valuable and stressed repeatedly throughout the semester.

Discussion of grammar or surface-level errors appeared frequently in students' writing group logs. One student remarked, for example, that while "everyone [in his group] was a little tensed" about reading their papers aloud to the group, the comments group members received helped them to "learn more about the proper form of a correct essay." For this student and many others in the class, "good" writing is identified with specific text features and conventions—a "proper" five-paragraph theme that is also grammatically perfect, or correct. Another student in this same writing group reiterates concern about grammatical correctness noting that "my partner read my paper helping me on punctuation and spelling points. Also to stay in the same tense."

A writing group log written during week eight reveals similar definitions of literacy and appropriate teacher-student relations. The writer confesses that "it's kind of hard being critical of someone else's work when I feel that my own writing skills are not up to par," but he admits that he "must be learning because every week I'm finding a couple of more little things wrong with the person's paper that I'm revising." In each of these excerpts, the language of functionalist or skills-based literacy predominates. Literacy, these students tell us, is about "punctuation and spelling," about errors hunted and found, about mistakes made and corrected. In context, these concerns are hardly unusual: after all, literacy as correctness has had a "long and tenacious history in American schools" (Flower), and it was from the legacy of such schools and classrooms that these students entered first-year composition.

The departmentally-mandated exit exam worked to maintain these students' belief in text-based literacy and undermine my own attempts to call this definition of literacy into question. While evaluation criteria don't exist in any kind of written form passing essays are, above all, grammatically correct. For students in this context, being judged acceptable, whether because one is literate—has passed the exit exam—or morally reformed, is all consuming. Students in English 101 quizzed me almost weekly about exit exam procedures, methods of assessment, repercussions of failure. They also refashioned writing groups to meet the demands placed on them by competing images of literacy. They met with one another, they talked with one another, they collaborated with one another—my vision of literacy instruction—yet they talked about grammar, mechanics, correctness and form—the official curriculum's vision of literacy. The end result was a hybridized version of writing groups that would allow them to meet multiple demands.

Conclusion

Unique as they may appear to be, students' responses to and experiences with writing groups in this setting actually tell us a great deal about collaboration in free-world classrooms as well: what goes on in the prison writing classroom—the extremes in attitude, behavior, and ideological constraint—helps us to resee the activities and tensions in writing classrooms on the outside, classes we have fooled ourselves into believing are familiar, predictable, and firmly within our control. One of the most important things these students tell us is that collaborative pedagogies are never ideologically neutral, despite what idealized portraits of collaboration and community would have us believe. Like all classroom practices, collaborative pedagogies advance a particular view of students, teachers, classrooms, and schools—about how students learn, about what they should learn, about appropriate teacher-student and student-student relations. To learn, students must interact with peers; to become literate, students must learn to negotiate rhetorical contexts; to learn and become literate, students must become active participants rather than passive recipients, must talk and wrangle, negotiate and affirm difference.

As students' responses to writing groups so clearly suggest, however, collaboration isn't, and perhaps shouldn't be, the only legitimate game in town. For some students, individual, rather than collaborative, learning may work best. And in some contexts, individual, rather than collaborative, pedagogies may be the only way of ensuring students against bodily harm. I think of David Bleich's observation that "increasingly diverse populations evince distances among students" and that "working with their colleagues under these circumstances has taught many students that 'sharing' often is not a safe activity and that hostility, malice, and withdrawal, when appearing in 'collaborative' situations, can spoil any chance for doing productive schoolwork" (43). Bleich concludes that "for any one group, working together may not, finally, be the right thing" (43). As teachers we must learn to read the broader social networks within which our collaborative practices will be situated and which will, in turn, shape our students' experiences with collaboration. Put simply, we must acquire what Akua Duku Anokye has called "teacher literacy," an ability to "read the cultural text." Here is a place to begin.

Works Cited

Anokye, Akua Duku. "Culture as Text." Paper delivered at the symposium Rewriting Literacies: Changing Communities, Shifting Discourses in the Twenty-first Century. Texas A&M University, Bryan, Texas. 22 Oct. 1999.

Bakhtin, Mikhail. *The Dialogic Imagination*. Trans. Caryl Emerson and Michael Holquist. Ed. Michael Holquist. Austin: U of Texas P, 1981.

Bishop, Wendy. "Students' Stories and the Variable Gaze of Composition Research." *Writing Ourselves Into the Story*. Eds. Sheryl I. Fontaine and Susan Hunter. Carbondale: Southern Illinois UP, 1993, 197–214.

Black, Laurel Johnson. *Between Talk and Teaching: Reconsidering the Writing Conference*. Logan: Utah State UP, 1998.

Bleich, David. "Collaboration and the Pedagogy of Disclosure." *College English* 57.1 (1995): 43.

Brooke, Robert. "Underlife and Writing Instruction." *College Composition and Communication* 38.2 (1987): 141–53.
―――――. *Writing and Sense of Self.* Urbana: NCTE, 1991.
Clark, Suzanne, and Lisa Ede. "Collaboration, Resistance, and the Teaching of Writing." *The Right to Literacy.* Eds. Andrea A. Lunsford, Helene Moglen, and James Slevin. New York: MLA, 1990, 276–85.
Flower, Linda. *The Construction of Negotiated Meaning.* Carbondale: Southern Illinois UP, 1994.
Foucault, Michel. *Discipline and Punish.* New York: Vintage, 1979.
Freire, Paulo. *Pedagogy of the Oppressed.* New York: Continuum, 1987.
Gergits, Julia, and James Schramer. "The Collaborative Classroom as a Site of Difference." *Journal of Advanced Composition* 14.1 (1994): 187–202.
Goffman, Erving. *Asylums: Essays on the Social Situation of Mental Patients and Other Inmates.* New York: Anchor, 1961.
―――――. *The Presentation of Self in Everyday Life.* New York: Doubleday, 1959.
Harris, Joseph. "The Idea of Community in the Study of Writing." *College Composition and Communication* 40.1 (1989): 11–22.
Leverenz, Carrie Shively. "Peer Response in the Multicultural Composition Classroom: Dissensus—A Dream (Deferred)." *Journal of Advanced Composition* 14.1 (1994): 167–86.
Perelman, Les. "The Context of Classroom Writing." *College English* 48 (1986): 471–79.
Schwalbe, Michael. "Goffman Against Postmodernism: Emotion and the Reality of the Self." *Symbolic Interaction* 16.4 (1993): 333–47.
Spellmeyer, Kurt. "On Conventions and Collaboration: The Open Road and the Iron Cage." *Writing Theory and Critical Theory.* Eds. John Clifford and John Schlib. New York: MLA, 1994, 73–95.
Stewart, Donald. "Collaborative Learning and Composition: Boon or Bane?" *Rhetoric Review* 7 (1988): 58–83.
Thomas, Jim. "The Ironies of Prison Education." *Schooling in a "Total Institution."* Ed. Howard Davidson. Westport: Bergin & Garvey, 1995.
Tobin, Lad. *Writing Relationships: What Really Happens in the Composition Class.* Portsmouth: Heinemann-Boynton/Cook, 1991.

CHAPTER THREE

ᔛᘏᕉ

Wrestling With the Angels:
Writing Groups, Messy Texts,
and Truly Collaborative Writing

Thomas K. H. Piontek
The Ohio State University

In an essay on the theoretical legacies of cultural studies, Stuart Hall proposes a new way of thinking about the relationship between theory and praxis: "the metaphor of struggle, of wrestling with the angels." Hall elaborates: "The only theory worth having is that which you have to fight off, not that which you speak with profound fluency. My own experience of theory … is of wrestling with the angels—a metaphor you can take as literally as you like" (266). This essay constitutes an attempt to apply Hall's metaphor to an examination of the ways in which writing groups functioned in a first-year writing course I recently taught in the Honors Program at The Ohio State University. Because I wanted to find out how students come to understand themselves as writers through their participation in collaborative writing projects, I set up my class so that students would be "wrestling with the angels." In addition, I was also interested in the role the specific nature of the assigned texts plays in this process.

Two interrelated factors made this class different from and more successful than first-year composition classes I had taught in the past. First, I realized that traditional collaborative writing models differ from most writing groups. In the traditional collaborative writing model, the writers collaborate to produce one text. In most writing groups, however, each writer is working on his or her own piece of writing, and the group responds to it. Recognizing this inherent contradiction between group work on the one hand and individual projects on the other, I decided to experiment with both approaches in my class. During the first five weeks, students worked

31

individually on several incidental writing assignments as well as their first essay; during the second half of the ten-week class, I assigned group projects, in which students collaborated in workshops to produce one text per group. In addition, each student was required to write an individual account of his or her experience in the writing group and the contribution he or she had made to the group project.

Another element that made a decisive difference in the students' attitude toward the process of writing was the selection of required readings for the class. I had deliberately chosen two nontraditional nonfiction books that engaged students in debates about identity, authorship, and the process of writing, rather than asking them to emulate the presumably "good" writing selected for them by the editors of composition textbooks. All too often instructors in composition classes assume that the most effective way to teach students to write well is to provide them with a model of what we consider to be "good writing" in the hope that students will not only recognize the qualities that we value in a given text but will also eventually learn to reproduce these qualities in their own writing. This was the way that I was instructed in composition, and, in spite of the large number of theoretical interventions into the field, this approach to the teaching of writing is still very much alive today. Mary Alexander, for instance, in an essay titled "The Art of Teaching Students to Think Critically," maintains that "by studying what I consider to be good examples of films, television shows or journalism, students get a glimpse of how to do things well" (B9). While I share Alexander's goal—teaching students to think critically—I have reservations about the methodology she proposes in the passage I quoted.

Along similar lines, Elizabeth Penfield writes in the preface to the latest edition of *Short Takes: Model Essays for Composition*, a collection of short essays organized according to the rhetorical modes—description, narration, example, definition, division and classification, comparison and contrast, process, cause and effect, and argument—that the essays collected in this anthology "serve as illustrative models of organization and stylistic techniques available to the writer" (xx). In spite of this kind of approach, which invites first appreciation and ultimately imitation, Penfield voices her hope that the essays will also "serve as sources of invention, as jumping-off places for students to develop their own ideas in their own styles" (xxi). It is this approach, in which an ideal text serves as a model for students to emulate, that I want to take issue with here.

First, I have my doubts about the fruitful coexistence of *prescription* and *creativity* posited by Penfield. What I am concerned about is the possibility that textbooks such as hers may be more likely to cater to the intellectually lethargic student (who spends way too much energy trying to figure out what the teacher wants) than to inspire the students' inventiveness and critical thinking. I agree with Deborah Britzman, who, in a recent paper on the psychological aspects of education, argues that "the act of prescription forecloses conflict." It is this conflict, which can be made productive in the teaching of many topics, including, of course, the teaching of writing. Furthermore, this approach to composition—"Here are several modes of writing; choose the one most appropriate to your purpose and imitate it"—seems to contradict current ideas about the pedagogy of writing. If we take seriously the idea most forcefully presented by Peter Elbow in *Embracing Contraries* that not only writing but also learning and teaching themselves are messy occupations and that, via this messiness, real cognitive growth occurs, then it would appear that the imitative approach is entirely too mechanical. Furthermore, it seems problematic to me because it focuses attention on the finished product and thus runs counter to the by now widely accepted definition of writing as a process, in which revising and redrafting are valued as much as the finished product. Do we not ultimately compromise the goal of making students critical thinkers when we simply ask them to emulate "good" writing—especially when we have preselected that "good" writing, letting them know, implicitly, that they aren't wise enough to select what's "good"?

Rather than ideal texts, the two books I assigned were postmodern or what George Marcus calls "messy" texts (567–68, passim) in that they foreground both questions of authorship and a definition of writing as a deeply relational rather than individual process. James McBride's memoir *The Color of Water: A Black Man's Tribute to His White Mother*, for example, establishes important connections between the stories we tell and the stories of those around us. The printed text stages this interrelatedness by alternating between chapters of McBride's autobiography, printed in a standard font, and his mother's reminiscences, printed in italics. To some extent, his mother's story seems to interrupt McBride's narrative, withholding narrative closure in his own story by taking us back in time to his mother's youth and the early years of her married life. McBride refers to this technique in the preface to *The Color of Water*. He represents his book as the result of a fourteen-year endeavor to "unearth" his mother's "remarkable story" and concludes, "Here is her life, as she told it to me, and betwixt and between the pages of her life you will find mine as well" (xvii). To be sure, McBride does give pride of place to his mother's words by printing them in a more flashy font and by choosing to inaugurate the structure of alternating chapters with his mother's recollections. Nonetheless, what the writer considers a tribute—and what critics and reviewers have called a biography and a memoir—ends up telling us at least as much if not more about the writer of the biography as about its subject. McBride's methodology highlights that writing never takes place in a vacuum, that every text is, in some way, both a response to and a prompt for someone else's text, part of an ongoing conversation. As it turns out, his mother's anecdotes ultimately shape the way we make meaning of his autobiography.

For some of the students these ideas were quite difficult to grasp, considering that they had had virtually no previous exposure to a discussion of genre or the creative process. As a matter of fact, early on in the quarter most of the students referred to McBride's book not as memoir, biography, or autobiography but as a novel. Perhaps it could be argued that the students were not that far off the mark, if one considers that several of the initial reviews of the book emphasized the narrative qualities of the text, claiming that it was as lively as a well-plotted novel. Students generally shared this appreciation of McBride's narrative talent, frequently commenting on how well he tells his family's story. This commentary in turn led to a debate about the differences between fiction and autobiography. What were the things we valued in these two forms of writing? How did categories such as invention and truth influence our judgment?

Discussions of genre also led to the first research project. I told students that I had noticed that although some of them referred to McBride's text as a novel it had been classified as biography in the catalogue of the Library of Congress. So was *The Color of Water* a novel or a biography? How could we tell? And why did it matter? Students went to the library to look up *biography* and related terms and to see what distinguishes this type of writing from the novel or from fiction in general. They did a very good job of identifying what distinguishes fiction from autobiographical writing, and also—and more importantly, perhaps—complicated the results of their own research. Thus, several students noted that they had come across types of writing that combine elements of both genres. *Fictional autobiography* and *autobiographical fiction* were the terms they discovered repeatedly in the reference works they consulted. This nomenclature alerted them to the fact that literary terminology, far from reflecting clear-cut and definitive differentiations, merely provides a system of classification that is supposed to facilitate the study of literature by breaking it down into a number of *supposedly* distinct types of writing. A student voiced her opinion that perhaps works that do not neatly fit the given categories may in fact be more interesting and worthwhile. This notion was seconded by a couple of students who reported that a text they were reading in a literature class, Maxine Hong Kingston's *The Woman Warrior* (1975), was considered a memoir by some of the critics whose essays they were using as secondary sources, whereas others considered the work a novel, albeit with an autobiographical slant. A good part of our subsequent conversation about *The Color of Water* centered on generic differences. That was no small task. It required students to grapple with some very subtle distinctions.

After several in-class discussions and a series of informal writing assignments, students began to prepare a critical essay about *The Color of Water*. They wrote their proposals as well as several drafts of their essays in groups of four to five. Students read each other's work and commented on it using group critique sheets I had prepared for them (see Appendix A). These handouts asked them to first restate the essay's thesis in their own words and subsequently to respond to the argument the writer was making. Responses were organized into three columns: things they liked or appreciated about the essay (+), things they thought did not work quite so well (–), and things they found confusing or that raised questions in their minds (?). During the initiation of the writing groups, I encouraged students to jot down keywords for each of their remarks so that writers would be able to identify the particular passage to which their comment pertained, and to make a minimum of two entries in the "+" column so that writers could more readily accept the criticism and questions contained in the "–" and "?" columns. Initially, some students resisted the peer review process. They doubted that fellow students could comment on their work with any kind of authority. After all was said and done, it would still be the professor who would assess and grade their essays, and how could the other members of the group possibly know just what kind of a paper I wanted them to write? After they had worked in groups for the first time, however, most of the students were quite relieved to find that their peers' feedback was actually quite helpful in revising their rough drafts. Once they finished workshops on their interim drafts, I collected those as well as the group critique sheets they had received. I commented extensively on their drafts, told them what I thought worked well in their essays, pointed out remaining problems, made suggestions for revisions, and returned the complete packages to them for final revisions.

Not surprisingly, perhaps, those writers who had paid close attention to their classmates' comments and questions and addressed them in the revision process revised their drafts quite substantially. Generally speaking, they did much better than the few students who had only minimally revised their rough drafts, apparently paying very little attention to the feedback they received from their peers. I shared this observation with them when handing back their interim drafts and pointed out that, for the most part, there was considerable agreement between the students' commentary and my own. Students proudly received this information, reading it as a confirmation of their growing expertise in a field that they felt they had entered as laypersons. One student actually stated that the group work had helped her to become a better reader, which in turn also helped her to improve as a writer. "I'm beginning to feel like I know what to look for in an essay, what makes an essay work." She added that it was much easier to figure this out reading someone else's draft because she had "some critical distance" to her peers' work, which, after working on her essay for weeks, she felt she no longer had to her own project. At the same time, the writing group allowed her to "borrow the other group members' critical distance to *my* work" and to use their constructive criticism in revising her essay. This experience of the synergy operating in their writing groups strengthened the students' confidence in the group process and prepared them for the second half of the course, in which I would ask them to collaborate not just by reading each other's work but by composing one text as a group. I have more to say about this later. Now I consider the students' success in writing their first essay in connection to the particular kind of messy text they examined in their papers and the considerable amount of time we had spent talking about literary terminology, a topic seemingly unrelated to a first-year course in expository writing.

After reading their final drafts, I was delighted to find that most students had produced quite sophisticated arguments about various aspects of McBride's text. The majority of the essays focused on the question of whether McBride's mother was at fault for not telling her children about her Jewish background or that they were biracial. Student opinions were split down the middle. Interestingly, those who blamed Ruth Jordan McBride for some of the problems her children suffered as a result of her secrecy as well as those who maintained that she did the right thing by shielding her kids from information they could not have digested at an early age made equally strong arguments. Students on both sides of the issue made their case by appealing to the text. Those who blamed Ruth Jordan McBride for her children's problems quoted more from the chapters chronicling the early years of the McBride family. Those who reasoned that the ultimate success of the children as adults proved that their mother made the right decision by withholding information from them quoted primarily the later chapters of the memoir chronicling the achievements of James McBride and his siblings. The group critique sheets reflected this seemingly paradoxical situation: readers would frequently express their disagreement with the opinions expressed by the writer, while at the same praising the author's persuasive use of textual evidence with comments such as "Great quotes!" or "You do a good job of supporting your argument." That one could write a strong essay—and get a good grade—no matter what side of the issue one came down on taught students a valuable lesson about the relative nature and the strategic use of textual evidence and convinced a few diehards that it really was not worth the time or the effort to figure out what the teacher wanted to hear.

Students' self-confidence grew further as they began to realize that critical thinking does not mean simply arriving at some foregone conclusion. This realization—and that they had worked up a critical apparatus and acquired a theoretical language with which to talk about this book—rightly made them feel like experts. This sense of empowerment in turn allowed them to make critical judgments with self-assurance based on the knowledge they had acquired. Students appeared to be more at ease in the writing groups. Their observations of their peers' essays became more substantive, and group critique sheets for the interim draft on the average contained twice as many comments as the critique sheets for the rough draft. The improved group work in turn had a definite impact on the quality of the finished essays.

Students not only backed up whatever claims they made about *The Color of Water* with frequent short quotations from the text—which alone would have filled the writing teacher's heart with joy—but they also substantiated their reasoning about McBride's quest for identity with discussions of how this pursuit shaped the text he produced. The texts of son's and mother's lives—his autobiography and her biography—are, as it were, folded into each other as we read alternating chapters of their life stories. Literary terminology, far from being a matter of mere formality, was linked back to the text in the students' sophisticated discussion of the connections between content and form, between the formation of McBride's identity through the discovery of his mother's history and the dialogical structure of the text.

The connection between content and form and the relational nature of writing also were topics of central importance in our discussion of the second assigned text, Patti Lather and Chris Smithies's *Troubling the Angels: Women Living with HIV/AIDS*. The heart of the book consists of five sections, clusters of stories with such titles as "Life after Diagnosis," "Relationships" and "Living/Dying with AIDS." The stories narrate the day-to-day realities of living with AIDS and trace patterns and changes in the ways these women have made meaning of HIV/AIDS in their lives. The individual stories were transcribed from support group meetings and their poignant titles were chosen from the words of the women—for example, "I'd Probably Be Dead If It Wasn't for HIV" and "It's Taken Me Years to Get Here," the latter referring to a local support group. Each story series is followed by intertexts on angels, which chronicle the social and cultural issues raised by AIDS. As the authors explain, the "angels of the intertexts are intended to serve as both bridges and breathers as they take the reader on a journey that troubles any easy sense of what AIDS means" (xvii). Across the bottom of most of the more than two hundred pages, Lather and Smithies provide a running commentary on their research methods, the theoretical frameworks, and their experience as coresearchers. Through the split-text format Lather and Smithies add to the women's stories "our stories of listening and then telling their stories." They comment on the women's narratives as well as their experience in gathering and digesting the "data" for their study. Scattered throughout the book are some of the women's own writings—poems, speeches, letters, and e-mail—along with angel images and what the authors refer to as factoid boxes, which contain information on such things as the worldwide demographics of HIV/AIDS, gynecological signs of HIV infection in women, and suggestions for further reading. The book concludes with an appendix that includes demographic data on the women as well as a list of references and resources.

As the list of contents suggests and the elaborate page layout attests, Lather and Smithies gather a complex and complicated representation of women with HIV/AIDS in *Troubling the Angels*. As the authors explain in the preface, there simply was no other way for them to put the book together because they no longer felt confident of the "ability/warrant to tell such stories in uncomplicated, non-messy ways" (xvi)—hence the book's postmodern appearance to which I referred previously. Students met this messy text with a great deal of resistance. They felt that the angel intertexts were extraneous and complained that the split-level text and the many inserted factoid boxes were distracting and made any linear reading of the book very difficult and time-consuming. Although to some extent I shared the students' experience of reading *Troubling the Angels* as disjointed and time-consuming, I did not share their sense of frustration. To me it rather seemed like the inevitable and logical result of the author's conviction that it is no longer possible to tell a simple, straightforward story about women with AIDS. I was faced with the difficult task of letting students know that I appreciated their sense of frustration while at the same encouraging them not to mistake the observation that it took a long time to read the book for a critical judgment of the text. Students, it seemed to me, needed to gain additional information to make more informed judgments about the book. How could the students' critical skills be developed without changing the focus of this class from writing and critical thinking to one on postmodern theory and the crisis of representation?

Since the publication of their book, Patti Lather, co-author of *Troubling the Angels*, has published several articles on the theoretical implications of her research on women with HIV/AIDS ("Drawing the Line"). These essays, I felt, provided valuable background information and could help us better understand some of the methodological choices Lather and Smithies made in the course of their study. On the spur of the moment I called Lather, who also teaches at Ohio State, and asked if she would consider talking to my class about her research and the process of writing *Troubling the Angels*. Rather than assigning another library research project, I decided to have students talk to one of the authors directly and to write a critical essay based on their reading of *Troubling the Angels and* the exchange of ideas with its coauthor. To my delight, Lather agreed immediately.

To prepare for Lather's visit, I divided the class into five groups, one of which was to conduct a formal interview with the author during the second half of her visit; the other groups would each write a collective essay presenting a critical analysis of one or more issues that their engagement with *Troubling the Angels* had raised for them. These assignments and the group structure initiated a flurry of in-class activities, which was soon complemented by students meeting outside of class or following up on in-class discussions via e-mail. The interview group needed to brainstorm issues they wanted to raise and to get input from the essay groups. Members of the groups working toward a research paper, in turn, had to make some preliminary decisions about the general direction of their projects so that they could let the interviewers know which kinds of questions they wanted them to pose to Lather. Although members of the interview group at times complained about the amount of time they had to invest in their project at this preliminary stage, they also appreciated the result of this labor-intensive project. Thus, one group member noted: "We all had different ideas about what should be included. There was lots of discussion and compromise, which eventually led to great questions." Another student reported that the group functioned like "a committee without a chair." Although he admitted that this democratic approach "increased the overall time we worked," he proudly concluded that the group process produced an interview "that [did] a very nice job of representing all of our voices." Given this solid preparation, the class was thrilled at the prospect of meeting a "real author," and whatever anxiety students may have had about the anticipated encounter was far outweighed by the sheer excitement the imminent visit generated.

Lather began her class visit with an informal talk about the years of research that eventually resulted in *Troubling the Angels*, which already answered some of the questions students planned to ask. They were quick to think on their feet, however, and began their interview with a series of questions concerning an issue that had surfaced time and again in our discussions of the book: the disjointed nature of the text. Students voiced their opinion that the angel intertexts felt extraneous to a book about women with HIV/AIDS and merely added to the already confusing makeup of the text. In addition, students wanted to know what the women thought of how their stories were represented. Lather freely acknowledged the resistance of some of the women she had interviewed to the format of the book, their insistence on what they called a "K-Mart book," a book that is so accessible to a general audience that it could even be sold at a low-end department store. Although the women did not exactly get their wish, Lather reminded her audience that the book they read was in fact the second text to come out of her involvement with the various support groups. While Lather and Smithies tried to find an academic publisher for their book, they self-published a preliminary version with a less-complicated page layout—but already with the split-level format—at the insistence of some of the women who wanted to see stories in print: "Where's the book? Some of us are on deadline you know."

In spite of what the authors call a member check, giving the women the "opportunity to edit us and themselves" (215), Lather acknowledged that final editing decisions were made by the coauthors. Dissenting voices, however, were not silenced. In fact, the criticism voiced by some of the women became part of the dialogic structure, which actually foregrounds disagreements and conflicts. As the authors put it in their preface, they are well aware that "[t]his is not, perhaps, the book that any of the women would write, but it is an effort to include many voices and to offer various levels of knowing and thinking through which a reader can make their own sense" (xv). As Lather elaborated in her presentation, this approach is a result of their effort to gather a complex representation of women living with HIV infection, rather than deliver the women to the reader in a linear narrative that can be easily consumed and digested. She explained that ultimately the text seeks to create critical awareness in the reader, rather than merely generating empathy for women with HIV.

The students seemed impressed with the amount of thought that had gone into the design of a book, which they, for the most part, had experienced as chaotic. They were perplexed when Lather told them that their frustration at the nonlinear nature of the book was exactly the readerly response the authors had hoped for and that, like them, many other readers and reviewers had been, as Lather put it in the title of an essay about the reception of the book, "drawing the line at angels." That the book was planned confusion rather than arbitrary chaos, however, did not stop students from asking more critical questions about the many stumbling blocks that they felt interfered with their reading of the women's stories.

I was relieved to find that the students also maintained their critical stance as they embarked on their writing projects. I must admit that I had some serious misgivings after one of the groups working on a critique of *Troubling the Angels* informed me that they were changing their thesis. "The group has done a complete 180 after they heard Lather," a spokesperson for the group told me in class. It had not been my intention to get students to toe a party line, to overcome their own objections to a book that I had picked for them and considered to be interesting and worthwhile. Yes, I intended for the author visit to provide them with some important background information on the authors' methodology, but the result I had hoped for was a more informed critical stance, not that nebulous thing still called appreciation in the context of many college courses.

My worries proved to be unwarranted. Perhaps I had simply underestimated the complex influence the structure of *Troubling the Angels* was to have on group discussions and ultimately on the structure of the groups' critical essays. One thing students had definitely learned from the way that disagreements get negotiated between the women and the researchers, as well as among the authors themselves, was that conflict is nothing to be afraid of. This became most evident in the students' statements about the writing process in their groups and the contribution they made to the group essay. On the one hand, these (self-) assessments acknowledged what I have referred to as the synergy effect of writing groups. Thus, one student explained that "[w]riter's block was not a major problem because if we got stuck, one of us was sure to have an idea." On the other hand, these statements also spoke without restraint about their frustrations with the collaborative process, which one student characterized as "much more stressful than doing an individual paper." Another student stated quite bluntly that "it is hard for four people to write an essay when each individual has their [sic] own ideas." The difficulty of condensing several different opinions into just one paper was particularly severe in one particular group, which started with four full-fledged individual papers and then tried to shape these individual efforts into one group paper. Group members, fairly entrenched in their respective positions, initially were not willing to give an inch. One of the members of this group admits that due to the group members' "desire to stick to our own thes[e]s, we made little progress the first week." Eventually, the group decided to scrap their individual essays. The next time they met, each group member brought no more than a page of notes, which they discussed, much like the other groups, as a committee of equals, before they began to compose one collaborative essay. This shift in approach did not resolve all problems, but it minimized frustration and allowed them to fulfill the assignment in a manner that both they and I considered successful. Getting to this point, however, was difficult for each of the groups. One student put it plainly when she stated that "when four people are arguing over the contents of one paper, it is difficult to determine what goes in and what gets left out." She reported that her group "sat down together and discussed the wording and content of every sentence," and she freely admitted that she was "annoyed that not everything I wanted to include could be put in." Nonetheless, this lengthy, time-consuming, and at times frustrating process in the end made for what she proudly called "a better finished product."

In an interesting way, this description of the group process echoes Lather and Smithies, who write in their running commentary that coauthoring a book has not obliterated the differences between them. As Smithies explains, for instance, Lather "writes to expose and confound the complexities of HIV/AIDS; I write to make them more manageable. Ultimately, this book is a manifestation of both of us, and I believe, better for it" (219). It certainly was ironic that although most students wholeheartedly disagreed with this assessment, discussions in writing groups were very much shaped by the author-implied model of collaborative writing. Yet it was precisely this model that helped students to realize that producing a joint text does not necessarily presuppose a consensus, let alone a unanimous stance, on the issues being discussed.

Ultimately, I was quite impressed with the complex structure of the arguments the individual groups presented. All essays had a clear and specific thesis, and, in addition, the authors managed to include opposing points of view, albeit only to discredit them and to ultimately make their arguments even stronger. I also noticed that the initial description of the text as merely chaotic was gradually replaced by a quite sophisticated discussion of feminist research strategies with citations of elements in Lather's work that seemed to illustrate such practices. Two representative examples will suffice to illustrate the sophisticated way students integrated the additional information they received from Lather's visit and some of her essays that they obtained from the library on their own.

One group made comparisons between the strategy employed in *Troubling the Angels* and the use of alienation effects in epic theater and particularly in the work of German playwright Bertolt Brecht. Importantly, however, that they now understood, as one student put it, "where the authors were coming from" did not mean that students approved of their strategies or deemed them successful. Students acknowledged that the additional information they had received helped them to understand the theoretical underpinnings of the book. At the same time, however, they questioned what would happen to other readers who did not have the advantage of gaining insight into the authors' motivation for deliberately making their book disjointed and difficult to read. Many students admitted that if they had not been required to read the book for class—and write an essay on it—they most likely would have put it down in frustration after a few dozen pages. They used this frank admission to initiate a complex argument about the importance of audience and the ways in which the book's format, while making sense in terms of the theory behind it, actually runs contrary to the uppermost goal of the authors: to inform as many people as possible about the lives of women with HIV/AIDS. They argued quite persuasively that "if the format of the book is causing the public to discontinue reading the study after just a few pages, the authors will not attain their objectives." After all, what good is the best theory if your audience either does not get it or simply does not care enough about it enough to commit themselves to the frustrating experience of reading a text shaped by this theory?

Another group took issue with Lather's notion that the book's layout—the split-level format of the text, the angel interchapters, and the factoid boxes—was ultimately successful because, rather than merely generating empathy for the women and their stories, it fosters the readers' critical engagement with AIDS as a global social problem. These students took issue with this argument on both counts. They argued that the readers' critical awareness was hindered rather than encouraged by the text's layout. Thus, they noted that although PCP is first mentioned on page 21, it is not defined as a form of pneumonia associated with AIDS until page 97 and dryly concluded that "[a] fact box containing this definition would be useful on the page where PCP is first mentioned." Citing this and similar examples, the students contested the idea that the text's postmodern layout necessarily helped them to produce critical awareness.

More important, however, they also took issue with the idea that generating empathy for the women represented in *Troubling the Angels* is inevitably a bad thing. They agreed that "[a]s the reader becomes emotionally involved in the women's stories, he/she finds it distracting to stop and read the other sections" of the text. Citing their own experience as readers, however, they argued that this "distraction," far from making them want to engage the text on a more intellectual level, actually made them want to put down the book altogether. Their essay makes a passionate case for the distinction between empathy and pity and argues that "empathy with the women" was their way of approaching the topic of AIDS, a problem they freely admitted none of them had thought about much in the past. The solution they suggested both surprised and delighted me. Rather than wanting to do away with the extraneous and distracting material altogether, they proposed reorganizing the book "into three different parts": "The commentary, in its entirety, should be presented first, followed by the support group interviews. Finally, the facts and statistics should conclude the study." Although the majority of group members were not particularly interested in the first and third parts of the suggested structure, the group as a whole nonetheless recommended that these components be retained for those who might be interested in them and have more use for the information contained in them. They carefully and conscientiously engaged Lather's explanation of her research methodology and the theoretical underpinnings of the study. They responded to Lather's ideas by suggesting a more democratic organization of the material, which differs decisively from the way of reading the authors seek to impose through the layout of the book. This reorganization of the material, they maintained, would cater to a more diverse audience—including, I might add, those well versed in AIDS discourse or the critique of empathy in the humanities and the social sciences as well first-year college students for whom empathy constitutes a valid and valuable approach to the AIDS problematic. Rather than swallowing the theory they were fed, they were doing battle with it. Instead of speaking theory "with profound fluency," they were wrestling with the angels in more ways than one.

The nature of the two assigned texts, and of *Troubling the Angels* in particular, illustrated for students how questions of authority, ownership of ideas, and writers' goals can be negotiated in productive ways. Thus students were quick to make connections between the disagreements between the coauthors of *Troubling the Angels* and among the authors and the women whose stories they tell on the one hand and their own negotiations in the writing workshops on the other. "We argued at least as much as Lather and Smithies argued with each other and the women in their book," one student wrote in her reflective statement, "but we made it work." A central aspect of their formation as writers was the connections students made between their experience as readers of messy texts and their experience as members of a writing group working on a collaborative project. An ideal text speaks in a unified voice, which obliterates any trace of its own genesis. In contrast, the messy texts I assigned make the disagreements and conflicts that occurred in the course of their production a central part of the stories they tell. This had a direct impact on my students. Rather than being afraid of differing opinions and potential conflict, they learned how group goals get negotiated within a writing group setting by reading books, which modeled different kinds of conflict resolution for them. The text they produced may have been more traditional than the assigned reading, but students did not shy away from the messy process it took to compose their texts.

Although teaching messy texts may be one way of honoring what Elbow has called the "rich messiness of learning and teaching," collaborative writing projects are perhaps the best way to make this messiness productive in the teaching of writing. In many ways, the students' praxis constitutes their attempt to apply the theoretical ideas they gleaned from their study of messy texts to their own practice as writers. The quality of their essays as well as the ideas expressed in their reflective statements on the group experience suggest that we need to both reconsider the practice of teaching "ideal texts" and to reconceptualize writing groups to facilitate not just group critiques of individual work but also groups working together on collaborative writing projects.

Works Cited

Alexander, Mary S. "The Art of Teaching Students to Think Critically." *Chronicle of Higher Education* 6 Aug. 1999: B9.

Britzman, Deborah P. "On the Difficulties of Education from the Vantage of the Klein/Freud Controversies." Lecture given at The Ohio State University. February 11, 2000.

Elbow, Peter. *Embracing Contraries: Explorations in Learning and Teaching*. New York: Oxford UP, 1986.

Hall, Stuart. "Cultural Studies and Its Theoretical Legacies." *Stuart Hall: Critical Dialogues in Cultural Studies*. Eds. David Morley and Kuan-Hsing Chen. New York: Routledge, 1996, 262–75.

Kingston, Maxine Hong. *The Woman Warrior: Memoirs of a Girlhood Among Ghosts*. New York: Vintage, 1975.

Lather, Patti. "Drawing the Line at Angels: Working the Ruins of Feminist Ethnography." *International Journal of Qualitative Studies in Education* 10.3 (1999): 285–304.

Lather, Patti, and Chris Smithies. *Troubling the Angels: Women Living with HIV/AIDS*. Boulder: Westview/Harper, 1997.

Marcus, George. "What Comes (Just) after "Post"? The Case of Ethnography." Eds. Norman K. Denzin and Yvonna S. Lincoln. *Handbook of Qualitative Research*. Thousand Oaks: Sage, 1994, 563–74.

3. WRITING GROUPS, MESSY TEXTS

McBride, James. *The Color of Water: A Black Man's Tribu*
New York: Riverhead, 1996.
Penfield, Elizabeth. *Short Takes: Model Essays for Compo*
Longman, 1999.

Appendix A

Honors English 110: First Year Composition
Group Critique Sheet

Author: Essay #:
Respondent:
Draft:

The thesis of this essay is:

+	−	?

CHAPTER FOUR

༄༅

Bringing the Writing Center
Into the Classroom: A Case Study
of Writing Groups

Julie Aipperspach Anderson
Baylor University

Susan Wolff Murphy
Texas A&M University-Corpus Christi

Humble Beginnings

At the end of "A Defense of Dualism," reprinted in *Landmark Essays on Writing Centers* (1995), Dave Healy raises the possibility of using writing center tutors in classroom workshops: "Why can't some of what tutors do with writers take place in the composition classroom? On writing workshop days, tutors could join the instructor in circulating around the room and doing short conferences" (189). Healy suggests that this process will reduce the distance between the writing center and the classroom. When we began working on a writing group outreach project in the spring of 1998, our initial desire was to address the writing concerns of students in an introduction to literature course. What we realized as we implemented the writing groups program in other writing classes is that our program meets the needs of students even as it increases the visibility of the writing center's mission. We believe that our writing center workshops are successful for several reasons: students' power as writers is increased, tutors are able to gain classroom experience, and teachers become informed of writing center practices and are encouraged to use these practices in their own classrooms. Fundamentally, these workshops expand the relationship between students and teachers to include writing center tutors, and because tutors apply writing center theory in the classroom, they replicate the non-

47

judgmental and nonthreatening environment of the writing center that encourages students to express their writing concerns. As important as it might be for the writing center to be distinct and separate from the authority and organization of the traditional classroom, creating opportunities of communication between teachers, students, and tutors benefits all in the long run. Bringing the writing center into the classroom encourages students to access the center and encourages teachers to trust the center and, perhaps, use tutoring techniques with their students. This program also encourages tutors to build relationships with more students and to recognize the different dynamics involved in group tutoring and one-to-one tutoring. This study provides both the practical and pedagogical background that writing centers need to implement writing groups as a successful program of any writing center.

Scholarly Context

Using writing groups in the classroom has become an increasingly popular teaching strategy during the last thirty years, but as Anne Ruggles Gere points out, they are "both old and new" (4). Writing groups have existed inside and outside the classroom for hundreds of years in a variety of forms to serve a variety of functions (Gere 11). In the last thirty years, however, there has been an increasing amount of agreement concerning the socially constructed nature of knowledge and thus a rise in the popularity of strategies (including writing groups) that allow students to negotiate meaning in a community. Bruffee argues that working in groups on their writing allows students to operate in the social context of conversation to improve their writing processes, to become fluent in the academic conversation, and to construct meaning together. This action by students somewhat decenters the teacher's authority, so students learn by teaching each other, discussing ideas, and debating issues. Gillespie and Lerner, in a brief overview of movements and shifts in composition theory, state quite succinctly, "[W]riting and learning require us to interact with others" (13). Peer response groups allow in-class time for students to practice their critical thinking strategies in conversation prior to putting them in writing.

Yet some teachers take issue with Bruffee's claim that "[students] converse about and pursuant to writing" (94). Teacher frustration may stem from students resisting the idea that meaning is socially constructed or that their view of reality is not the only right one. Students' frustration, their resistance, or both, may actually result from an inability to converse productively about writing. Regardless of the cause, however, lack of student cooperation in groups creates a lack of focus that may cause chaos, bruised egos, lack of progress, and more student frustration. Bringing writing center tutors into the classroom to facilitate peer writing groups is one answer to these problems. Tutors can model the process of peer critiquing, can keep the conversation focused on the writing activity, and can empower students to revise. The authority of the tutors is undeniable; it helps them keep groups on task. Still, tutor authority can be mitigated by strategies such as Brooks's minimalist tutoring or those outlined in Gillespie and Lerner's *The Allyn & Bacon Guide to Peer Tutoring*.

Using writing center tutors in the classroom can emphasize process as long as the tutors are trained to work with writers and their skills rather than on the finished product. Increasingly, the focus of many writing centers has shifted from correctness and grammar instruction to writing as process—teaching students how to write academically on their own rather than to be dependent on the center. Tutors trained in minimalist tutoring strategies (Brooks) can start at the student's point of need and insist on student-focused and student-directed interaction, while restricting that focus to writing and the written product under investigation. To prevent tutors from being teachers, they must use nonprescriptive, minimalist tutoring strategies to distinguish their authority from the teacher's authority.

Writing centers have used classroom workshops to a variety of ends; they usually entail an effort to publicize the writing center's availability to a greater number of students by addressing a specific teacher's or course's need. A few of these are described in Kinkead and Harris's *Writing Centers in Context*, which demonstrates the primary characteristic of writing centers: they are all unique. Most of the workshops discussed seem like hosted mini-lessons on writing, taught by either writing center administrators or tutors. Thus, although these examples do introduce writing centers to students, the tutors in these programs maintain an instructor's status as writing expert, and thus maintain their distance from students. The workshops in Kinkead and Harris do not seem to be writing groups like ours that incorporate tutors as pseudo peers to model and facilitate the group's processes within the classroom.

Method

Because this study has been a process of retrospection and reflection, and not a predesigned case study, the method is constrained by factors of time, distance, personnel changes, and lack of audiotapes of groups. When this book on writing groups was proposed, we sat down and constructed from memory the workshop's development in the writing center at our university during the past two years. To augment our memories of the evolution of the workshop program, we interviewed a random selection of the tutors and the coordinators who had participated in the program from its inception. We also spoke with the faculty director concerning the program's history and reception. Unfortunately, we were unable to contact any students from the first semesters of the program's development. However, informal feedback from students, via tutors and instructors, indicated that students found the workshops beneficial.

In addition, we referenced the writing center database for the actual (as recorded) numbers of students served, workshops held, and so on (see Appendix A). We reviewed writing center theory about group tutoring, taking the writing center into the classroom, and how issues of authorship and authority are negotiated in consultations. By these methods, we hope to triangulate our account of the workshop development with the perspectives of other members of our department and writing center. Although we do not have a specific means to measure the success of the workshops, our measures of success primarily can be divided into the following six categories:

1. Demand for workshops by instructors
2. Return visits to writing center by workshop participants
3. Testimony of tutors involved in workshops
4. Testimony of instructors requesting workshops
5. Our observation of workshops
6. Meeting of writing center and teacher goals during workshops

The testimony and observations are measures in at least two ways: they say the workshops are successful, and the reports of events demonstrate whether or not writing center goals, teacher goals, or both, are met.

Program Development—First Year

We have been graduate student coordinators of the writing center, tutors, teachers of the introduction to literature course, and teachers of rhetoric and composition. At the time of this study, the writing center is located in the department of English in a large south-central state university. It is staffed by graduate students of English, who occasionally have been teachers of rhetoric and composition, technical writing, or introduction to literature. Although these tutors are invested with the authority of being English graduate students (and sometimes part-time teachers), they are trained in Brooks's minimalist tutoring techniques and thus attempt to be nondirective in their tutoring interactions. The writing center has a faculty advisor (director), but his purpose is primarily one of oversight. The majority of the daily administrative work is handled by the two graduate students, who apply for yearly appointments to be writing center coordinators.

During the spring of 1998, Julie was teaching an introduction to literature course, and, although her students should have met the prerequisite of rhetoric and composition, most of them were not prepared for the writing assignments. After a concise overview of basic writing issues, she realized that her students needed specific assistance with their papers—attention that could only be gained from one-to-one conferencing. Due to time constraints and the large number of students, she could not meet with each one of them in this manner nor could she require each student to arrange for writing center tutoring (it's against the writing center policy to require attendance at a tutorial). When we talked about these students' writing concerns, we realized that we could bring the writing center into the classroom by combining peer workshops with writing center tutorials.

The primary pattern for all the workshops was established in an introduction to literature class in the spring of 1998. The students were organized into groups of four or five with one writing center tutor. After the students read aloud a complete draft of their papers, they could express any concerns that they had with these papers. Each peer in the group was required to provide at least two positive comments and two constructive criticisms. The peers could immediately address the issues that the author expressed, or the peers could respond to other writing issues. Since the peers did not have copies of each paper, they were encouraged to take notes on the thesis, organization, and strength of the argument. All the peers were required to respond to the paper before the writing center tutor did, but the peers could ask the tutor for advice or clarification as the peers responded. So the tutors (at least theoretically) worked from the minimalist perspective to ensure that the students maintained control over the writing groups. Once all of the peers offered their criticisms, the tutor could provide a wrap-up of the discussion and note any major issues that the peers did not mention. In this way, the tutors could offer end notes to each paper as a means of transitioning from one student's essay to another's.

Program Development—Second Year

The success of the workshop pilot in the spring of 1998 encouraged the writing center coordinators to advertise the workshops in the fall of 1998 to the English department as a whole. The writing center sent out a memo describing its workshops. Five instructors held eight workshops that semester (see Appendix A). Each served between 20 and 32 students. Out of a total of 660 students (in 1,025 sessions) that semester, 137 were participating in workshops; 35 students followed up with a voluntary visit to the center. However, the writing center was not prepared for the glitches (particularly in staffing and preparation) it encountered when the program was broadened and the number of participants was increased so dramatically. These glitches are discussed more fully in the "Lessons Learned" section of this chapter.

In spite of the program's growing pains, the writing center continued to offer workshops (now in the absence of either of the authors as administrators) during the spring and summer of 1999. In the spring of 1999, the writing center held 24 workshops, serving 321 students. Despite the writing center having a very limited staff in the summer of 1999, it participated in 7 workshops. Out of 468 visits (235 students) during the summer, 239 were workshop sessions (134 students). Graduate student coordinators during the spring and summer commented primarily on the difficulty of accommodating the demand for workshops (a factor we discuss later).

Program Development—Continuing Without Us

Workshops are now an integral aspect of the writing center's services. Based on our experiences during the development and introduction of our first semester of writing workshops, the writing center has created standard forms for soliciting writing workshops (such as introductory memos and a handout for the writing programs office to include in the standard syllabus for writing classes) and for recording tutor and student participation in the workshops. The current writing center coordinators are committed to training teachers and tutors, so the workshops are as successful as possible. The writing center is overwhelmed with requests for writing workshops from both first-year and experienced teachers to such an extent that the workshops have affected their hours of operation and staffing. As expected, students who participated in workshops during the first few weeks of the semester are seeking the assistance of tutors outside of the classroom. Again workshops are apparently esteemed by teachers and students as a valuable service of the writing center. As seen in Appendix A, the workshops have been very successful in terms of numbers. What we want to share now are the lessons we learned from this program that the numbers cannot tell.

Lessons Learned

In determining how to describe the lessons that we have learned in the process of institutionalizing this program, we are using workshops that have been marked by either their success or disaster (a perception by either tutors, teachers, or writing center administration). Primarily, we are addressing three categories: (1) teacher and tutors agreeing on goals for the workshop, (2) administrators adequately staffing workshops with tutors, and (3) tutors performing inappropriate roles in the classroom.

One of the first lessons we learned concerning the workshops is the agreement between teachers, tutors, and students about goals for the workshops. For example, one of the five teachers who held the most successful workshops during the fall of 1998 came to a writing center staff meeting in advance to speak directly to the tutors who would be visiting her class. We believe that the agreement between instructor and tutor feedback after the workshop was guaranteed to occur because the instructor provided the tutors with specific goals. At the staff meeting, she announced that she was dividing her students by preparation level, and she surveyed tutors to see who preferred working with a complete draft versus an outline or brainstorming. Rather than a general goal being defined for the entire class, each group defined its own goals by its level of preparation. The success of this workshop, however, was in effect guaranteed because teacher, tutors, and students shared common goals that were explained before the workshop.

In contrast, a less successful workshop occurred at an even earlier stage of development. In the first class to use our model, the immediate response to one of the workshops by one tutor and her group of students was quite positive. When the instructor evaluated those students' papers for a grade, she realized that global issues (both content and writing) had not been addressed by the writing group (the students later informed the instructor that the group had worked only on editorial concerns, and it was never clear how much the students learned from this emphasis on local revision). Thus, from the instructor's perspective, that particular writing group was not as successful as other writing groups that dealt with global issues. Perhaps, had agreement between teacher and tutor goals been established before the workshop, the teacher could have emphasized her interest in her students' global writing concerns.

The second lesson that we learned as we expanded the program to meet the needs of more instructors each semester is specific to small or smaller writing centers. Providing tutors for workshops can deplete the writing center of one-to-one tutoring time. In fact, scheduling continues to be one of the most difficult administrative aspects of running this program; most of the graduate student coordinators, past and present, stated this as their primary concern. A current coordinator says that his most stressful administrative hazard is simply "coverage of bodies/man hours available," to cover the demand for workshops (Cornish). The writing center faculty director makes the following comment:

> [Workshops] take staff away from our primary mission which is face to face [tutoring] ... when you get a lot of requests, you can't turn people down. But to have one person in the writing center and everyone else at a workshop [is not acceptable either]. We need to find a way to balance workshops with face to face stuff so the face to face is weighed more heavily. (Holcomb)

The number of tutors that our writing center has changes each semester, and often there is not enough staff to keep the writing center open while classes are hosting workshops. Thus, the writing center is often closed when it would normally be open.

A fall, 1998, workshop demonstrates the importance of the first two lessons; when we evaluated this workshop in terms of its success, there was an interesting disparity between teacher and tutor feedback. The instructor requested four tutors, and we could supply only three. There were, then, five groups in the class, two led by the instructor (she bounced back and forth), and three led by writing center tutors. The tutors claimed that the students left alone were not productive, but the instructor seemed very pleased with the outcome. The disparity between tutor and teacher assessment was partly based on their lack of established goals for the workshop. This factor was noted by one of our most experienced workshop tutors: "Teachers should prepare the classes before the tutors arrive. They should have their students do group work at least once. Teachers should model the kind of behavior they want [to see]" (Cardenas). This tutor's observations illustrate the necessity of teachers and tutors to communicate the goals of each workshop before tutors come to the classroom and the importance of adequate staffing. Despite these complications, tutors still participate in as many workshops as possible, perhaps because, as a previous coordinators comment, tutors have "higher morale [after workshops] than during regular sessions" (Weber) and "[workshops are] a really good deal for everyone concerned" (Cornish). This attitude by tutors and administrators encourages both to overcome the limitations of the developmental nature of our workshop program. Naturally, there are also situations that should be avoided.

The convenience of having tutors in the classroom may encourage teachers who are uninformed about tutoring practices to ask tutors to participate in unpleasant experiences of exploitation. When tutors are asked to perform inappropriate roles in the classroom during workshops, students, tutors, and even teachers can become very frustrated. For example, one instructor asked the tutors to act as substitutes for her class, which the coordinators prevented at the last minute. This substitution is problematic because the authoritative nature of the teacher's role contradicts the tutor's role in the writing center. In addition, many tutors are inexperienced as teachers and are not comfortable assuming this authoritative position. Another example of such exploitation occurred when a teacher asked the writing center tutors to workshop with students just after she handed back graded papers. She asked the tutors to act as interpreters for her comments and grades to help the students begin their revision processes, but one tutor described this as, "traumatic and not very helpful" (Sherwood). These situations led us to develop policies for teacher training by the writing center before workshops occur to ensure that tutors would not be placed in uncomfortable or inappropriate situations.

Requisites for Successful Workshops

The success of the writing center workshops is not the sole responsibility of the students, the teacher, or the tutors. When one of these participants doesn't know what to do before, during, and after the workshop, the workshop can be a disaster for everyone. As Appendix B demonstrates, hazards are as numerous as benefits. Therefore, it is important for administrators to focus on training and communication with teachers. For writing center workshops to be successful all three participants must be trained and prepared: the students, the tutors, and the teachers.

Before a workshop can be successful, the teacher must practice certain pedagogies that create an environment that builds the necessary relationships for group work. A teacher must begin establishing relationships between students prior to the introduction of writing center tutors to the classroom. For example, students could regularly work in groups to discuss the readings before the lecture. Because students would be required to teach the rest of the class about their responses, they would become accustomed to staying focused on their group's assignment. How an instructor teaches a class to value and use group work is an individual decision. But when students are used to working in groups, they learn to depend on each other to share the work load and to trust each other to provide good work. Also, the more experience they have working in groups, the better their analysis and generative skills become. Of course, an instructor does not need to use group work at every class session, but she must do so often enough that the students are comfortable with the instructor's expectations and are not discussing weekend plans or tests in chemistry.

Like the students, tutors also need special training for a successful workshop. This training must come from two directions: the writing center administration and the teacher. The workshops are based on a minimalist tutoring philosophy. The tutor should encourage the peers to discuss the writing issues with the author before offering any comments. Sometimes, the tutor can generate questions for the peers to answer to help the peers get started on their critiques. Once the peers have demonstrated that they are finished, the tutor provides the author with a summary of the writing issues discussed and how the author can begin the revision process. The tutor can also make suggestions for the paper that the peers did not mention as additional feedback.

The tutors are meant to be guides for the peers; the tutors can be pseudo peers in the group and model constructive criticism. For example, if peer response to the first student paper is minimal to nonexistent, the tutor can ask the peers generative questions to encourage discussion, such as, "How is the thesis sentence specific?" or "How are the paragraphs related to the thesis?" After a tutor has modeled this exploration of one student paper, the tutor can request that the peers replicate the processes demonstrated. However, the tutor should not be directive, except in prodding the peers to offer solid criticism. In this manner, the writing center tutors maintain the nonevaluative role in the classroom that they demonstrate in one-to-one sessions in the writing center.

Tutors also have better experience with writing workshops when they have some training in teaching strategies. Many of our writing center tutors have not taught before, and, although they are very excited to be in the classroom, they also are very aware of their own limitations. Practically, tutors need training in how to offer generative discussion questions when the peers are unable to offer specific feedback on a paper. Tutors also need to be prepared to handle time constraints. In our writing center, most tutorials last almost an hour. When the tutors are working in writing groups, they need to know how to focus on a student's paper quickly and provide the best feedback to ensure that each student has equal time during the one-hour workshop. Or tutors need to be prepared to keep students occupied for the entire length of the workshop so that their group does not disrupt other groups that are still reading and analyzing papers. These are strategies that teachers with only one or two semesters' worth of experience should know how to handle without thinking, but tutors without teaching experience may be uncertain of their authority to keep students on track and productive.

The tutors also need training from the teacher hosting the writing center group. Depending on how the instructor sets up the writing groups, all members of one group of students may be less experienced writers, whereas another group may consist of more experienced writers. Also, tutors are not provided with the same information about the classes' writing concerns or issues that the teacher knows firsthand from evaluating essays. Thus, tutors need to know what global writing issues to emphasize in the peer groups. Teachers should also inform tutors about their grade criteria, the requirements of the writing prompt, and the parameters of the writing assignment. To prepare tutors, we request that instructors meet with the writing center staff to describe the following three items:

1. The specific writing needs of their students
2. The expectations of the assignment
3. The goals for the workshop

We also ask for a written handout of their requirements or goals for the day that can be distributed to students and tutors. Students who have not learned to value the contributions and opinions of their peers in group work generally do not come prepared, resist input of their peers, and rely too heavily on the feedback of the tutor. The more informed the tutors are concerning the writing process that is occurring in the teacher's classroom, the better the tutors can help students succeed on the assignment and become better writers.

Just as tutors and students need to be prepared for successful writing center workshops, so do the instructors who host the workshops. Much of this training can come from writing center administration. During our writing program's orientation for new graduate teachers, the writing center informs the new teachers of the various services available to them. For example, the writing center staff demonstrates how the tutorial process works in the writing center and describes the procedure for organizing writing workshops. The combination of presenting these two services together allows teachers to see how their students will be tutored both in and out of the classroom. However, teachers also need to be taught how to divide their students into groups, how to prepare their students for group work, and how to prepare their students for giving constructive peer feedback during a writing workshop. Teachers also need to visit the tutors before a writing center workshop so that tutors are aware of the writing issues (both of content and form) that shape the assignment and goals of the class.

Appendix C provides a brief listing of guidelines that demonstrates one way to establish effective communication by teachers and writing center tutors and administration. Appendix D may be used by tutors or teachers during a workshop to record student attendance and provide helpful hints and directions for the activity. These forms can obviously be modified to meet the needs and preferences of individual instructors and writing centers.

Implications

Perhaps one of the best advantages of the workshops is that they provide the writing center with some form of assessment early in the semester. The return of workshop students to the writing center (see Appendix A, Column 5) and the requests from teachers for a second or third workshop provide positive feedback (as indicated by Appendix A, Columns 3 and 4, the number of workshops is always more than the number of teachers requesting them except in one instance). These workshops can also contribute to a professional development program for tutors; as one writing center coordinator notes, "The groups are training for the consultants who will become teachers" (Cornish). The tutors gain class-room experience, which some may not have.

Bringing writing center tutors into peer groups facilitates the writing and revising process without subverting the students' control of the groups. We believe that writing groups are an effective means for modeling the kinds of critiques (positive feedback, generative questions, content and form comments) that students need to learn how to give each other and which they must also learn to apply to their own papers. Constructing writing groups with minimalist tutors allows students to gain and maintain authority over ideas and language. By defining the tutors' positions in the classroom as writing center staff, teachers can participate as tutors as well when they become a tutor for a writing group. By establishing clear goals for the workshops, teachers and tutors narrow the gap between traditionally isolated sites of learning—the classroom and the writing center. When writing center pedagogy and practice are blended in a classroom, students have greater access and opportunity to become better writers. Teachers, also, gain access to these writing center principles that they might otherwise not have encountered. Like all writing center activities, introducing workshops into the classroom is not a static structure but a dynamic interaction that begins at the teacher's, tutor's, and student's points of need.

Works Cited

Brooks, Jeff. "Minimalist Tutoring: Making the Student Do All the Work." *Writing Lab Newsletter* 15.6 (1991): 1–4.

Bruffee, Kenneth A. "Peer Tutoring and the 'Conversation of Mankind.'" *Writing Centers: Theory and Administration*. Ed. Gary A. Olsen. Urbana: National Council of Teachers of English, 1984. 3–15. Rpt. in *Landmark Essays on Writing Centers*. Eds. Christina Murphy and Joe Law. Davis: Hermagoras, 1995. 87–98.

Cardenas, Diana. Personal Interview. September 27, 1999.

Cornish, James. Personal Interview. September 27, 1999.

Gere, Anne Ruggles. *Writing Groups: History, Theory, and Implications*. Carbondale: Southern Illinois UP, 1987.

Gillespie, Paula, and Neal Lerner. *The Allyn and Bacon Guide to Peer Tutoring*. Boston: Allyn and Bacon, 2000.

Healy, Dave. "A Defense of Dualism." *Writing Center Journal* 14.1 (1993): 16–30. Rpt. in *Landmark Essays on Writing Centers*. Eds. Christina Murphy and Joe Law. Davis: Hermagoras, 1995, 79–190.

Holcomb, Chris. Personal Interview. September 27, 1999.

Kinkead, Joyce A., and Jeanette G. Harris, eds. *Writing Centers in Context*. Urbana: NCTE, 1993.

Sherwood, Matthew. Personal Interview. September 27, 1999.

Weber, Ellen. Personal Interview. September 27, 1999.

Appendix A

TABLE 4.1
Writing Center Records

Semester	Total Students[1]	Students in Workshops	Total Workshops	Number of Teachers	Repeat Students[2]
Spring 1998	343	49	4	2	10
Summer 1998	94	21	1	1	0
Fall 1998	660	137	8	5	35
Spring 1999	903	321	24	13	79
Summer 1999	235	134	7	4	29
Totals	2235	662	44	25	153

[1]This figure reflects the total number of students who attended the writing center.

[2]This figure is the number of sessions held in the writing center with students who had attended workshops in their classes.

Appendix B: Benefits and Hazards

Benefits

- Creates a team between teachers and the writing center
- Introduces students and teachers to specific writing center consultants, thereby reducing the distance between classroom and center
- Intervenes on site in the writing process
- Allows tutors to model peer critique, spotting which issues have been avoided or missed by the students' peers
- Keeps students on track, making sure everyone participates and comments before the tutor contributes; turns questions back to the group

- Introduces students (and sometimes teachers) to the nonjudgmental (friendly) tutoring strategies of a writing center, reducing the fear of remediation or simply exposing a draft to public view

Hazards

- Students need to be trained to work in peer response groups before workshop groups will be effective (student driven)
- Tutors cannot be brought in to interpret teacher grades or comments(thereby becoming the voice of the teacher and not a consultant)
- Tutors cannot act as substitutes for an absent teacher
- Teachers must make the goals of the session clear to both students and tutors (brainstorming, thesis statement, final editing)
- Tutors are not full participants in the collaborative process because they do not bring their own writing to the group
- Insufficiently trained tutors might try to be friends rather than guides, allowing the writing task to be set aside in favor of casual conversation (in a repeated group this might work, but not in a one-time visit)

Appendix C: Introducing Workshops

1. Address staffing issues. Make sure you can spare three to four tutors during tutoring periods. Tutors will probably volunteer times they do not normally work and take themselves off the work schedule for time worked outside the center.

2. Train tutors in peer group (as opposed to one-to-one) conferencing. Teach them time management to ensure each student gets equal time. Give them ideas on how to keep groups that finish early working so they don't disturb the other groups.

3. Train tutors in teaching strategies (if strategies are not normally discussed) that can make class time productive if the group does not have paper drafts to read. For example, groups can brainstorm ideas and thesis statements and outline, read, and synthesize source material, or free write or draft individually. If groups finish early, tutors can work one to one while other students begin revising.

4. Have inexperienced tutors observe peer workshops run by experienced tutors.

5. Announce the workshops on a limited basis at first to work out the kinks. Suggest that teachers do peer group work first to get their students used to the process.

6. Have teachers meet with tutors to discuss the goals of the assignment and the workshop and the class's writing concerns.

7. Use whatever forms are necessary to keep track of the workshops, number of students helped, and the tutors involved.

8. Announce the workshops more broadly, but do not overextend your center or your tutors. Have workshops filled on a first-come, first-served basis. It is better to say no than to provide poor service and damage the writing center's reputation.

Appendix D: Sample Writing Workshop Consultant Worksheet

Student Name	Student ID	Points

For attendance, credit for homework, and writing center records, please record the name of the students in your group and determine the amount of work completed by each student on the drafts. Give 5 points for complete drafts, 3 points for approximately one half of a draft, and 1 point for an outline and thesis statement.

Student Name   Student ID

Points

_____   _____

_____

_____   _____

_____

_____   _____

_____

Workshop Directions

- A student should slowly read his or her paper aloud to the group.
- The reader should offer at least one strength and one weakness of the paper. While the student is reading, peers should note aspects of the paper that they like, ones they feel need improvement, and any questions the paper leaves unanswered. They should record their observations on a copy of the draft (if provided) or on a separate sheet of paper.
- Each peer should respond to the reader's paper by offering at least one strength and one weakness. Each peer's response must be different and specific.
- After the peers have evaluated the paper, the consultant should respond to any comments that need reinforcing and also provide one strength and weakness.

Helpful Hints

- Make sure each student's paper receives equal time. The 8 a.m. class ends at 9:15 a.m. and the 9:35 a.m. class ends at 10:50 a.m.
- Keep the students focused on content and writing issues rather than grammatical concerns. Answer their grammar questions, but emphasize the importance of their logic, credibility and support.
- Students with the most amount of writing completed should go first, and students with the least should go last. If a student does not have a draft or has written very little, help the student brainstorm ideas and even ask the student to write for five minutes and then continue with the consultation.
- If the students finish early, have them begin revising their drafts. You may also work with them one to one.

CHAPTER FIVE

ಬಬ

Sponsoring Student Response
in Writing Center Group Tutorials

Magdalena Gilewicz
California State University, Fresno

Talking about writing [in the writing center] gives us more so I kind of know what to talk about.

—student

We can think because we can talk, and we think in the ways we learned to talk.

—Kenneth Bruffee

In writing center group tutorials, where involving students in collaborative negotiation of feedback is one of the fundamental goals, students, not just the tutor, are placed in the role of responders. What we ideally envision in a group setting is a community of writers engaged in an examination of writing, sharing their reactions, asking questions, discussing ways to improve writing, and offering strategies for revision. This is why in classroom instruction we put students in peer group workshops, and this is why in a writing center we may move from one-to-one interchange to, let's say, a three-students-and-one-tutor group, as is done at California State University, Fresno. Group negotiation of writing in a tutorial can be seen as the most vibrant enactment of theories of collaborative learning, where the entrance to the academic discourse takes the form of a more individualized approach than the classroom can offer, more collaborative approach than one-on-one tutoring provides, more mediated approach than peer groups give, and more peerlike interaction than a conference with the teacher offers. If the rationale for tutoring students in groups is to tap into pedagogical advantages the other kinds of instructional settings cannot as successfully address, then the most generalized statement of purpose for tutoring

63

students in groups would be to enhance the teaching of writing by having students learn to respond to each other's work in progress under the guidance and instruction of an experienced writer trained as tutor.

Our current writing pedagogy is based on the assumption that talking about writing will help students produce better writing and become more effective and conscious writers. Response to writing, therefore, has been seen as a valued activity that makes visible the communal or social nature of the construction of meaning, especially if it is based on live interaction, rather than just written response. As teachers and tutors learn how to engage students in the process of writing and how to respond to enhance learning, not as much attention has been paid to teaching students how to respond to writing. Student-teacher conferences and one-on-one tutorials can be seen as modeling of questioning and response that students then would carry over to peer groups (Sullivan 49–52). Those settings, however, do not put the student actively in the position of a responder but only in the position of a recipient of response. Classroom peer group workshops and group tutorials demand that students become active responders. The focus of this paper is the group tutorial, a hybrid species that can be viewed as a cross between peer groups and one-on-one tutorials that dominate as models of peer response in the classrooms and writing centers. In such a tutorial, students not only follow the model of response offered by the tutor but also are offered a chance to practice actively such response by asking questions of each other in a negotiation facilitated and mediated by the tutor.

Since in this kind of tutoring students are exposed to each other's writing, and by design need to get involved in response, how much they know about writing and how much they know about talking about writing are issues that come strongly to the fore. However, because tutoring is most often seen as a one-on-one engagement, tutoring manuals do not address how, together with the writing ability, tutors are supposed to assess and enhance the students' ability to respond. Therefore, the issue of what and how students learn in group tutorials extends beyond the process of writing and involves examination of student reading and responding, both of which demand to be seen, examined, and taught as processes as well.

My observations and findings are based on my work at a writing center at California State University, Fresno—a tutorial service with a twenty-year-old tradition of employing group tutorials where three students from various courses work under the guidance of a tutor in semester-long, twice-weekly, fifty-minute interactions. The rationale for creating this kind of set-up was originally to have students "learn from each other's mistakes" as they looked for surface errors in each other's writing and did grammatical exercises. As the function of writing centers changed across the country from fix-it shops to places where students learn how to become better writers, the role and workings of our writing center were re-examined, and new questions have been asked of the choice of group tutoring as a way to enhance the instruction of writing. However much the decision to base the writing center on groups, rather than individual interaction with a tutor, might have been originally dictated by budgetary and administrative concerns and enrollment advantages, we view the group tutorial now as a collaborative environment where students improve their writing, develop the ability to examine writing critically, and acquire and practice the language of response.[1]

How Student Writers Read and How Student Readers Respond

The ideal for a group tutorial is the same as the one described by Sullivan for peer groups: "Students help students, everybody participates, the writing process is illuminated, products improve dramatically and the community thrives" (58). The mere act of putting students into groups, however, to have them discuss each other's writing will not turn groups into "Burkean Parlors" (to use Lunsford's term), with students, as Gere and Stevens idealistically claim, providing accounts of writing "as teacher comments can at best imitate" (103).[2] We cannot assume that student discussions about writing will produce response for revision. The reality shows us that often not much is accomplished if students are not first actively taught how to read and talk about writing.[3]

Early last semester, Adam, one of the students in my tutorial group, initially denied the need for any help with a draft he had written because, as he said, he had already received feedback from his classmates and knew what he needed to change. When asked what the classmates had suggested, he replied that they praised him for "good details" and told him to correct some grammatical and spelling mistakes. He was satisfied with the response—in fact, the response had confirmed what he had expected— and didn't see the need to put the draft up for another discussion. When he finally agreed to read and let us discuss his draft, it became evident that the paper was a typical first draft limited to the recounting of an event

---

[1]Bruffee's admission that "[f]or American college teachers, the roots of collaborative learning lie neither in radical politics nor in research ... [but rather in] a pressing educational need" holds true as the rationale for establishing CSUF's group tutorial writing center in 1980, however attractive and tempting it may appear to justify its pedagogy now by the validation of collaborative learning by social constructionist theories (Bruffee 637).

[2]Gere and Stevens's study of fifth and eighth graders showed textual concerns similar to those discussed further in this piece (i.e., local issues dealing with word choice and unclear statements) and didn't show any evidence of rhetorical concerns as the researchers claim. If the kind of student response is impressive at an elementary school level, what do we say to the realization that beginning college writers respond basically in the same way?

[3]Spear's extensive study of students' responses in unmediated peer groups strongly supports my observations.

(slashing two friends with a thumb tack and being suspended) without any discernible purpose, reflection, or conceptual context or any conscious awareness of an audience—in a word, it was what Newkirk discovered students called a "story"—that is, "a presentation [not necessarily a narrative] of facts and experiences in which the shaping hand of the writer is not explicitly evident" ("Direction" 307). The other two students in the group duplicated the feedback the writer had already received by pointing out some surface errors and praising him for interesting content. When, as a tutor, I tried to bring in genre concerns and asked the group, "What is the difference between the recounting of events and an essay?" they replied, there wasn't any, stating "An essay is a story." This was on the heels of a two-session discussion of another group participant's paper reflecting on Cynthia Ozick's essay defining this very genre. None of the students in the group, including the student in advanced writing class who wrote on Ozick, could apply the knowledge about the genre to measure the success of the narrative draft. They could not place Adam's writing in such broader discourse context. They resorted to affective identification. When the author ducked my questions about what the experience had taught him, why it was important for him to tell it, and so on, the other two students came to his aid by assuring me that what he described "*really* happens in high schools" and that they knew what feeling peer pressure was like. They identified with the content, which was presented clearly, and didn't see the need to "mess it up." They reaffirmed their entrenchment in the content, superficially answering my questions about audience and purpose by telling me, "He wrote it so that others wouldn't do it and wouldn't be suspended." The questions I posed, which were meant to lead to rhetorical concerns, were deflected by solipsistic responses. My attempt to elicit and then model response for rhetorical concerns was not sufficient. At this early point in the semester, students were not yet willing nor knew how to examine their writing and their reading in new and difficult ways, even though those new ways had been already discussed in their classes and techniques of responding were modeled by the teacher.

My students' inability to adopt the rhetorical concerns I was trying to discuss was related to their lack of knowledge and practice of those conventions of academic literacy. Even though they had been already introduced in their classes to such notions as purpose, main idea, and purposeful organization, those notions were abstract, not internalized as their own concepts and experiences as readers. They did not have the same expectations of the text as readers as I did as a tutor, nor did they have the language to engage these issues in their collaboration. Grimm advocates unmasking what academic culture sees as "natural practices" to help students revise: "When writing center workers learn to address cultural expectations directly and explicitly so that students can understand the values at stake, students can make more informed decisions about how they want to perform" (34). Explaining to my students, however, that those conventions were accepted and expected practices in the academic setting was not enough. The writer chose not to "mess it up" himself—perhaps because he was reassured in his stance by the other two students in the group, perhaps it was easier not to engage my questions, perhaps all three of them refused to move from the clarity of what was already on paper because they didn't know how to make clear what was emerging as potential messiness, and perhaps because they experienced my questioning as unsupportive and not nice, as not the kind of response they would use themselves. The two students (responders) in the group allied themselves with the writer and did not engage his writing seriously as readers.

If we base our classroom and tutoring pedagogy on the assumption that reading and discussing other's writing will help students detect and revise their own, we need to examine what kind of reading ability they bring with them as we put them in peer workshops in classrooms or in group tutorials, heeding Bizzell's call that we need to find out what the students know before we ask them to collaborate (5). Tutors have to be aware of how much students know about the processes of writing, reading, and responding—how students are used to writing and reading, and how they talk about it—before they can consciously involve students in learning how to read each other's writing and in practicing response. Knowledge of how students read will lead us to answer the question of why students initially cannot go beyond global praise and surface corrections.

How Students Read

First, and most obviously, most students who come to the writing center are novice writers, for the first time consistently exposed to and actively practicing the full range of writing tasks that make up the writing process.[4] Whether on the basic or freshman writing level, students are still learning what Phelps calls the "formative attitude" of seeing text as "evolving," open to revision, rather than "self-contained," completed to be evaluated (48).[5] Because they are still seeing text as a product, even when they are told they are dealing only with first drafts, as readers students focus their attention

---

[4]It needs to be noted that many of the generalizations in my paper are based on the student population that the CSUF writing center serves. According to a demographic survey I conducted in the fall 1998 semester, 60% of the students were in the freshman class, 54% were taking a remedial (basic) writing course, 78% were twenty years old or younger, 63% spoke English as a second language, 53% were native born, and for 40% the highest level of at least one parent's education was elementary school, for 22% high school.

[5]Faigley and Witte, Anson, and Chenoweth, among others, discuss inexperienced writers' chief interest in improving mechanics in writing.

on surface-level, local, lower-concern types of problems. Their impulse is to "fix" what they read. Deeper concerns of revision, such as choice of and focus on the topic, purpose, structuring, and so on are not within their field of vision. What they do to their own writing and what they notice in others' writing is propelled by a vision of a final text unfolding linearly, in one direction in time. This one-dimensionality and single-directionality of conceptual perception does not allow them to look much beyond sentence progression. This vision may also encompass skeletal notions of structure, such as thesis presence and placement, paragraph transitions, and minimal audience awareness formed by questions concerning the effectiveness of introductions to "grab" the reader's attention and of conclusions to give the reader a sense of closure. They may also address spots of confusion that require localized attention. Teaching students to consider more global concerns of revision is a long and difficult process both for teachers and for tutors. Therefore, we cannot expect students to discuss these issues spontaneously and without mediation.

Second, most student writers have a very limited repertoire of rhetorical strategies, and as readers they cannot recognize such deep features themselves; therefore, they cannot engage such issues in group discussions of their own writing. Cognitive research into reading processes confirms this experiential claim. In their study of experienced (graduate students) and inexperienced ("average freshman") readers, Haas and Flower found that novices focused their attention primarily on content and their own affective reactions, whereas experienced readers read for content, function, and the rhetorical design of the text. The results showed that whereas both kinds of readers paid about an equal amount of attention to "content strategies" (answering the question "What is the text about?"), and "feature strategies" (concerns dealing with identifying introductions, conclusions, examples), the novices employed "rhetorical strategies" only in 1% of their reading protocols, compared with 13% of the protocols of experienced readers. What the researchers classified as rhetorical strategies were issues of purpose, context, and effect on the audience—deep features of the text that appear as clues and are drawn from the reader's "knowledge of discourse situations [used] to recreate or infer the rhetorical situation of the text [being read]." The researchers also suggest that "[t]here is some indication that these strategies were used to help readers uncover the actual 'event' of the text, a unique event with a particular author and actual effects" (Haas and Flower 251).

The same study also showed interesting findings concerning the readers' ability to recognize stated and implied claims. Of the inexperienced readers, only 33% recognized the claim (main point) as it was explicitly stated in the text for the first time, and all of them recognized it as it was repeated in the following segment of the text. None of the readers in this group, however, recognized the implied claim. In contrast, all of the experienced readers inferred the stated claim by the segment of the text that preceded the actual statement of the claim, and all of them inferred the implied claim by the end of the reading. At the end of their article, Haas and Flower suggest possible parallels between the content ("knowledge-getting") concerns of student readers and the content and information ("knowledge-telling"— Bereiter and Scardamalia's term) concerns of student writers. The study clearly suggests that if students are not familiar with and not able to recognize rhetorical strategies, they will not use them purposefully in their own writing, and as readers and responders in peer or tutorial groups they will not be able to comment on those features of the text.

Because students neither as readers nor as writers are aware of rhetorical features, they are preoccupied primarily with content. Similarly to Haas and Flower's findings, Newkirk establishes that "willingness to identify with the author is a powerful determiner of student response" ("Direction" 304). This "relating" to the author through identifying their own knowledge with the paper's content corresponds to Haas and Flower's affective response and concentration on content-related issues. What students valued and praised was their familiarity and identification with the issues presented in the paper; they approved of its content because it was in some way about them and read in information using their own background, therefore perceiving complexity where it was not to be found. By asking his student subjects to predict the teacher's preferences, Newkirk also discovered that students could not foresee the teacher's judgments and mistakenly saw elaboration (Adam's "good details") as a category most valued by teachers. In response groups the tendency that Newkirk observed results in praising work that deals with familiar topics in familiar ways and in requests for elaboration that does not lead to more complex thinking but only adds bulk.

This preoccupation with content and inability to handle rhetorical material was critically demonstrated in a group I recently tutored. Gerry's essay on what influenced her educational choices ballooned from the required three pages to thirteen as she dutifully addressed all of the questions the teacher raised in margins and in conference and peer students asked in class. The tutorial group discussion, during which both I and the other two students tried to sort through the material to give the paper some focus and direction, was misread by her and contributed to even more elaboration. In another group, Yosef, aware of his peers' tendency to ask indiscriminately for more detail, refused to engage any questions aimed at providing some needed material for clarity of meaning because he predicted that if he answered them, peers would ask him a dozen more questions for details and thus derail his focus. These facts from research and practice leave us with questions about the validity of student response when it comes to dealing with deep textual features required by academic discourse. They also direct our attention to the responsibility tutors working with groups have not only to incorporate such concerns into tutoring of writing itself but also to teach students to become more discerning readers of their peers' papers and more effective responders.

As the last example shows, many students are well aware of the limitations of their own reading and response. In a survey I conducted at the writing center during the tenth week of the Fall 1999 semester asking students to compare their work in tutorials with unmediated peer groups in their classes, students raised the same concerns with peer response researchers raise. In addition to negative general statements about peer groups, such as "students may not know what they are talking about," "we talk about nothing," "[t]hey don't know nothing," students pointed out that their peers "just talk about our grammar errors," "… just correct the work that we did already," "I'm told that I have a great paper with lots of detail and that I only have a few grammar and spelling mistakes." Students also commented on unfounded global praises ("They only tell me it's good," "I get only good comments, not honest") and much lesser engagement with analytical questions: "It [work in peer groups] is easier, it's not as intense as it should be. I think it's because we don't really analyze things carefully enough." On the other hand, they pointed out that, while working in a group with a tutor, their papers are "deeply looked at": "structure," "how to improve ideas," "exploring different routes," understanding the demands of an assignment, and addressing "the whole paper" were the foci they valued. Although this kind of survey may have little research validity, it attests to the gap that students perceived between their own demands for more complex feedback and their peers' preoccupation and comfort with surface-level issues they saw addressed and could themselves address.

Tutor's Roles in a Group Tutorial

The challenge for tutors in group settings becomes threefold. In addition to helping students improve their writing ability, tutors have to monitor and affect the way students read each other's writing and the way they respond. The purpose of my rather lengthy consideration of the ability of students to read and form responses has been to establish some basis that would give tutors an idea of how prepared students are for response in group tutorials: what practical knowledge of process they have, how they construct meaning as they read and what kind of meaning that is, what practice of response they bring from peer groups. A student profile formed by answers to these questions enables the tutor both to make use of the abilities students bring with them and to set goals for actively teaching students how to read and respond, as well as help teach them to become better writers. What sets writing centers that use the group tutoring model apart from the ones that are based on one-on-one tutorials is exactly the opportunity and responsibility to teach and engage students in collaborative response. Since group tutoring writing centers are a rare breed, no specific guidelines exist concerning the training of tutors for running writing response groups. In existing scholarship, what is being said about peer groups, one-on-one tutoring and teacher-student conferencing has to be examined, and whatever is found applicable needs to be applied to fill this gap. As a long-term goal, a group tutoring writing center should also generate its own pedagogical and theoretical discoveries specific to its own species. For now let us look at the implications of the previous discussion for training tutors.

It needs to be stated and taken for granted that the rich pedagogy and ethics developed for one-on-one tutoring (and presented as textbooks and resource books for tutors by Harris, Meyer and Smith, Murphy and Sherwood, Gillespie and Lerner, among many others) in a great measure apply to tutors who work with groups and need not be repeated here. In a group, however, the role of the tutor should evolve from that of the most experienced responder and model to initiator and facilitator of student response and finally to moderator and equal participant in collaborative negotiation. In terms of instructional responsibility, unlike in an individual tutorial, the tutor in a group needs first to help the students become more effective readers, then responders, and eventually step away from the instructional role and become a participating audience member on similar terms with the other students, or perhaps even a mere observer. This gradation of functions implies that, progressively, the tutor needs to let the students become more independent as they learn about writing and the range of revision strategies, as they become better readers of each other's drafts, and as they learn effective response.

From the beginning, students see the tutor in a special role. The survey of students I mentioned earlier in relation to their work in peer groups also showed trust in and comfort with the authority and knowledge of the tutor: "Without my tutor we would not work as hard. I would not put the time and effort to it"; "I feel like I am around a person that knows what they are talking about and have enough knowledge to help me out." Students also stated the tutor's presence made the group focus the discussion on specific writing issues; they perceived the tutor's ability and effort to address higher-level concerns and provide them with strategies for revising: "With a tutor present we are able to see more clearly and find solutions that make our paper better." The tutor's presence gave them license to express their criticism openly: "Maybe [in peer groups] we are afraid to make the person feel bad," "It's hard for me to comment or suggest something on a paper that sounds good to me. It looks way better than mine that I think how could I suggest something when I have very bad paper." The students also noticed the emergence of their own questioning self ("She asks me questions about my paper that I could ask myself to improve the paper") and the emergence of their own language of response ("Talking about writing here gives us more so I kind of know what to talk about"). The tutor in this kind of group setting then is not a co-equal, an equally "knowledge-able" peer, as Lunsford advocates, nor is the tutor in the role of helping the student "find her own answer by questioning rather than telling and explaining," as Harris would see it. The tutor is in the position of a more experienced and knowledgeable reader and responder with the potential to transfer those skills to the other group participants. To involve the group in a productive discussion of each other's papers, the tutor needs to be aware of the reading abilities and habits students bring to the table and consciously undertake the task of teaching students how to become better readers to make them competent responders.

Application

To help students become more effective readers, tutors first need to know how their students read. The most obvious and fundamental step is the same as in helping them become better writers: as readers, too, they have to see writing as a dynamic process, not as a finished product, to move away from mechanical concerns and learn the depth of issues and questions that lead to effective writing. Studies like the one by Haas and Flower show tutors that students already know how to read for content. With novice responders, the danger of stopping with content concerns is, as Newkirk and Spear observed, identification with the paper's content, which leads to unexamined acceptance and global praise or haphazard requests for elaboration not guided by rhetorical concerns with purpose, focus, leading idea, or audience. To steer students away from the pitfalls Newkirk's study implies, and yet still capitalize on their interest in content, tutors need to teach students to embrace the content of the whole paper and move away from local concerns of language surface (spelling, grammar, word choice) and format mechanics (transitions, introduction, conclusion, placement of thesis). Embracing content of the entire paper and its development is a crucial step. It is what experienced readers do in the moment after reading the last words of a paper and before verbalizing a response. It allows for a detachment from the text, holding it and turning it in our minds, taking stock of what is offered. Students must learn to do it too before they can be expected to address issues of rhetorical effectiveness and consider suggestions for revision. This is the foundational step in teaching students the process of forming and articulating a response.

The techniques I examine now that teach readers most effectively to pull away from surface concerns and help them embrace the whole text to examine its workings come from Elbow and Belanoff's *Sharing and Responding—*

a unique and invaluable resource for training both tutors and students in the practice of reading and developing response.[6] The first step is to ask students to verbalize detailed summaries, or what Elbow and Belanoff call "sayback" (22–24), which moves students toward consideration of writing as an extensive utterance, rather than a patching of details they can pounce on. A variation on this technique is moving through the paper and relating what each paragraph "says"—a portion of Bruffee's "descriptive outline" (40–43). These stock-taking responses help students observe writing as a meaning-unfolding event. In my experience, tutors need to insist on getting such content overviews and other kinds of response in writing. Oral responses in a group let students push the responsibility onto others, verbalize in fragments, or abandon the activity altogether. In my survey one student said that the presence of the tutor "gives us a sense of order and inpresinmnet [sic] where you write, think, write, talk then write." To develop actively the language of response, students need to practice it in writing, and tutors need to incorporate writing into tutorials. The presence of a tutor for this practice is important to model the activity of writing the response, to join in as a responder, and, if necessary, to urge the students to write and then share their responses. In writing, students have time and space to articulate their responses individually before they use them as a springboard for group discussion. Even in experienced, well-functioning discussion groups this stock-taking step should not be ignored. In addition to teaching students how to form perceptions of the whole text, it fosters trust in readers as attentive, reliable listeners and allies.

The next step is to observe and describe the effects writing produces in readers. A form of feedback that transitions between the embracing of the whole content and describing how it works on the reader is "metaphorical description" (35–36). Here, students are asked to draw pictures of the writing, give images of the "writer-to-reader relationship," and compare the piece of writing to animals, persons, or weather. It invites playfulness and is initially seen by students as foolish and corny, yet it produces serious and often striking results. Here is an example of one student's

---

[6]In my many years of teaching students how to give feedback, I have found *Sharing and Responding*, which expands on many of Elbow's techniques presented in his *Writing with Power*, to offer the most systematic, practical, and comprehensive gradation of methods to engage students in revision and response. Unfortunately, a valuable section entitled "How a Writer Might Think about This Feedback" was eliminated in all editions following the first one. This section, while perhaps not served by the best examples, pointed to an important step a writer needed to take while engaging in the revision process. What *Sharing and Responding* in its present form lacks is teaching student writers how to analyze and evaluate feedback offered by readers, as well as an illustration of revision decisions made by writers based on received feedback, especially concerning macrostructural issues. My study addresses these issues very briefly; a more sustained study and pedagogy need to be developed regarding feedback reception and revision decisions both for tutoring and classroom settings.

free-written response, followed by consideration of what the image of writing as a meal suggests:

> OK, so I need to decide what kind of a meal this was. It wasn't a special treat at a great restaurant. It was a meal at home, by myself, not any celebration, just everyday meal. The food was not spicy or with any special flavor. The taste was mild, even, no surprises. I see a piece of something covered with white sauce, a lot of white sauce. So much white sauce I'm not sure what's underneath.

> So what does it tell me about this piece of writing? It is clear, I can follow it, but it tells me more or less what I already know. It is very personal, talks about something very dear and expresses the wish of having a friend and that's a feeling I share. But I would like the writing to surprise me more, or tell me something I haven't thought about, give me something new to take from it, some surprising taste, not just that white sauce.

Another student in the group compared the writing to a "burrito filled with refried beans," and the writer herself saw it as a meal she "whipped up quickly" using "whatever [she] found around." If not treated as a game played for its own sake, this kind of response helps students to create three-dimensional images of writing and to see writing as an event. It can also move students toward consideration of rhetorical factors, such as the writer's attitude toward the topic and task, of audience and purpose. Writing and sharing of such feedback anchors the discussion it further generates, justifies comments and suggestions, and provides distance from both the author and the text.

One of the most powerful and extensive ways to record the readers' reactions is through "movies of the reader's mind" (Elbow and Belanoff 30–35). In this feedback readers are asked to record their reactions ("what's going on in their heads") as they go through the text. It makes them see writing as "doing" something to them, realize their expectations, predictions, identify their stance toward the text, locate areas that cause given reactions (like confusion), as well as substantiate a general sense of satisfaction or dissatisfaction with the text. These and other excellent forms of reader-response-based feedback Elbow and Belanoff propose train students to become careful, discerning readers conscious of how the writing works on forming their reactions and responses. They lay a deep and solid foundation for collaborative discussion of writing in a group tutorial, systematically teaching students to become perceptive readers, helping them develop the language of response they then further apply and practice in discussion.

Such extended forms of descriptive response help the tutor and students eventually get at the difficult rhetorical concerns of establishing purpose in writing, finding and controlling focus, negotiating needs and expectations of the audience. The tutor needs to help the group extend descriptive feedback into such rhetorical questions and strategies for revision, help them build what Flower, Hayes, Carey, Schriver, and Stratman call "strategic knowledge" (226). The food metaphors, for example, initiated a complex discussion about why the writer chose her best friend as the topic, how she could address the audience's negative reactions, what material was worth keeping, what others could learn from her piece, and so forth.

Addressing rhetorical concerns, what Flower et al. call "macrostructure issues," requires the presence of a tutor. The difficulty of examining such issues by inexperienced writers and readers by themselves makes them abandon the task before it is examined in depth, either because of frustration or because they cannot gauge at what point an issue is satisfactorily exhausted. The tutor in a group monitors and focuses students' progress with such demanding issues, pursuing questions until the author and the readers are able to arrive at a solution. Involving other students in such questioning pursuit, having them witness where it leads and how far it can be extended helps them repeat such procedures later. Adam, the author of the thumbtack-slashing paper I mentioned earlier, who refused to engage the question of purpose initially, brought up the concern himself later in the semester. Practiced in descriptive responses, he was now part of a discussion where I as a tutor was pursuing the issue of purpose with another student. Having a much broader and richer sense of himself as an audience, he was participating in a discussion aimed at helping another writer realize purpose in her writing. The crucial moment for Adam's development as a writer, as well as a reader, came when in the middle of our group negotiation over another student's paper he discovered that the questions we were asking of the author were the same questions that I had tried to apply to his paper earlier in the semester without success. Playing now actively the part of an audience, he realized the relevance and need of addressing the same questions in his own writing. That's when he made the most substantial revision in his own paper—after he became a more experienced and demanding reader, conscious of what writing contains and how it works on the audience.

As students become aware of the importance of rhetorical issues, they need crucial help from the tutor in deciding where and how in their writing such issues need to be addressed. Dealing with this issue in a discussion also shows the tutor how deeply the students have internalized those concerns. Three quarters through the semester, having been exposed to macrostructure issues, another student in a group I observed assessed her learning in the following way:

> I feel that my writing has changed a lot. I can tell because when I write, I look more into what I am writing about, not just grammar and run-on sentences but if my paper makes sense. Do I have a purpose and if I do what is it? ... I also

try to stay on topic .... I look at who is going to read the essay and what they would get out of it.

A follow-up piece she wrote during the same tutorial revealed, however, that she still did not understand how and where in her writing the questions of purpose, expression of focus, and validity for the audience need to be addressed. When asked what she still needed to learn, she delegated those issues to her introduction and conclusion:

> I need to work on my introduction and conclusion. I never realized how important they are till I came to college. The intro helps the reader understand what the rest of the story [sic] is all about and why it is important and the conclusion helps the reader understand what I have learned from the story. I feel that those are my weak points because I don't really know how to start my intro and what needs to be there. For my conclusion I don't really know how to end it, because sometimes I don't learn anything from what happened.

What a group discussion led by the tutor needs to address for this student is why she mechanically ascribes the function of carrying out the macro-structure concerns to the introduction and conclusion. In addition, the discussion needs to address how to work the macrostructure concerns into the entire fabric of the paper, considering through readers' responses the readers' needs for the expression of such rhetorical concerns.

In semester-long, systematic practice with working on improving their writing, learning how to become more effective and demanding readers, students become more independent in negotiating revision, and the tutor then needs to monitor his or her own role in discussions to allow students more room to exercise their knowledge and skills. Decentering the group is an important goal to allow the students in their collaboration to take on the questioning and suggestion-making role of the tutor. In the group I described earlier whose suggestions Gerry was taking only to interpret them as requests for more material and quadrupling the size of the assignment by adding more bulk, Zoua stepped in toward the end of the semester and started to show Gerry how to sort out her material once the group took stock of what was in the draft. In her own two papers, Zoua learned to cut out extensively and add new material to accommodate and realize the focus and purpose she discovered for her writing through group discussion. In helping Gerry, she did what I as a tutor would feel uncomfortable with. For a while she appropriated Gerry's shapelessly swollen draft, showed her what to discard that did not serve the focus, pointed out where the paper should begin and what order it needed to follow. Her moves were based on the negotiation the group had together, whose suggestions Gerry herself helped form and articulate but was afraid to carry out. Therefore, Zoua was not imposing her own vision on the paper but was showing Gerry how to execute solutions Gerry accepted and wanted to make but was not able to. She shared with Gerry the skill she developed more quickly and was comfortable with. I sat for about twenty minutes watching the collaboration, contented as Joyce's artist paring his fingernails while watching the performance. I knew I could back off because Gerry trusted Zoua and understood her actions as coming from her concern as a deeply interested, affected reader and a struggling writer herself. Gerry's learning throughout the semester, her active responses as a reader to the others' papers showed me that what she needed was a push to break free of the fear that taking charge of the material could "mess up" her writing. Zoua's decisive moves showed her how revision needs to be done. They were the result of a strong foundation these students built as readers and responders in the tutorial.

Tutoring in small groups offers a unique educational setting where students learn to collaborate while working on their skills as writers and readers. Students witness and influence each other's processes of revision, develop into active and effective readers, and assume the role of responders as they acquire and exercise the skill and language of response. The presence and involvement of the tutor assures them of learning that goes beyond the knowledge they bring with them. This, in turn, builds trust in the workings of the group to move toward more effective solutions and strategies arrived at by the group under the sponsorship of the tutor. The model of tutoring I described in this chapter by using my own observations and applying research and methods developed for classroom teaching, peer groups, and one-to-one tutoring, requires research, methods, and theories of its own. By drawing on strengths of other writing settings, it turns peer interaction in small groups into effective collaboration and active learning by providing the expertise and moderation of a more experienced writer and reader trained as tutor; it gives students intense, focused individual attention that turns into negotiated knowledge. It can be seen and needs to be studied further as perhaps the most powerful enactment of theories of collaborative learning.

Works Cited

Anson, Chris M. "Response Styles and Ways of Knowing." *Writing and Response: Theory, Practice and Research*. Ed. Chris M. Anson. Urbana: NCTE, 1989. 332–66.

————, ed. *Writing and Response: Theory, Practice and Research*. Urbana: NCTE, 1989.

Bereiter, Carl, and Marlene Scardamalia. "Cognitve Coping Strategies and the Problem of Inert Knowledge." *Learning and Thinking Skills: Research and Open Questions*. Eds. Susan Chipman, J. Segal, and Robert Glaser. Hillsdale, NJ: Lawrence Erlbaum Associates, 1985. 65–80.

Bizzell, Patricia. "Academic Discourse: Taxonomy of Conventions or Collaborative Practice?" *College Composition and Communication* (1986): ERIC ED 279806.

Bruffee, Kenneth. "Collaborative Learning and the 'Conversation of Mankind.'" *College English* 46 (1984): 635–52.

Chenoweth, A. "Recognizing the Role of Reading in Writing." CCCC paper (1995).

Ede, Lisa, ed. *On Writing Research: The Braddock Essays*. Boston: Bedford/St. Martin's, 1999.

Elbow, Peter. *Writing with Power: Techniques for Mastering the Writing Process*. New York: Oxford UP, 1981.

Elbow, Peter, and Pat Belanoff. *Sharing and Responding*. 3rd ed. Boston: McGraw-Hill, 2000.

Faigley, Lester, and Stephen Witte. "Analyzing Revision." *College Composition and Communication* 32 (1981): 400–14.

Flower, Linda, John R. Hayes, Linda Carey, Karen Schriver, and James Stratman. "Detection, Diagnosis, and the Strategies for Revision." *College Composition and Communication* 37 (1987). Rpt in *On Writing Research: The Braddock Essays*. Ed. Lisa Ede. 191–226.

Gere, Anne Ruggles, and Ralph Stevens. "The Language of Writing Groups: How Oral Response Shapes Revision." *The Acquisition of Written Language: Response and Revision*. Ed. Sarah Warshauer Freedman. Norwood: Ablex, 1985. 85–105.

Gillespie, Paula, and Neal Lerner. *The Allyn and Bacon Guide to Peer Tutoring*. Boston: Allyn and Bacon, 2000.

Grimm, Nancy Maloney. *Good Intentions: Writing Center Work for Postmodern Times*. Portsmouth: Heinemann-Boynton/Cook, 1999.

Haas, Christina, and Linda Flower. "Rhetorical Reading Strategies and the Construction of Meaning." *College Composition and Communication* 39 (1988). Rpt in *On Writing Research: The Braddock Essays*. Ed. Lisa Ede. 242–59.

Harris, Muriel. *Tutoring Writing: A Sourcebook for Writing Labs*. Glenview: Scott, Foresman and Company, 1982.

—————. "Collaboration Is Not Collaboration Is Not Collaboration: Writing Center Tutorials vs. Peer Response Groups." *College Composition and Communication* 43.3 (1992): 369–83.

Lunsford, Andrea. "Collaboration, Control and the Idea of the Writing Center." *The Writing Center Journal* 12.1 (1991): 3–10.

Meyer, Emily, and Louise Z. Smith. *The Practical Tutor*. New York: Oxford, 1987.

Murphy, Christina, and Steve Sherwood. *The St. Martin's Sourcebook for Writing Tutors*. New York: St. Martin's P, 1995.

Newkirk, Thomas. "Direction and Misdirection in Peer Response." *College Composition and Communication* 35 (1984): 301–11.

Newkirk, Thomas, ed. *Nuts and Bolts: A Practical Guide to Teaching College Composition*. Portsmouth: Heinemann-Boynton/Cook, 1993.

Ozick, Cynthia. "SHE: Portrait of the Essay as a Warm Body." *Atlantic Monthly* Sept. 1998, 114–8.

Phelps, Louise Wetherbee. "Images of Student Writing: The Deep Structure of Teacher Response." *Writing and Response: Theory, Practice and Research*. Ed. Chris M. Anson. Urbana: NCTE, 1989. 37–67.

Spear, Karen. *Sharing Writing: Peer Response Groups in English Classes*. Portsmouth: Heinemann-Boynton/Cook, 1988.

Sullivan, Particia A. "Charting a Course in First-Year English." *Nuts and Bolts: A Practical Guide to Teaching College Composition*. Ed. Thomas Newkirk. Portsmouth: Heinemann-Boynton/Cook, 1993. 17–42.

CHAPTER SIX

ʦʑ

Shaping Writing Groups in the Sciences

Sharon Thomas
Leonora Smith
Terri Trupiano Barry
Michigan State University

Overview

In the fall of 1997, on the basis of a pilot project conducted in the summer of 1996 and in concert with a faculty member from zoology, we received a Fund for the Improvement of Post-Secondary Education (FIPSE) Grant to establish writing groups for graduate students in the colleges of Natural Science, Engineering, and Agriculture and Natural Resources. Graduate students in these disciplines, who were currently at work on a significant writing project, such as a research proposal, part of a thesis or dissertation, or a manuscript for publication, could enroll for credit in a graduate-level course. Students were organized into small groups based on similar disciplines and related research projects. Each group also included one graduate assistant from the FIPSE staff (the writing person) and a volunteer faculty member (the science expert).

In both the original project and in the current course, procedures are modeled on those found in many creative or professional writing groups. At the first meeting of the semester, each participant describes the nature and goals of his or her research project. Then, each week, one or two students present drafts of their current writing projects. Prior to the weekly meeting, all participants read the work to be discussed. Students present their work every other week on a rotating basis.

Over the project's first seven semesters, we—and 24 volunteer faculty from the sciences—provided writing groups for 152 graduate students (and a few postdocs) from 31 different fields, ranging from agricultural economics to zoology. We also collected information on the work of these writing groups through questionnaires, audiotapes, student reflections, field notes, interviews, faculty focus group meetings, and follow-up questionnaires. Along the way, we identified some provocative areas of tension.

Evolution of the Model

In the spring of 1996, a faculty member from biochemistry came to the Writing Center in search of a way he and his graduate students could write more quickly to move from research to manuscript to publication more efficiently. Although the idea of a writing workshop was new to him, he agreed to the experiment, and we established a professional writing group for the faculty member and the four graduate students working in his lab.

The Associate Director of the Writing Center and a graduate student in composition and rhetoric also participated in this group. We knew, as outsiders to the field, that we could not manage a successful writing group in biochemistry; we needed the professor to supply the disciplinary knowledge. At the same time, we were aware that becoming an expert in a particular field is not solely based on the accumulation of facts. Rather, writing like an expert includes both mastery of facts and "attention to the rhetorical processes by which these facts are created and disseminated in texts" (Geisler 210). Because content knowledge and rhetorical moves are the woof and warp of the fabric of scientific writing, the presence of an expert from the sciences and an expert from composition and rhetoric became a key feature of our emerging model.

In the initial meeting with this group, we were introduced as the writing specialists. Our exact role at this point was not clear, but we knew we did not want to limit our contributions to comments on surface-level issues, so even though we found the texts difficult to understand, we attempted to comprehend the content as well as pay attention to the rhetorical markers that might indicate the structure of the argument. Often, however, because the content was so foreign, we were reduced to clinging to any rhetorical language that could provide a life raft in what seemed to be a sea of scientific jargon. Surprisingly, this language was often missing.

For example, in the following draft of an introduction, the writer has written a text in the language that she might use to talk about her work at a weekly lab meeting with the professor and other graduate students working on the same or related research projects:

> Bean common mosaic is a widespread and economically important disease, caused by the virus (BCMV). Bean lines which are resistant carry a dominant gene called *I* gene. A single RAPD marker (OW-13690) has been found to be tightly linked in coupling with the *I* locus in five segregating populations

(2.5–5.8 centimorgans). This marker was shown to be useful for indirect selection criteria for pyramidng epistatic BCMV resistance genes. (FIPSE Project, Summer, 1996)[1]

Although this shorthand language might suffice, and might even be an efficient manner of communicating among the people working in the same
lab on the same or related research projects, it leaves outsiders like us
stranded. Therefore, we often came to the group meetings full of questions,
such as the following:

- If the *I* gene confers resistance against BCMV, where is the problem?
- What is the importance of the single RAPD marker?
- What are indirect selection criteria?

In this case, we had difficulty determining what problem the student
was attempting to address, and we could not see a strong argument for the
research she was conducting. In her final draft—after several revisions
based on discussions in the writing group—the student added both the information and the rhetorical markers that readers need to be able to understand the text.

Move 1: Establishes
a territory (by
summarizing
previous research).

Move 2: Establishes
a niche (by indicating
gap in current
knowledge).

Move 3: Occupies the
niche (by announcing
current research).

Bean common mosaic virus (BCMV) is a widespread
and economically important pathogen of common
bean (*Phaseolus vulgaris L.*). The only effective way to
prevent the occurrence of the disease caused by this
pathogen is to develop genetically resistant cultivars
(Kelly et. al, 1995). Bean cultivars that carry the dominant *I* gene are resistant to all known races of BCMV.
However, when bean plants are infected with strains
of bean common mosaic necrosis virus (BCMNV), the
presence of the *I* gene causes a lethal hypersensitive
reaction in the plant (Haley et. al, 1994a). Combining
the *I* gene with other strain-specific recessive resistance genes (*bc-1, bc-2, and bc-3*) would protect the
plant against BCMNV. However, using disease strain-
ing, it is not possible to detect the presence of the *I*
gene in the *I/bc-3* gene combination (Morales and
Kornegay, 1996), because the recessive *bc-3* gene
epistatically masks the action of the *I* gene (Kelley
1995). **Hence**, a reliable and specific molecular
marker that can be used to indirectly select for the
hypostatic resistant I gene is needed to breed for
BCMV resistance. (Melotto et al. 1216)

---

[1]We are grateful to Maeli Melotto for allowing reproduction and discussion of her text.

Even as outsiders, once we knew that "the very same *I* gene which confers resistance against BCMV causes a lethal reaction when plants are infected with a second virus, BCMNV," we were able to grasp the problem. Then, when she explained that "while a combination of resistance genes would protect the plant against BCMNV, ... using [visual] disease screening, it is not possible to detect the presence of the *I* gene in the *I/bc3* combination," we could begin to understand why her research was important. In addition, the writer added some "text connectives," such as "however" and "hence" (Vande Kopple), that guide the reader through the text. And, in this final version, she accomplishes the three rhetorical moves Swales considers necessary in an introduction: she establishes a territory; then, she describes a niche or gap in that territory; finally, she shows how her research can occupy that niche. She can now devote the remainder of her introduction to describing the specific genetic research needed to develop "a reliable and specific molecular marker" (FIPSE Project, Summer, 1996).

Audience

As Gopen and Swan pointed out, one of the problems writers face is that they often "underestimate the difficulties and ambiguities inherent in the reading process" (356). How much information the reader needs was an early issue in the project and has continued to be so. When graduate students in the sciences mistakenly assume the audience for their writing has the same knowledge as the colleagues in their laboratory, their texts miss the mark.

However, just how much information a particular audience (members of a thesis committee or readers of a particular journal) might need is difficult to determine. Initially, many graduate students seem inclined to brush aside our questions by claiming that the information we seek is "common knowledge," but, when we make requests for clarification, the discussion almost always turns to the question of how much information to include. The ensuing conversations help the writers to determine their specific audience and what that audience needs to know.

The first writing group, situated in the biochemistry professor's lab, turned out to be the pilot study that helped us understand the complex relationship between content knowledge and rhetorical processes. Frequently, those areas that we, as the writing specialists, found difficult or lacking in some rhetorical move turned out to be the same places the biochemistry professor also noted as deficient, though he generally commented on some part of the science that seemed to be missing. These junctures almost always prove to be pivotal points in the texts and the ensuing conversations are often of great importance, because they are the conversations that allow us to explore the ways in which content domain and rhetorical processes are woven together. Once we locate these points, we can begin to ask questions about how the argument ought to be structured for the particular discipline and for a particular audience within that discipline.

The questions put forth by the writing facilitators can help make implicit rhetorical knowledge explicit, both for professional disciplinary faculty who are sharing their expertise and for the would-be professional students who are developing expertise of their own. As Bazerman pointed out, rhetorical conventions may be so thoroughly submerged in the day-to-day practices of scientists that the rationale underlying them becomes concealed. Experts tend to codify rhetorical conventions in their own discipline and treat them as merely formulaic so that they are often unaware of the role these conventions play in their own writing and are, therefore, unable to teach them to others.

Better Writing; Better Science

Even though the graduate students sometimes found our questions annoying, we continued to ask them, and, in the end, they performed another important function. We have learned, over the years, that when the graduate student (usually in frustration) picks up a pencil and paper or moves to the chalkboard, we have cleared a significant hurdle. When they resort to drawing to help us understand, they also begin to produce the language they need to explain the research they conducted. Once they produce a satisfactory oral explanation, we can usually work as a group to compose an appropriate written version.

As soon as they begin to revise their writing, they begin to look back at their research. They discover they must flesh out background, prior research, context, details of the methods used, and so on. The writing groups spawn a cyclical pattern in which the experience of writing up their results for an audience of peers begins to have an impact on the way they design and record their research. As one student pointed out, "When I do my experiments, I now think about what details [will] need to be included in the writing" (FIPSE Project, Fall, 1997).

The cyclical pattern continues when the graduate students return to the writing. Over the past three years, we have watched many students discover how effective writing can foster better science. Many of the students claim the writing groups have helped them to become aware of the link between doing science and thinking and writing about it. A number of students have stated that they learned that "writing and good science are interrelated" and that the course "led to deeper critical thought as a scientist." For example, one of the students made the following comment:

> You cannot learn to write from grammar books or by reading ...; you have to discuss each other's thinking and writing. I learned to write in an active way

and to avoid vague thought. I think this is very important in the sciences. (FIPSE Project, Summer, 1996)

The student's professor added this evaluation:

This student was very tentative in her writing, unsure of the type and depth of information that should be included. Based on the workshop, the student has become very confident, more expressive of her ideas, and is quite an accomplished writer. The manuscript she authored has already been accepted for publication. Clearly the workshop was extremely valuable to the student, instilling in her confidence which she will effectively display in her future scientific work and writing. (FIPSE Project, Summer, 1996)

At the end of that first semester, the biochemistry professor made the following report:

Our writing group has been a tremendous success. Even the most skeptical student is now pleased with the results of our sessions. We have learned to work cooperatively towards evaluating and improving a manuscript. In [one student's] case, the end result was a thesis that was a pleasure for the committee to read and the final defense was a thorough investigation of the data and its relevance rather than a lengthy criticism of writing style. (FIPSE Project, 1996)

The response was a pleasure for us as well. For this group, the transition to the writing group model was very smooth. The professor and his students already held a lab meeting every week, and we simply turned every other meeting into a writing group meeting. As a result of this experience, we believed we had found a model that could easily be transplanted from the humanities to the sciences. When the next professor (a zoologist) arrived on our doorstep, we thought we had a useful and collaborative model to offer her.

Needs Assessment

The zoology professor was initially motivated by her own students' writing difficulties; however, based on conversations with other faculty, she knew this problem was occurring across the sciences, and she was determined to find a method that would get to the heart of the problem. As she phrased it, "These students can't write." Later, this professor became a partner in the FIPSE Writing in the Sciences Project. Early on, she developed a questionnaire designed to assess how science faculty at our university currently managed their graduate students' writing and what they perceived to be the common problems associated with the written work of their students.

This survey revealed a management problem. Virtually all of the faculty surveyed (95%) dealt with the writing of graduate students on a one-to-one basis, a time-consuming and often repetitive process. Asked how often they responded to a given piece of writing, 69% of the faculty fell into the two-to-five times category, with some faculty giving feedback as many as twenty times on a particular piece of writing. That the faculty members in science are often coauthors on the pieces their students write explains some of this intensity. Nevertheless, science faculty were clearly making a huge investment in the activities of one-on-one feedback and conducting conferences with graduate students about their writing. We suggested a writing group approach as more efficient and cost-effective than their current one-on-one writing instruction.

The survey also gave us some insight into the difficulties graduate student writers were experiencing, at least as perceived by the faculty who worked with them. In their responses to a series of open-ended questions, science faculty exhibited concern about graduate students' generally poor writing skills, fear of writing, lack of understanding of the length of time required to produce a well-written text, the problems international students face, the belief that the facts speak for themselves, and what they perceived to be a general lack of critical thinking and organization.

At first, the zoology professor suggested a course in which we would teach the graduate students what goes into various parts of a research paper, and we would teach them how to "fix" their writing. Her response to the problem was not unusual and is no doubt familiar to anyone who has worked in writing across the curriculum or writing in the disciplines. We respected the faculty member's analysis of student writing problems. As Russell pointed out, the process of learning to write in a discipline is a "gradual and subtle" one, "bound up with the activity of the discipline"; therefore, "faculty have tended to mistake the inevitable struggles of students to acquire rhetorical conventions of a discipline for poor writing or sheer ignorance" (18). On the other hand, situated as we were in another discipline, we were inclined to interpret the writing "problems" of these students in a way that was more contextually constructed.

We tended to explain the students' difficulties in producing texts and their hesitation as writers as markers of the transition they were making as they negotiated their way from the subordinate roles of student and novice to the role of professional expert. To construct the kinds of arguments their professors and future colleagues find acceptable, graduate students must develop sufficient discipline-specific expertise. Given, however, that most graduate students are novices lacking sufficient knowledge in both content domain and rhetorical processes to be able to write as experts, crossing the divide between novice and expert is a difficult step.

We argued for writing groups, similar to the one in our pilot project, facilitated by experts with both disciplinary and rhetorical knowledge. Here, students could work on authentic writing projects in conjunction with other graduate students working on similar projects in similar areas,

Organizational Issues

In the summer of 1996, with support from the Graduate School, we implemented a larger pilot project. The zoology professor advertised our writing groups to science faculty across the campus and twelve students asked to participate. These groups differed in an important respect from our biochemistry group: they were not composed of graduate students all working in a particular lab with a particular professor. Instead, the groups in the second pilot project were composed of students from many different disciplines. The zoology professor provided all the science expertise and the Associate Director of the Writing Center worked as the writing facilitator. Later, the zoology professor joined us to write a grant proposal for the Fund for the Improvement of Post-Secondary Education—a proposal reviewed and commented on by our own writing group.

When we received the grant to continue this project, we had already learned that too much disciplinary diversity within a group presented some challenges. However, while we preferred the professor-and-students-from-the-same-lab model, we knew this model was not possible if we were going to offer writing groups to all interested graduate students from any of the programs in any of our three science colleges. Consequently, we decided to group students in professional writing groups according to related research areas, based on information gathered at the initial organizational meeting. Our zoologist partner then contacts faculty with suitable expertise who are willing to volunteer as facilitators.

Of course, these faculty are not intimately familiar with the research of the four or five students in their group in the way the biochemistry professor knew the research of the students working in his lab. However, even though the science faculty facilitator sometimes has to stretch to cover all the areas represented by the student writers, this arrangement does have its advantages. Many students, we have discovered, prefer to work with colleagues and faculty outside of their own lab so that they can revise and polish their work before they present it to their major professors.

In some ways, the more divergent backgrounds of the students are also an advantage, because such groups provide a more realistic audience for the works in progress. Even though we were able, during the initial years of the project, to hire graduate students from composition and rhetoric to work with the groups, the burden of asking for clarification was not always on their shoulders. Often the graduate student peers saw the same areas of concern as the writing teaching assistants but were able to frame more scientifically focused questions.

A New Context

Soon after the project began, we discovered several aspects of the lives of graduate students in the sciences that would have a significant impact on the work of the writing groups and which were not familiar to those of us from the humanities. For example, funding for graduate students in the sciences comes mostly from grants that are tied to specific research projects being carried out by particular professors in those professors' labs. In some other ongoing projects, we had worked with graduate students from the liberal arts, the social sciences, and education. Most of these graduate students also had funding of some kind, but their funding changed from year to year, and it was seldom tied to a research project conceived and supervised by a faculty member. Graduate students outside the sciences often select their research topics fairly late in their studies and usually can choose their own topic of interest as long as they can assemble a committee that will approve it. In the sciences, graduate students usually begin doing research in their major professor's lab as soon as they enter graduate school. If the funded research goals of the lab change, the graduate student's research must change as well, and most of their work is published with at least their major professor as a coauthor, and possibly several other coauthors as well. These constraints had a powerful impact on the work of the graduate students and on the writing groups.

Some other characteristics of writing in the sciences were not as complex; nevertheless, they contributed to the way these students work as writers. For example, those of us from the humanities continually encouraged the science writers to expand their descriptions, to add to their arguments, to make their papers longer. On the other hand, the faculty volunteers from the sciences frequently suggested breaking complex syntax into shorter, more simple sentences and cutting out transitions and other words we considered pivotal to the argument. Only later did we learn that scientists generally pay by the page (subventions) for the publication of articles accepted by leading journals. Thus, they continually try to pare down sentences to save money. As readers from outside these disciplines, we did not expect to understand fully the content of the students' papers. Still, we often felt as if we were reading shorthand. Once we discovered the economic cause, we could work with students (and faculty) to focus first on communicating the message and, later, on condensing that message.

In the humanities, graduate students move from novice to professional in a fairly autonomous manner. Students in these disciplines frequently become published writers by revising seminar papers, most often on their own or with assistance from peers. In the sciences, graduate students work in the lab of a particular professor whose research fits their interests. Any writing the student does for publication must, necessarily, meet with the approval of the professor, because his or her credibility and future funding are at stake.

Because these graduates immediately embark on one or another of the research projects underway in that lab, even first- and second-year master's degree students often have opportunities to become listed as coauthors on research papers published by their labs. This practice of multi-author research articles poses problems for graduate student writers in the sciences. Even very early in their programs, some graduate students may be asked to "write up" the results of their part of the research project. The final document, however, is generally written by the faculty person listed as the primary investigator (PI) on the grant proposal. These opportunities to publish, then, are often not actually occasions to write for publication; rather, they are opportunities to prepare a lab report that someone else incorporates into an article for publication.

By the time these students come to the end of the program, their responsibilities as science researchers and writers increase. Eventually, their particular research project becomes the subject of a major paper, and the graduate student is listed as first author, along with faculty connected to the research project. Even in this situation, however, the PI has a vested interest in the results published and may exert considerable pressure on the graduate student to shape a document in a certain way. Even if the graduate students manage to retain sole propriety over the manuscript, they may be surprised to find that their writing, which in the past was simply integrated into the PI's article and received few, if any, comments, suddenly is deemed inadequate for "professional" writing.

The Level of the Claim

The writing of a professional-level piece of work, such as a dissertation or a thesis, or an article for publication, represents a move toward equal participation in the professional conversations in the student's field. The difficulty of this move is evident in the problems students have in determining how they should insert themselves into ongoing discussions. Not yet experts in either the content or the rhetorical moves of the disciplines, these graduate students, nevertheless, must figure out how to situate their work in a larger body of research.

Sometimes these students are too tentative. For example, phrases such as "based on the assumption that" and "tried to" are often flagged by faculty facilitators as being imprecise and not aggressive enough. Other times, students are too assertive. In these cases, the writing group members may suggest that the writers lower their sights. For example, the student who wrote "We present a real-time automated surveillance system" in the first draft, had revised that statement to "We are developing a real-time automated surveillance system" in the final draft (FIPSE Project, Summer, 1999). He had been counseled to make clear that this system was only under development, not an already proven product.

Based on a study he did of two biologists and the research proposals they were writing, Greg Myers argued that all researchers have to make decisions about the level of their claims. The complexity of this decision is described by Swales as follows:

> The higher the level of claim the more likely that it will involve contradicting large bodies of the relevant literature and will challenge assumptions embodied in important ongoing research programs. On the other hand, the lowest level claims may contradict nothing, but may also add very little to what is accepted and established within the given research field. (117)

Concomitant with determining the level of their claims, graduate student writers must also determine the use of what Vande Kopple describes as epistemological markers, sometimes called shields or hedges, that writers use to indicate how committed they are to their claims. According to Vande Kopple, these markers occur in surprisingly high numbers in scientific writing, and they are used to indicate "cautious commitment" or to reduce the "degree of liability" (5).

For example, one student wrote this phrase in his first draft: "The susceptibility to fungal pathogens is the primary obstacle to [*Pao annua's*] use as a desirable turf grass. Diseases that cause widespread damage are often investigated as potential biological controls." In the second draft, the writer had already begun to hedge a bit on his claims by changing "use" to "acceptance" and adding "suggests" and "might be." The second draft read as follows: "This susceptibility to fungal pathogens is the primary obstacle to [*Pao annua's*] acceptance as a desirable turf grass and suggests that it might be amenable to biological control" (FIPSE Project, Fall, 1998).

Because their projects are tied to the research of a professor whose funding for future research depends on timely completion and publication of current research projects, graduate students in the sciences are often thrust into the position of having to make and defend claims before they have acquired the necessary background knowledge in their field's research literature.

If the ability to determine how strong the claim can be rests on whether or not the results can "contradict" and "challenge," only those researchers with considerable knowledge of the literature and current research projects in that field can make such judgments. Even the experienced researchers in Myers's study had difficulty determining which level they could claim. Certainly, graduate student writers—who, in most cases, are novices—will experience even more difficulty determining scientific importance, which Myers has defined as requiring "both that the work be original and that it be closely related to the concerns and methods of current research" (225).

Tensions

Other constraints in this new context soon became apparent. We discovered, for example, that interchanges around the workshop table are frequently microcosms of the much larger tensions and controversies in the contexts in which the texts are being produced. It is not a surprise that academic work is the site of contentions; it is what we argue with and argue about. But the way in which these tensions play out often bring to the fore the way in which particular bits of text function as parts of an ongoing larger argument or dispute. The interrelated issues of autonomy, authorship, and distribution of power frequently affect how the writing groups function; indeed, they often dictate what the groups need to do to facilitate a particular student's writing.

For example, Hannah[2] (FIPSE Project, Fall, 1998), a graduate student in animal science, brought to her writing group an article for publication on her research project on serum markers in bone and cartilage metabolism. Because of the nature of her research, two faculty members were listed as coauthors. Unfortunately, they had conflicting ideas about how much and what kinds of detail ought to be included. In her attempt to please both faculty members, Hannah had inserted several asides in the discussion section, distracting the reader and impeding the flow of ideas. When the group suggested places where Hannah might cut what seemed to be extraneous information, Hannah referred to the particular faculty member who wanted the information included. Although Hannah agreed with the group that certain pieces of information were not really necessary, she was hamstrung by the conflicting requirements placed on her by her coauthors. Part of the problem stemmed from the complexity of the serum marker calculation for cartilage, a calculation with a host of variables. One professor felt Hannah needed to detail explicitly all these variables; in the process, Hannah confused readers, who had a difficult time determining the actual results of her study.

In trying to please two advisors with conflicting ideas about how much and what kinds of detail were necessary to constitute "good writing," Hannah was unable to produce any good writing at all. The group suggested that Hannah take control of the writing. She was listed as first author, she had done all the actual research, she had studied and prepared the literature review; therefore, the group suggested she should be prepared to support her own decisions about her writing. Later, Hannah did take control of the writing and was able to produce a well-written manuscript, one

[2]We wish to extend our sincere appreciation to all the students and faculty who have participated in this project, and especially to those whose work is included here. To preserve anonymity, names have been changed unless the author granted us permission to use his or her name.

that satisfied both professors and was eventually accepted for publication. Even though she had little experience as an author, Hannah was eventually able (with the group's support), to act as the single author and take control of the situation. In cases like this one, the writing group becomes a sounding board, as well as a springboard to professionalism.

In some instances, however, the tensions that are played out over a particular text are more deeply rooted. Amy, (FIPSE Project, Fall, 1997) a PhD student working on breast cancer research in a lab of some distinction, had successfully grown multilayered human breast cells, which differentiated and grew into "organoids." These organoids were capable of replicating certain functions of human breast cells. This procedure for growing cells was a recent development made possible because of a new medium for growing cells (Matrigel). Prior to this development, studies of human breast cancer were based on cells grown on plastic, which only form monolayers, or on animal models. One of the members of Amy's committee had built her career on animal model studies, and Amy did not want to antagonize her by discrediting animal studies, which could only approximate human models. Thus, in the introduction section of an early draft, she mentioned the animal studies only in passing. Amy did not point out the problems with these studies that could be overcome by the new approach she had developed. Amy's avoidance of any mention of the problems associated with animal studies resulted in the omission of an important step in her argument. In Swales' terms, she had left out step number two: raising a crucial question about the existing research.

In early drafts, Amy avoided this move, even though members of the writing group urged Amy to explain more fully why she had chosen Matrigel. Instead of pointing out the difficulties with the current approaches based on animal studies, Amy limited her comments to the following: "This type of in vitro system [Matrix] lends itself to a lesser degree of complexity and greater controllability than animal studies" (FIPSE Project, Fall, 1997).

The group continued to point out that research on breast cancer would not have progressed to its current state without animal models; therefore, Amy was not so much discrediting animal models as she was building on prior research. Finally, in draft six, Amy produced the following revision:

> At present, the best tools we have to unearth the basic mechanisms involved in protective and risk factors implicated epidemiologically for breast cancer that approximates the in vivo condition are the animal models. However, the cellular and hormonal relationships in these animals are different from those of a human being. Matrigel, a substratum for plating cells, has emerged recently that has great promise in this respect .... We propose to elaborate the use of this extracellular matrix substratum, by characterizing the behavior of the normal human breast epithelial cells plated on it. (FIPSE Project, Fall, 1997)

Here, Amy completes all three moves. She describes the present research tools (move one). Then, she points out the problem with this approach ("However, ….") so that she can create a space for her own research niche (move two). Finally, she occupies that niche (move three) by describing the promise of this new approach. Later in the introductory paragraph Amy found a way to give credit to her professor's work by stating, "This type of in vitro system [Matrigel] might provide the link needed by animal studies for extrapolation to the human condition" (FIPSE Project, Fall, 1997).

In both of these cases, the problems in the texts were almost directly the result of tensions in the context in which the texts were being produced. The position of graduate student novices working with professionals in positions of power, who can affect the outcome of their research, substantially affects what they include, or omit, in their writing. The group's implicit understanding of the reality of the distribution of power is always at the fringes of the conversation in writing groups in the sciences.

Conclusion

As of this writing, we have concluded the evaluation and dissemination phases of the FIPSE grant and have secured funding from the Graduate School and the colleges of Agriculture and Natural Resources, Natural Science, and Engineering to continue the writing groups as a regular offering for graduate students in the sciences. Initially, our project had three goals: to promote graduate students' understanding of discipline-specific writing in the sciences, to provide faculty with an alternative model for handling their students' writing (instead of the widespread practice of editing and revising students' writing on a one-to-one basis), and to establish a culture of writing in the sciences at Michigan State University. We have made significant headway on all three.

A vast majority of the students who participated in the groups have successfully completed their master's or doctoral theses or had the sections of the projects on which they worked approved so they could move on to the next step. Others have completed and published articles. The chairs and committee members of these students rated the quality of their first to last draft significantly improved, and they made positive comments about the role of the groups in the way in which graduate student writing is managed: "Faculty time spent on student writing reduced"; "Would save the committee several rewrites." As of this writing, 530 students from 43 departments/units have taken the course, and 98% of these students have said they would recommend it to other graduate students.

We continue to study our practice closely through follow-up of former students as well as through close examination of successive drafts, student interviews, faculty rating of early and later drafts, and faculty focus groups. Our results suggest that the groups have been successful in helping disciplinary faculty develop a more dynamic notion of writing as inextricably intertwined with the domain knowledge of the sciences. In addition, our work has reminded us that importation of any model or structure from one circumstance to another must always be responsive to the particulars of the situation—the popular notion of reproducing best practices not withstanding. What to us is most emblematic of the project is that, like the initial FIPSE grant, our work is created and sustained by our own cross-disciplinary collaborative process. If "writing people" in higher education are to help improve writing on an institutional level, they must welcome and seek out partnerships with disciplinary faculty and be fully open to the mutual nature of these arrangements. We see such interdisciplinary collaborations as powerful locations for initiating and sustaining projects of institutional change.

Acknowledgments

This project was funded by the U.S. Department of Education (FIPSE Award No. P116B70442). Additional financial support was provided by the colleges of Engineering, Natural Science, and Agriculture and Natural Resources, the Graduate School, and International Programs at Michigan State University.

Works Cited

Bazerman, Charles. *Shaping Writing Knowledge: The Genre and Activity of the Experimental Article in Science*. Madison: University of Wisconsin Press, 1988.

Geisler, Cheryl. *Academic Literacy and the Nature of Expertise*. Hillsdale: Lawrence Erlbaum Associates, 1994.

Gopen, George, and Judith Swan. "The Science of Scientific Writing." *American Scientist* 78 (1990): 550–58.

Melotto, Maeli, Lucia Afanador, and James Kelly. "Development of a SCAR Marked Linked to the *I* Gene in Common Bean." *Genome* 39 (1997): 1216–19.

Myers, Greg. "The Social Construction of Two Biologists' Proposals." *Written Communication* 2.3 (1985): 219–45.

Russell, David. *Writing in the Academic Disciplines, 1870–1990: A Curricular History*. Carbondale: Southern Illinois UP, 1991.

Swales, John. *Genre Analysis: English in Academic and Research Settings*. Cambridge: Cambridge UP, 1990.

Vande Kopple, William. "Refining and Applying Views of Metadiscourse." Conf. on Coll. Composition and Communication. Phoenix. 12 Mar. 1997.

CHAPTER SEVEN

ᘓᘛ

Reciprocal Expertise: Community Service and the Writing Group

H. Brooke Hessler
Oklahoma City University

Amy Rupiper Taggart
North Dakota State University

When we informed our Director of Composition that we wanted the sophomore students to exchange texts with third graders she asked, "What's in it for the third graders?" The third grade teachers asked, "What's in it for the college students?"

My sophomores figured it would be an "easy A"—after all, how tough could it be to write to a bunch of kids?

Combining elementary and college writers into a writing group involved taking a risk, trusting that what began as a form of mentoring would evolve into collaboration: for the program to work, "pen pals" must become "writing partners." I could see my students making that transition—but could they?

Peer beneath the surface of any writing group established as a form of community service and you are likely to find a microcosm of collaborative social action, reaction, or inaction. In this chapter we attempt to demonstrate how community service writing groups afford a unique opportunity for academic writers to collaborate with people whose authorial expertise is manifestly different from their own. Building on such pedagogical strategies as community literacy (Peck, Flower, and Higgins) and community-engagement writing (Hessler), the instructors who developed the Writing Partners approach are seeking to make the writing group (and the partnerships within it) a hub of collaborative inquiry and literate action by writers who are ordinarily distanced from one another by campus or convention. Like many community service writing programs, Writing Partners is rooted in an academic writing curriculum: writers join the writing groups in partial fulfillment of a course requirement, and their work is ultimately graded by an instructor. These students form partnerships with writers from a community beyond their campus, such as an elementary school or community agency, engaging in writing projects that encourage them to share and use the group's diverse perspectives and experiences as they develop their texts. The key pedagogical challenge for this approach is reciprocity. Without the recognition, respect, and exchange of one another's authorial expertise, the writing group ceases to become a partnership and may easily lapse into a perfunctory academic exercise—or worse, a performance of "charity"—for the college students and an awkward institutional obligation for the community partners (Cushman; Flower; Herzberg).

The intercultural and interdisciplinary features that make community service writing such a rich site for writing groups also pose the greatest challenges to reciprocity. To gain a more sensitive understanding of the ways reciprocal learning may be fostered and inhibited by the community service writing group, we draw an initial comparison to its kindred academic form, the classroom-based peer response group. We examine how issues of authenticity and authority complicate reciprocity and explain how community-engagement pedagogies such as community service writing attempt to resolve some of these issues. Community service writing is the pedagogical framework of our case study, the Writing Partners program. We draw on this case study to present a series of concerns and recommendations for constructing community service writing groups. Finally, we discuss how such an approach extends current concepts of the writing group.

Reciprocity and the Academic Writing Group

Although a vast range of community service writing groups exists—from Web-based discussion threads on neighborhood crime to creative writing workshops at a local library—the practices employed within these groups are often informed by the customary activities within the academic peer response group. This influence is not surprising because academic writing instructors contribute directly to community service writing across the curriculum and within their own programs. Common classroom strategies for collaborative writing and learning are readily adopted for projects and programs that invite community writers into the classroom or transport the writing group off campus. Yet, although a writing group composed of student peers faces many of the same difficulties as a community service writing group, the latter group's complexity is magnified by the implications of its successes and failures, which reach beyond the classroom via its members. Stretching the peer response model to accommodate this complexity can alter the fabric of reciprocity by challenging students to sincerely and constructively engage alternative perspectives as credible sources of expertise.

When a class of college writing students is combined with a group of non-college-student writers, of whatever age or level of writing experience, the second group is inevitably perceived by the first as outsiders. The writing practices and perspectives of the college writing group are aligned with an elite institution; those of the off-campus writers (particularly off-campus writers who are not college-educated) are, in the eyes of the college writer, practices and perspectives not customarily rewarded in the college classroom. Even when the off-campus writers demonstrate superior expertise as nonacademic writing professionals (such as business or technical writers), college students are likely to be skeptical about the extent to which these writers can help the students earn a desirable academic grade on their compositions. In practical terms, off-campus writers are not the ones grading the writing, and often the knowledge they bring does not reflect the academic knowledge and skills that students are asked to perform for their college instructors. A similar condition holds true within traditional, classroom-based, peer response groups. Writing students who are best able to replicate the traditionally rewarded models of academic discourse, such as English majors or peer tutors, are insiders whose expertise is most likely to be respected within the academic writing group (Leverenz).

This gravitation toward homogeneous writing practices is sometimes disrupted by student enrollments (or instructor interventions) that mix students of very different writing abilities into peer writing groups, creating a condition of "heterogeneity" that, at its best, can sensitize writers to diverse discursive practices and often overlooked forms of authorial expertise (Elbow "Writing Assessment"). As James Moffett observes, such peer groups present writers with a "natural audience" for their writing, an audience that is more realistic and authentic because it more closely resembles the discourse occurring in the world beyond school and beyond the peculiar demands of the writing instructor (193). Yet though the instructor may recognize the authentic worth of the peer writer's expertise, the college student is less concerned with "realism" than the instructor's evaluation of the text. Because such graded, classroom texts are above all "words-for-teacher," Joseph Petraglia argues that the peer response group is actually a source of pseudotransactions in which student writers provide responses as if they were the text's real audience despite that the text's only true audience is the instructor (26). Such gamesmanship is, Petraglia maintains, an inevitable consequence of an inauthentic composition context. In this light, bringing more diverse writers into the writing group is unlikely to inspire students to value a different authorial expertise.

In her peer writing group study within a multicultural classroom, Carrie Shively Leverenz challenges the authenticity of peer response in a context carefully constructed to validate lived experience and differing perspectives as sources of expertise. Composed to foster "a rhetoric of dissensus" (Trimbur 610) through which students can recognize and explore difference, this classroom appears to offer its peer writing groups an ideal opportunity "to critique the ways in which established knowledge-making communities ignore or erase difference in order to maintain a single, authoritative, 'normal discourse'" (Leverenz 168).[1] Whereas class discussions are animated by multiple perspectives, the writing group observed by Leverenz is clearly dominated by a single student who exhibits mastery in conventional academic discourse. Peer response defers to this student, whose representation of institutional authority silences the "abnormal discourse" of the other writers in the group. Unable to recognize the importance of his or her colleagues' authorial perspectives, the conventional student nonetheless receives a positive evaluation for his or her group work and an A in the class. Echoing Petraglia (31), Leverenz concludes that student writers must negotiate a fictional realm of nondomination within the classroom because, with or without pedagogical attempts to distribute authority or privilege diversity, the institutionalized context remains, and the instructor retains the voice of that institution (184–85). Facilitating authentic reciprocity requires a learning environment in which writers perceive a real shift in academic authority, and instructors are "intense listeners" to different and dominant discourses (185).

Community-engagement pedagogies attempt to achieve at least a partial shift in authority through the collaborative development of texts. With an emphasis on constructive communication—the use of writing to engage social concerns and build understanding—community-engagement strategies urge students to reach beyond the classroom for insight and expertise. Generally speaking, community engagement is an umbrella term for pedagogies such as community service learning and participatory action research through which students engage contexts, audiences, resources, and constraints in unfamiliar discourse communities (Hessler). Because successful texts cannot be produced without the contributions of their community partners, students are placed in a position of need relative to people whose expertise they might not ordinarily seek, and instructors are required to challenge their own preconceptions of authority as they facilitate and evaluate the work of these writers.

Community Service Writing
and Community Service Writing Groups

To provide a framework for our case study, we must first clarify the difference between what we see as community service writing and community

---

[1]The concepts of normal and abnormal discourse come from Richard Rorty's *Philosophy and the Mirror of Nature*.

service writing groups. Generally speaking, community service writing encompasses a wide variety of writing activities (including reflection journals, reports, newsletters, and professional documents developed for community organizations) that is largely individually authored and occasionally collaboratively authored by students. There are five basic models of community service writing, which Paul Heilker describes as follows (74):[2] The first treats community service as a topic. Students work at agencies, not engaging in any writing until they return to the academic environment. They then typically reflect on the work they've done in a journal to reach a better understanding of their work and, potentially, of associated social issues. One of the potential pitfalls of this model is the students' lack of truly critical understanding due to minimal contextualization and broader classroom discussion. In the second community service possibility mentioned by Heilker, students use their service as a research source. The service constitutes field research and finds its way into a works cited page in an essay on a related topic (homelessness, hunger issues, public policy, and so on). Service learning linked to critical pedagogy, a third version, combines service with active dialogue regarding social injustice. Radical critique in reading, writing, service, and discussion is the modus operandi in such a course. A fourth model eschews the overtly critical and social goals of the critical pedagogue for more traditionally academic goals. Service here allows students to write in the "real world," not to improve social situations but to improve their understanding of and skill in writing. Finally, Heilker adds a fifth version of community service writing, "writing as social action." Although socially active writing is more closely tied to community agencies—students write texts useful to the agencies' goals, such as newsletters, grant proposals, and brochures—the textual exchange is still unidirectional.

---

[2]Tom Deans proposes an alternate taxonomy for understanding service-learning's goals and structures in *Writing Partnerships: Service-Learning in Composition*: writing for the community, writing about the community, and writing with the community. When writing for the community, students do much of their learning at a nonprofit agency because they produce documents that the agency needs, using the discourse conventions of the agency. The goals of writing for the community include learning to negotiate the move from academic to workplace discourse, reflecting on service to learn more about social issues, and aiding the agency through text production. When writing about the community, students learn primarily in the classroom, create documents for classroom use only, and use academic discourse. The goals here include reflection on service experiences, critical consciousness raising, and the production of academic texts. Finally, writing with the community places students' learning primarily in a community center of some sort; the documents produced may have a variety of purposes, including attaining academic and social goals, and the discourses are varied. Writing with the community potentially achieves collaborative social action, negotiation of difference, and a re-creation of university and community connections. Linda Flower's composition textbook, *Problem-Solving Strategies for Writing in College and Community*, demonstrates how this taxonomy relates to specific academic and community writing strategies (328).

Through his concept of writing as social action, Heilker seems to create a more authentic and ethical relationship between university and community. However, his discussion falls short of Ellen Cushman's complex understanding of the power and agency issues so crucial to community engagement. Cushman addresses the issue of reciprocity which, for us, is central to the community service writing group. She claims, "Reciprocity includes an open and *conscious* negotiation of the power structures reproduced during the give-and-take interactions of the people involved on both sides of the relationship" (our emphasis 381). Reciprocity acknowledges the social nature of community service writing groups. Each member of the group shares expertise on the subject at hand. However, just as critical consciousness is not a guaranteed result of service learning (Herzberg 59), reciprocity also does not naturally happen in every community service classroom. We believe it can be cultivated pedagogically. This is where writing group pedagogy becomes necessary.

We define the community service writing group as a writing group composed of two or more authors within and beyond the classroom who are mutually invested in the development of texts that serve community needs. The writing group's work constitutes literate action because writers are applying their literacies as agents of social change to accomplish objectives beyond individual educational purposes (Flower "Literate Action"). All group members simultaneously develop individual and sometimes group texts, which may ultimately merge into a common document or address a common goal. As literate action, then, the texts may be placed on the Web to educate others, they may constitute action in the individuals' lives (in the form of a job or grant application), or they may initiate larger collaborative projects, such as a tenants' bill of rights or an activist newsletter. Though the line between community service writing and community service writing groups may blur, for this chapter we feel it is useful to differentiate the writing groups from other kinds of activities where the interplay of individual and collective authorship is less central to the purpose of the community writing project.

Fig. 7.1 offers comparative examples of community service writing and community service writing groups. Note the inherently collaborative nature of the writing in the right-hand column, as well as the reciprocity consciously built into the relationships of the group members. The community service writing group seems better suited to authentically reciprocal relationships.

To demonstrate our concept of reciprocal-expertise pedagogy for community service writing groups, we present a local case study. We believe this writing project offers multiple options for modeling effective community service writing groups. It also illustrates some of the difficulties of implementing a reciprocal-expertise pedagogy.

Community Service Writing	Community Service Writing Groups
A college writer studies intercultural discourse practices. She also performs community service work (such as helping to distribute a weekly newspaper produced by urban teens at a local high school) that enables her to spend time observing interaction between people from several different discourse communities (the various communities of teens and adults within the urban high school, as well as the local citizens who subscribe to the newspaper). The college writer reflects on her experiences in a journal and produces an academic essay analyzing the discourse practices she observed.	A college writer studies intercultural discourse practices and then enters a neighborhood community center to collaborate with an urban teen to develop a communication project that draws from the expertise of both, such as a newsletter article explaining the teen perspective on urban violence to a diverse audience of concerned citizens. As they work through the problem of engaging, educating, and motivating their audience, both writers become stronger collaborative problem solvers and communicators.[3]
Students interview residents of an eldercare center and write profiles of them. The profiles will be published in the eldercare newsletter and may help attract both funding and volunteer help, thereby serving an agency need.	Students and eldercare residents collaborate on a community document that consists of profiles of the residents (developed through simultaneous textual activities, perhaps also including participation of family and friends) and other relevant aspects of their community in the form of a scrapbook or an educational document for local school children (a text that profiles older citizens to teach local history to children). The authorship is overtly shared in a way that everyone recognizes.

FIG. 7.1. A comparison of projects developed through community service writing and community service writing groups, emphasizing reciprocity.

---

[3]This example is taken from the intercultural inquiry projects developed by Linda Flower and her colleagues at Carnegie-Mellon University and Pittsburgh's Community Literacy Center (Flower, "Partners in Inquiry").

Case Study: Writing Partners

Writing Partners is a program offered by Write to Succeed, a nonprofit organization begun by composition instructors at Texas Christian University.[4] The key elements of the Writing Partners program are as follows:

• The development and exchange of texts generates community engagement. (This process is approached as an experience of collaborative inquiry and literate action. In the spirit of Lisa Ede and Andrea Lunsford's dialogic model of collaboration, both process and product are valued.)
• Partnerships are composed of people from manifestly different discourse communities, which requires each writer to learn to collaborate with someone whose interpersonal expectations and experiential contributions are very unlike his or her customary peers.
• All partners are overtly learners and writers. (No group's expertise has greater value than another.)

In practice, Writing Partners may take many forms, though it has primarily functioned, thus far, as a pairing of college and elementary school classes. Throughout the spring 1999 semester, second- and third-grade students at Saint Peter the Apostle Catholic School and intermediate composition students at Texas Christian University exchanged letters, pictures, and stories, creating a relationship that enabled them to gain new perspectives on school, audience, and the importance of written communication. The ages and educational levels in this model served to separate the members in terms of discourse conventions. Members were challenged to adjust to their audiences and were influenced by the differing perspectives that came from discussing issues in a way they were not accustomed to speaking or writing. Because both groups exchanged texts and because each writer was exposed to someone outside his or her discourse community, the situation was ripe for reciprocal learning.

Writing was focused on topics arising from an exhibition at The Modern Art Museum of Fort Worth: Architecture of Reassurance: Designing the Disney Theme Parks, thus forming a sort of triangulated "partnership." Though texts were only exchanged by the elementary and college students, the museum provided docents for tours, an on-campus lecture about the exhibition, and celebration space at the museum for a capstone reception. The mu-

---

[4]Write to Succeed, Inc., is a nonprofit corporation founded in 1997 to enhance students' writing experiences, to expand the writing classroom to include the community, to foster collaborative learning and writing relationships, and to facilitate change through writing. The Write to Succeed mission is to create, fund, and implement educational programs on campuses and in the community to develop life and professional skills through writing <http:\\www.writetosucceed.org>.

seum's presence in the project offered a topic not owned by either the college students or the elementary students. The topic existed as a common ground, both in terms of struggling with new concepts such as "Imagineering" (imagination and engineering combined to create comforting and inspiring architecture, particularly at Disney's theme parks and planned communities) and in terms of the common experience of theme parks and Disney in the American cultural consciousness. The museum, in turn, was able to fulfill its mission to generate and maintain community interest in the arts. The project not only brought young people to the exhibition, giving them an early taste of modern art and museums, but it also brought their families and friends into the museum for the final celebration. The museum gained potential patrons and a deeper connection with the students in both age groups who had actively engaged with the art through several weeks of writing. In this way the museum becomes not just a field trip destination but a familiar, friendly resource for continued learning.

It is the letter exchange and face-to-face interaction, however, that provide the primary foundations for reciprocity for Writing Partners writing groups. The writing groups are initially formed as partnerships through letter writing, which both sustains the relationship and advances writing discussions. After the first, introductory letter, partners begin discussing the writing they do on an approximately biweekly basis; they engage in metadiscourse. The letter as text serves as a site for many of the practices in which traditional writing groups participate. Writers invent as they discuss their initial ideas, they refine their writing topics as they explain projects to another audience, and they offer feedback that may help their partners with development, organization, and revision.

For instance, during the Spring 1999 partnership, college students assigned to write memoirs about their childhood experiences turned to the elementary writers for inspiration and expertise: the younger students helped them remember what mattered to them most during that time of life—what brought them joy, frustration, and wonder; the children's stories and the tone of their second-grade language helped the college writers to recall significant moments from the past with vividness and with the understanding that sharing these kinds of stories can be important work. In turn, the college students helped the younger writers with their projects, such as the development of their own "imagineered" theme parks. They posed generative questions in their letters to the children: What will be the theme of your park? How do you want people to feel when they visit your park, and why? What kinds of activities, sights, and sounds do you think will give them that experience?

The letters divert the attention of peer writing groups from surface issues toward more substantive writing concerns. Because the genre is familiar to virtually all audiences, it provides a relatively neutral discourse zone as well, one not privileged overtly by one community or the other. The college students often demonstrate particular sensitivity to this kind of equity in many small but significant ways. For example, they tend to modify their use of language and technology to create a consistent field of interaction: using words that are accessible but precise; incorporating graphics, color, and other forms of visual appeal; and often composing letters by hand—a painstaking process for many—to make a more personal connection.

Face-to-face interactions strengthen the participants' relationships. This contact comes first in the form of a writing workshop hosted by either class. For example, college writers may facilitate a brainstorming session to help the younger writers develop a new project or revise an existing one. During the spring of 1999, one college class organized its workshop around developing introductions, conclusions, and descriptions. The younger students brought drafts of a paper in progress and worked in small circles (consisting of two pairs of writing partners) to revise their texts. The college students talked about their upcoming assignment, explaining the process they follow to develop their own writing and listening to similarities between writing for college and writing in an elementary classroom. These conversations—in person and in writing—challenged the college writers to explain complex concepts and arguments in language simple enough for a child to understand and respond to.

Whenever possible, the culminating event of a Writing Partners project is a public one, as in the spring of 1999, when teachers, students, parents, and other interested parties attended a publication celebration at the Fort Worth Museum of Modern Art.[5] The publications included a collection of writing, titled *Imagineers at Work*, and other projects produced by the elementary-college writing groups. Through this venue, students had another opportunity to bring their writing into the community; all were equally invested in the success of the event and the performance of the writing. The elementary students' creatively "imagineered" theme park projects were displayed prominently on tables surrounding the room, as were other projects developed throughout the semester—from memoirs to historiographies, all drawn from the activities of the writing groups. A short presentation by teachers and students enabled the guests to see how the semester's work in all four classes related and contributed to one another.

In sum, reciprocity is embodied in the Writing Partners pilot project in several ways:

1. The writing group itself assumes a two-way exchange of text.

---

[5]In subsequent semesters this event has been held on a university campus.

2. The letter exchange creates a textual common ground, a genre familiar to both groups of students.

3. The topic established by the museum exhibition constitutes a common focus and introduces yet another element of expertise and interdependence to the mix.

4. A face-to-face workshop reinforces the work already being done by all parties in letters and in separate classrooms.

5. Mutual investment in a public presentation of semester work motivates partners to attend to their audiences and to engage each audience as a group that matters beyond the instructor.

In addition to the elementary-college transactions of the initial Writing Partners projects, two other kinds of partnerships are currently under development: an online partnership of American and international students and a local partnership with a community service agency. Each new model of the basic partnership will test the reciprocal-expertise pedagogy and reveal new possibilities for the community service writing group. The online partnership is envisioned as a way to extend the reach of the collaborative program beyond the local community and also to explore the opportunities and constraints of web-based collaboration. To date, we have found that the promise of a face-to-face experience is by far the most motivating element for both classes of students. An alternative encounter for the online partnership could take the form of an Internet radio broadcast. In this model, students exchange texts throughout the process of codeveloping the radio station website and in creating social action texts that would ultimately be broadcast as Web-based radio commentaries. As in all Writing Partners projects, the central goal is to give students an opportunity to use writing as a way to build something that will bring them closer together. In a pairing of college students with community agencies, two-way textual exchange, letters, and interaction may also serve as a basic framework for reciprocity in writing. For instance, if a professor chose to frame his or her course as a community service writing group united with an area job- and life-skills training program,[6] potential projects could arise out of an initial letter exchange. Although college students might discover they need a stronger foundation for their analyses of work-related issues and texts (e.g., by reading works such as Bowe, Bowe, and Streeter's *Gig*, maintaining

---

[6]United Way agencies and other community organizations frequently offer these programs through homeless shelters and recreation centers. In 1999–2000, the Texas Christian University branch of the Writing Partners program developed this kind of agency partnership with area food banks, and with the Tarrant County Homeless Coalition. More recently, the Oklahoma City University branch has begun a partnership with the Oklahoma City National Memorial Museum.

work-experience journals, and studying work-related genres of writing), agency partners could offer their personal experiences and work documents for review. As the relationship continues, partners may discuss the problems, ideas, and concerns they have regarding their developing documents, receiving advice and feedback of all kinds as they proceed.

In Writing Partners projects, the assumption is that each partner brings unique needs, knowledge, and discourse practices to the relationship; when the groups are conscientiously facilitated, members may serve as valuable resources to one another.

Teaching Reciprocity—Cautions and Suggestions

Although there is still much to learn about fostering reciprocal learning in writing groups, the Writing Partners approach offers a few early insights into reciprocal-expertise pedagogy. In simple terms, this pedagogy is a matter of paying close attention to the relationships formed and maintained through participation in a writing group and encouraging group members to continuously recognize and use one another's expertise. The fundamental source of this expertise comes from the differing perspectives contributed by each member—differences manifested in their expectations, authorship, and reception of each text. Through our study of the Writing Partners program, we identified five primary elements that have become both obstacles and opportunities for reciprocity:

Resistance. As our opening quotations suggest, many educators and students question the feasibility of teaching academically valuable writing abilities through a program that pairs college students with writers whose expertise falls outside the realm of traditional academic writing. This question mirrors the more general concern about the academic value of any pedagogy that shifts student activity from the campus to the community. In *Where's the Learning in Service Learning?*, Janet Eyler and Dwight E. Giles, Jr. demonstrate that the academic outcomes for this kind of curriculum (including strengthened abilities in critical thinking, applied knowledge, communication, and problem solving) are enriched, not replaced, by social action. The Writing Partners case study described specific applications of the expertise exchanged with the community partners. When we turn to the broader academic objective of critical thinking, we can see benefits as well. Writers who seek expertise from community members rather than academic sources are challenged—often by sheer logistical necessity—to develop greater flexibility as researchers, collaborators, and communicators. Within the writing group itself, this challenge initially takes the form of an unfamiliar face, a stranger who must become a partner. This situation creates a disorienting dilemma: the participant is placed within a learning context that is distorted by the presence of people who are unlike his or her customary peers. Resolving this dilemma will require the participant to learn and interact in new and different ways (Palloff and Pratt 131). As Eyler and Giles explain, the disorienting dilemma requires students to critically examine their presuppositions and generate new understanding that transcends—but does include—their formal education (145–50).

Assessment. Often a teacher's nemesis under traditional classroom circumstances, assessment or evaluation can be even more difficult in a community service context such as Writing Partners. There are, in fact, more assessment issues raised by community service writing groups than we can possibly mention in this space. Centrally important to this study is the issue of assessing reciprocity. College students are unlikely to receive customary academic feedback from nonacademic writing partners, and the use of academic discourse conventions is not essential for a valuable and insightful response. The challenge, then, is to adjust our assessment criteria to represent our knowledge that the type of feedback and interaction received in this relationship differs from and is equally relevant to academic peer responses. We would, in essence, be creating the "context-specific criteria" Nora Bacon advises for all service-learning evaluation (52). For instance, we can note, along with Writing Partners instructor Carol Lattimore, that students use their partners' perspectives to invent more creatively. Lattimore's students wrote memoirs that looked back to the time when they were in second grade, their partners' age. They may not get "grammar advice" or even attention to formal organization from these partners, but they are challenged to step outside their discourse norms. Demonstrated success in entering another's discourse or challenging their own discourse thus becomes a primary criterion for grading students' work. A further criterion would be the negotiation of multiple audiences, since students will be learning to write to audiences other than the teacher, with the teacher as a secondary audience. When they learn to fulfill assignment requirements, satisfying the teacher while effectively addressing the immediate audience of the text (the partners), they have achieved the unique writerly goals of the community service writing group.

Authorship. A further assessment issue is highlighted by authorship theory. How do we place individual grades (the academic norm) on collaborative, reciprocal, relationship-building work? Candace Spigelman notes that most members of writing groups see themselves as "we" when they are in the group setting but revert to the language of individual ownership when referring to the text they will eventually be graded on. Individual grading constantly reminds students involved in writing groups of the prevailing academic notion of authorship—that is, single authorship. This tension may lead members of writing groups to dismiss the feedback they receive from others as negligible, particularly when their partners are not familiar with college writing and assessment procedures. In a dialogic, rather than hierarchical, approach to collaboration, both process and product are valued equally (Ede and Lunsford), which, if built into the pedagogy of the class, would place the grading emphasis back on the relationship-building process so central to the group. However, writing groups are seldom dialogically structured; that is, writing groups seldom allow for dialogue on every issue throughout the writing process. Rather, they are commonly the sort of collaboration in which a hierarchy emerges. The person whose name will appear on the top of the document contributes the most work time with the text, while members of the group periodically collaborate in developing, clarifying, redirecting, and prompting. We are left with the unanswered question: how can we grade process if we decide to place more emphasis on it?

Diversity. Throughout this chapter we emphasized diversity as a term for authorial perspective. That is, although an array of scholarship addresses the importance of diversity for the academic experience (see, e.g., Heath; Olguin and Schmitz), our research is specifically concerned with the way writers engage unfamiliar perspectives to acquire compositional insight or to take collaborative literate action. The disorienting dilemmas achieved through unconventional writing partnerships bring "perspective by incongruity" to the writing process. Kenneth Burke coined this term for the metaphorical strategy of examining a subject in terms of something that occupies a markedly different category (*Attitudes* 308). Thus, instead of studying "the piety of the saint" we might study "the piety of the sinner" or something even more incongruous, such as "the piety of the cobra." Burke introduces perspective by incongruity as a critical tool that enables us to transition from our customary orientations to new ones (*Permanence* 69). In traditional composition pedagogy, students regularly engage perspective by incongruity through metaphor; in reciprocal-expertise pedagogy the transformed perspective is initiated by interpersonal incongruity.

The Writing Partners program has experimented with several strategies for incorporating social diversity into its writing groups. One of this program's chief challenges has been to determine which kinds of diversity are most productive for reciprocal learning: age, social class, ethnicity, educational experience—all of these are, broadly considered, elements of cultural diversity that could be incorporated into a community service writing curriculum. Because this program originated at an institution whose undergraduate population is predominantly white, middle to upper-middle class, and of traditional college age, introducing diversity in any of the previously mentioned categories seemed desirable. As the program extended to institutions with more diverse student populations,[7] the instructors were

---

[7]For example, from 1999 to 2002 Writing Partners operated at Texas Wesleyan University, a "New Urban University" whose population is predominantly nontraditional, multicultural, first-generation and working students.

able to begin challenging and refining their initial strategy. For example, couldn't perspectives by incongruity be achieved without off-campus writing partners if the institution's student population is already diverse? What we have discovered so far is that the partnerships with children create a kind of difference that is particularly effective in the writing class. The college writers enter the writing group envisioning themselves as mentors, taking greater responsibility for the content and presentation of their texts. Because they are not intellectually intimidated by this audience, they are often more willing to take creative risks and discuss their writing process more openly. As they become more familiar with the children, they begin to take them more seriously as readers and writers—in short, the college writers experience a change in perspective as they become more sensitive to the children's contribution to their own texts.

Logistics. Not to be forgotten are the logistical challenges. These include effectively coordinating with other teachers, finding and gaining financial support, and facilitating face-to-face meetings. The first issue, teacher coordination, has been particularly difficult for a few reasons: elementary school teachers have very tight schedules and limited access to e-mail and telephones in their classrooms. To exchange letters, the college teachers often drive to the elementary schools. Regular communication is, therefore, inhibited, reducing possibilities for pedagogical collaboration and goal sharing. We recommend, at minimum, considering a foundations-intensive, pre-semester meeting at which the partnered teachers share their goals and pedagogical concerns. For the collaborative relationships to be productive for the students, the teachers need to share some common vision.

Finding and gaining financial support for simple things such as photocopying the students' work at the end of the semester, transportation from one school to the other, and the food and space necessary for a celebration requires grant writing—a process that consumes much time and energy. Furthermore, although some local businesses are glad to donate or reduce the costs for goods and services, such piecemeal financing does not advance the project in terms of day-to-day operations, curriculum development, expansion, and ongoing refinement.

Student transportation to and from museums, workshops, and celebrations not only raises financial concerns but also legal and logistical ones. Who is responsible for the students as they move from place to place? Do the field trips require extra chaperones? How much time is involved? Is there such a thing as a time and place when everyone—elementary and college students and teachers, parents, and our other community partners—can come together in person? We present this (much abbreviated) logistical litany to emphasize that in any community-engagement program logistical matters and pedagogical concerns are inseparable; creating and sustaining community service writing groups requires an infrastructure—one that invariably begins with reciprocal relationships between the instructors and community partners. To make this pedagogy work, we need them more than they need us.

Expanding Writing Groups Through Reciprocal Expertise

Traditional writing groups are based on a peer response model (Elbow *Writing Without Teachers*; Gere; Spear), but community service writing groups expand their membership to include those who do not commonly see themselves as peers. With expansion come new issues that, as we have demonstrated, are not easily answerable. Building writing groups on the basis of reciprocal expertise seems to be appropriate when we assume that reciprocal relationships are inherently more productive for members of a group than charitable or consistently hierarchical ones and when we assume that give-and-take is part of the writing group model. According to Gere, writing groups have historically fulfilled a multitude of functions for their members: entertainment (11); intellectual exercise (12); composition practice (14); pedagogical or classroom approaches (15); self-help (32); the intellectual development of women, who could not obtain such an education elsewhere (41); publication facilitation (46); and language development (77). The community service writing groups often embody many of these goals, while adding a more overtly social dimension: community service writing groups are implemented in favor of peer response groups to cultivate a critical consciousness (Herzberg), to engage in intercultural inquiry and literate action (Flower), and to collaborate for social change (Cushman). The community service writing group encourages reciprocity in ways that some forms of traditional community service, such as tutoring, do not. It is the onerous duty of teachers to understand the nature of reciprocity and the strategies that will help ensure its presence in the classroom and in the "community" of the community service writing group.

Works Cited

Architecture of Reassurance: Designing the Disney Theme Parks. Exhibition. The Modern Art Museum of Fort Worth, 1999.

Bacon, Nora. "Community Service Writing: Problems, Challenges, Questions." *Writing the Community: Concepts and Models for Service-Learning in Composition*. Eds. Linda Adler-Kassner, Robert Crooks, and Ann Watters. Washington DC: American Association for Higher Education, 1997. 29–56.

Bowe, John, Marisa Bowe, and Sabin Streeter, eds. *Gig: Americans Talk About Their Jobs*. New York: Three Rivers P, 2001.

Burke, Kenneth. *Attitudes toward History*. 3rd ed. Berkeley: U of California P, 1984.

————. *Permanence and Change*. 3rd ed. Berkeley: U of California P, 1984.

Cushman, Ellen. "The Rhetorician as an Agent of Social Change." *College Composition and Communication* 47.1 (1996): 7–28.

Deans, Tom. *Writing Partnerships: Service-Learning in Composition.* Urbana: NCTE, 2000.

Ede, Lisa, and Andrea Lunsford. *Singular Texts/Plural Authors: Perspectives on Collaborative Writing.* Carbondale: Southern Illinois UP, 1990.

Elbow, Peter. "Writing Assessment in the Twenty-First Century: A Utopian View." *Composition in the Twenty-First Century: Crisis and Change.* Eds. Lynn Z. Bloom, Donald A. Daiker, and Edward M. White. Carbondale: Southern Illinois UP, 1996. 83–100.

——————. *Writing without Teachers.* New York: Oxford UP, 1973.

Eyler, Jane, and Dwight E. Giles, Jr. *Where's the Learning in Service-Learning?* San Francisco: Jossey-Bass, 1999.

Flower, Linda. "Literate Action." *Composition in the Twenty-First Century: Crisis and Change.* Eds. Lynn Z. Bloom, Donald A. Daiker, and Edward M. White. Carbondale: Southern Illinois UP, 1996. 249–60.

——————. "Partners in Inquiry: A Logic for Community Outreach." *Writing the Community: Concepts and Models for Service-Learning in Composition.* Eds. Linda Adler-Kassner, Robert Crooks, and Ann Watters. Washington DC: American Association for Higher Education, 1997. 95–117.

——————. *Problem-Solving Strategies for Writing in College and Community.* Fort Worth: Harcourt Brace, 1998.

Gere, Ann Ruggles. *Writing Groups: History, Theory, and Implications.* Carbondale: Southern Illinois UP, 1987.

Heath, Shirley Brice. "Work, Class, and Categories: Dilemmas of Identity." *Composition in the Twenty- First Century: Crisis and Change.* Eds. Lynn Z. Bloom, Donald A. Daiker, and Edward M. White. Carbondale: Southern Illinois UP, 1996. 226–42.

Heilker, Paul. "Rhetoric Made Real: Civic Discourse and Writing Beyond the Curriculum." *Writing the Community: Concepts and Models for Service-Learning in Composition.* Eds. Linda Adler-Kassner, Robert Crooks, and Ann Watters. Washington DC: American Association for Higher Education, 1997. 71–78.

Herzberg, Bruce. "Community Service and Critical Teaching." *Writing the Community: Concepts and Models for Service-Learning in Composition.* Eds. Linda Adler-Kassner, Robert Crooks, and Ann Watters. Washington DC: American Association for Higher Education, 1997. 57–69.

Hessler, H. Brooke. "Constructive Communication: Community-Engagement Writing." *Coming of Age: An Advanced Composition Curriculum.* Eds. Linda Shamoon et al. Portsmouth: Heinemann-Boynton/Cook, 2000.

Leverenz, Carrie Shively. "Peer Response in the Multicultural Composition Classroom: Dissensus—A Dream (Deferred)." *JAC: A Journal of Composition Theory* 14.1 (1994): 167–86.

Moffett, James. *Teaching the Universe of Discourse.* Boston: Houghton Mifflin, 1968.

Olguin, Enrique, and Betty Schmitz. "Transforming the Curriculum through Diversity." *Handbook of the Undergraduate Curriculum.* Eds. Jerry G. Gaff et al. San Francisco: Jossey-Bass, 1997.

Palloff, Rena M., and Keith Pratt. *Building Learning Communities in Cyberspace.* San Francisco: Jossey-Bass, 1999.

Peck, Wayne, Linda Flower, and Lorraine Higgins. "Community Literacy." *College Composition and Communication* 46, 2 (1995): 199–222.

Petraglia, Joseph. "Spinning Like a Kite: A Closer Look at the Pseudotransactional Function of Writing." *JAC: A Journal of Composition Theory* 15.1 (1995): 19–33.

Rorty, Richard. *Philosophy and the Mirror of Nature*. Princeton: Princeton UP, 1979.

Spear, Karen. *Peer Response Groups in English Classes*. Portsmouth: Heinemann-Boynton/Cook, 1988.

Spigelman, Candace. "The Ethics of Appropriation in Peer Writing Groups." *Perspectives on Plagiarism and Intellectual Property in a Postmodern World*. Eds. Alice Roy and Lise Buranen. Albany: SUNY P, 1999. 231–40.

Trimbur, John. "Consensus and Difference in Collaborative Learning." *College English* 51, 6 (1989): 602–16.

Writing Partners. *Imagineers at Work*. Fort Worth: Write to Succeed, 1999.

ﬗﭲﭲ

Coauthoring as Place: A Different Ethos

Kami Day
Johnson County Community College

Michele Eodice
University of Kansas

> A place for us: that is all we seek. A place that allows full expression to the
> "you" and "me," the "we" of our commonality, a place where that abstract
> "we" discloses the traces that lead back to you and me.
>
> —Benjamin R. Barber, *A Place for Us*

Names and Places

Writers reading this essay will most likely recall Anne Ruggles Gere's in-
fluential work, *Writing Groups: History, Theory, and Implications* in
which Gere acknowledges that the "writing groups...phenomenon has
nearly as many names as people who employ it. The name, of course, matters less than what it describes, which is writers responding to one and
other's work" (1). Not surprising to us, Gere includes collaborative writing
among the eighteen different terms for writing groups she enumerates.
Muriel Harris defines collaborative writing as "involving two or more writers working together to produce a joint product .... Each may take responsibility for a portion of the final text [but each must take] some sort of
collective responsibility for the final product" (369). Priscilla Rogers and
Marjorie Horton acknowledge the broader definitions of collaborative writing that Gere and Harris speak of, but they extend the discussion to include
the possibility of a "fully collaborative enterprise involving coauthors who
plan, draft, and revise a document in a face-to-face context" (122). Gere and
others acknowledge a wide spectrum of ways writers work together, and we
would like to propose that collaborative writers, or coauthors, constitute

writing groups. In other words, all writing groups have in common writers responding to each other's work. Coauthors, among other things, certainly respond to each other's work; it follows, then, for us, that coauthors, whether they number two or thirty-two, instantiate writing groups. Just as Gere's history describes (literally and figuratively) the places writing groups—especially those marginalized by race, class, and gender—have carved out for themselves, through our research we have mapped the places where contemporary academic coauthors have created an ethos apart from mainstream academic authorship.

Studying Coauthors

Inveterate coauthors are a breed apart, a breed worthy of study. But even though coauthored texts represent a significant percentage of published work in the academy, few studies exist of the material practices and affective features that characterize collaborative text production. As coauthors ourselves, we have been studying other academic coauthors for the past several years.[1] We observe them as they write, but we also study the stories they tell about their work together. Included in their stories is often a description of the physical places in which these teams coauthor: hotel lobbies or hotel rooms, summer cottages, departmental offices, kitchens, back porches. We have been spotted huddling together over a laptop on a Burger King table at 3 a.m. in the Las Vegas airport. Of course, many coauthors are separated by miles and even time zones, so the place they meet in may not be corporeal; their writing space then becomes virtual, filled with e-mail exchanges and telephone conversations. However, the place that emerges as most significant in the stories they tell us is the place made possible by their desire to coauthor, their ability to coauthor, and their enactment of coauthoring.

Our qualitative study involved in-depth interviews with ten successful academic writing teams, representing a range of disciplines, experiences, and expertises. Several of the teams have coauthoring relationships that span years, but all teams had produced at least one joint text previously and were engaged in a writing project at the time of our study. As we collected and analyzed more stories of coauthoring, a pattern of interaction consistent with an ethic of care emerged. These coauthors choose to locate themselves in a place where respect, trust, and care make possible not only publishable products but also rich and rewarding personal relationships.

---

[1]Some data from our research interviews appear in this essay; to read our full study of academic coauthors, see our book *(first person)^2: Successful Coauthoring in the Academy*, Utah State UP, 2001.

Classical Conceptions of Ethos as Place

Stuart Brown, one of the experienced coauthors we studied, characterizes coauthoring as "a different ethos" (Brown). We too have come to see the space or place created by coauthoring as an ethos; our vision is based on the coauthors' perceptions of what their relationships evoke and on our own understanding of classical rhetoric. We have found some evidence to support a view that the classical idea of ethos conflates the concepts of character and place, and we start by describing the familiar conceptions of ethos, which primarily focus on the character of the rhetor.

In his *Rhetoric*, Aristotle identifies three modes of persuasion—ethos, pathos, logos—and the first, ethos, involves the personal character of the speaker; in fact, according to Aristotle, a speaker's "character may almost be called the most effective means of persuasion he [as far as Aristotle was concerned, rhetors were all men] possesses" (152). Edward P. J. Corbett, in his essay "The Ethical Dimensions of Rhetoric," stresses that Aristotle "affirmed that the ethical appeal was the most potent of all the means of persuasion" (256). However, scholars are perpetually challenged by the contradictions inherent in *Aristotle's* assertion that persuasion by moral character "must be due to the speech itself, not to any preconceived idea of the speaker's character" (17). Is ethos about being virtuous or about appearing to be virtuous? Corbett and others acknowledge the "ambivalence about the ethics of human conduct," which clouds Aristotle's definition of ethos; on the one hand, Aristotle describes ethos as putting the listener into a certain frame of mind to listen to the rhetor, and on the other hand, Corbett asserts, Aristotle is not "indifferent to the morality of the means one chooses to achieve an end" (261). Corbett is convinced that for Aristotle, "ethos was never a mere façade or veneer. It was the hard core of a person" (266).

However, Jasper Neel disagrees with this interpretation, using as evidence Aristotle's words from Book I of the *Rhetoric*: "Our discussion [of ethos] will at the same time make plain the means by which a speaker may produce in his audience the impression that he is of such and such a character" (qtd. in Neel 165). "In other words," says Neel, "virtue and goodness can be rhetorical effects, and by knowing how to produce these effects through the discourse, the rhetor can…assume a virtue not actually present in the rhetor's life" (165). Other scholars, such as George Yoos, agree that Aristotle taught that the speaker could "distort the audience's perception of his own personal qualities" (qtd. in Corbett 263) if that distortion meant the audience would be persuaded. When Jasper Neel or George Yoos insist that the speaker must be situated authentically in their discourse, they mean that the speaker's products cannot help but reflect the speaker's character. Neel proposes that the writer or speaker cannot live just "any sort of life while using rhetorical discourse to generate the effect of a moral, reliable ethos" (165).

We tend to align ourselves with Aristotle's critics, but, in the long run, it doesn't matter which interpretation we accept: when we read a text, we usually don't know anything about the writer beyond what he or she tells us. If the text appears moral, we don't know if the author is actually good or seems to be good. However, when we read a coauthored text, we know one thing about the writers: they write together. The implication for us is because they write together, especially if they choose to continue their coauthoring after their first project, the chances are good that these coauthors come from an ethical place, an ethos involving respect, trust, and care. Ethos has to do with both character and place. And the coauthors we studied come from a place created by their individual characters to another place that reflects their collective character: "a different ethos."

An etymological approach takes us from familiar notions of ethos as character to the notion of ethos as place. We turn to William M. Sattler, who explains that ethos is "derived from the Greek word for custom, habit or usage." He posits a close connection between this interpretation of ethos (a habit or custom) and the term *folkways*, which he defines as "accepted and approved practice" (55). Furthermore, he continues, folkways are often raised to the level of mores, which "concern conduct deemed so vital to the group that to violate group practice is considered to be destructive to the social welfare." However, for Sattler, "*ethos* is more inclusive than habit...and has a more comprehensive meaning than *mores*." Ethos subsumes custom, habit, and mores and "may be defined as totality of characteristic traits, rather than in terms of mere custom or morally approved habits" (55). It is this "totality of characteristic traits" that interests us and helps us move our understandings of ethos to ethos as place.

Another root meaning of ethos is found in H. G. Liddell and Robert Scott's *Lexicon*: "*êthea*, a plural noun meaning haunts or, more colloquially, 'hang outs.'" Susan C. Jarrett and Nedra Reynolds point out that "this etymology teaches us that customs are formed in places where one is accustomed to being" (48). To further the connection between habit and place and the Greek notion of ethos, S. Michael Halloran notes that one Greek meaning for ethos is "a habitual gathering place" (60). Karen Burke LeFevre extends that definition to depict a "socially created space...the point of intersection between speaker or writer and listener or reader" (45–46). Halloran evokes an "image of people gathering together in a...place, sharing experiences and ideas...[and claims that] to have *ethos* is to manifest the virtues most valued by the culture to and for which one speaks" (60).

Coauthoring In Academia

The coauthors we studied are members of a recognized culture: academia. But coauthors often struggle to "fit the square peg of multiple, polyvocal creativity into the round hole of singular 'authorship'" held sacred by the institutions in which they work (Lunsford 529). Consequently, they find themselves in a culture apart—their ethos (coauthoring) creates a place separate from the mainstream (academic) culture. We see parallels with the clubwomen in Gere's history of writing groups, *Intimate Practices: Literacy and Cultural Work in U. S. Women's Clubs, 1880–1920*: the writers in our study, by their actions, "critique the dominant culture ... [and] often move from critiquing to developing and implementing alternatives to the status quo" (53). Therefore, those who choose to coauthor do not necessarily or automatically reflect the values of the culture they publicly represent. Coauthors especially are seen not to "manifest the virtues most valued by the culture" of academia, a culture they are seen by some to resist, either because they consciously choose the square peg or find themselves unwittingly in the role of rebel.

Lisa Ede and Andrea Lunsford, two experienced coauthors in our study, told of the problems Ede had during her tenure review because of her coauthoring with Lunsford. After several years of productive coauthoring with Lunsford, Ede's publication record was called into question. Lunsford was even asked to provide "a line count of how many lines [she] wrote and how many lines Lisa wrote." Lunsford finally convinced the committee that a line count was impossible and Ede was tenured, although Lunsford "remember[s] the dean saying very specifically that if she [Ede] ever wanted to be promoted to full professor, she would have to do more singly authored work."

They also told the story of Edward P.J. Corbett's being "puzzled," "horrified," and "almost apoplectic" about their decision to coauthor an essay for Robert Connors's book on classical rhetoric and modern discourse, which was the first of their many coauthored projects. They thought Corbett would "think it was especially wonderful if they collaborated," but he cautioned them against it. Others cautioned them as well that they would jeopardize their tenure, expressing "shock, consternation, or dismay" at their coauthoring, and Ede and Lunsford admit they were at that time "naïve" in their belief that they "were not the odd ones...everyone in the world writes collaboratively" (Ede and Lunsford).

Also, several coauthors we interviewed explained that in their departments, points are awarded depending on author position on a publication; for example, a psychology professor revealed that she is awarded one hundred points for single authorship of an article, forty points if she is one of two authors, and five points if she is one of five authors. Many more stories circulate about practicing coauthors being challenged during merit review, especially in the humanities.

So, coauthors create their own "haunts" within the larger culture of the academy. Despite admonitions from the academy, more and more scholars are choosing to coauthor with peers, and their motivations run from the pragmatic to the personal. According to Frederick G. Reamer "there is some evidence that the pressure to publish may be leading to a rise in co-authorship" (130). Is it surprising then that Anne E. Austin and Roger G. Baldwin cite studies that indicate "a positive correlation between the number of authors on a paper and the probability that it will be accepted for publication" (31)? In the September 3, 1999, issue of the *Chronicle of Higher Education*, an annual survey entitled "Faculty Attitudes and Characteristics" showed that 66.5% of scholarly work is not conducted alone; the study also showed that 60% of the manuscripts submitted were accepted for publication. From these figures, we conclude that if we can assume writing is part of this study's definition of scholarly work, and if more than 66% of scholarly work is not conducted alone—is in fact collaborative—then a significant number of published texts are coauthored.

So where is this place the seemingly growing numbers of coauthors are accustomed to being, to hanging out? What *are* their customs and habits? And what are the virtues manifested by the coauthoring culture and its members?

Customs of the Coauthoring Culture

When we began studying successful academic coauthors, we expected them to talk about what they did: their material practices, how they negotiate what to include in the text, how they sit at a table together over a keyboard, and such. They did talk about their practices, but what struck us was their attention to—and sometimes almost reverence for—their relationships with each other. Like the members of writing groups Gere discusses in *Intimate Practices*, the coauthors in our study seem to value the relationship over the task, seeing their publications as happy by-products of their personal and professional associations. As they analyzed, some for the first time, their relationships, the words *respect*, *trust*, and *care* surfaced repeatedly. Among the issues raised spontaneously by these coauthors were first-author identification, promotion and tenure, cognitive gains, ownership, and the affective benefits of coauthoring; the elements listed previously—respect, trust, care—were integral to every discussion. These academics could not describe their acts of coauthoring and the attendant issues without using those words. It seems that the place these coauthors are accustomed to being, the ethos they have created, involves habits that reveal a respectful, trusting, caring approach to their work together.

First-Author Position

For instance, coauthors worked through the question of whose name would appear first on a publication by employing these elements. In reviewing studies of academic coauthoring, Austin and Baldwin point out that "conflict concerning the order of authorship can erupt" because "in a meritocracy like higher education, it is not sufficient to recognize all contributors to a joint publication. The system demands to know who contributed more and who contributed less to the collective endeavor" (67). Austin and Baldwin present some solutions to this problem, such as listing names in alphabetical order, attention to the significance of the contribution, and heed to seniority (68–69), and though some of the coauthors in our study acknowledged considering these solutions, most of them took a more nurturing stance, one that asks "Who *needs* to be first author?" This concern for the professional needs of each other is not even mentioned by Austin and Baldwin but is a primary focus for those in our study. For example, Duane Roen has coauthored more than seventy-five publications, often with graduate students, and he explained that "most often the first author has been the person who most immediately needs to have this publication...someone who is finishing a degree and is going on the market" (Roen). Michael Blitz and C. Mark Hurlbert have become accustomed to alternating first names on their coauthored publications, but Hurlbert admitted that when he became a full professor before Blitz, "We agreed...well we didn't have to agree...it just happened...that his name went first on everything...who needs it" (Blitz and Hurlbert). Several other coauthoring teams described their first-author decisions as context driven, based on a general concern for professional welfare, and primarily responding to the political implications of first-author status for untenured academics.

Once professional concerns were out of the way, most teams insisted that first-author position was arbitrary: it didn't matter. The teams we studied trust each other to honor their commitments, and they respect each other's work enough to hope for equal recognition of all team members' contributions by those who read and evaluate their writing. Consequently, first author is not seen to be about getting credit. When we asked Kathleen and Jim Strickland how they had decided who would be first author on their book *UnCovering the Curriculum*, Kathleen turned to Jim and laughed, "Ask him!" to which Jim replied, "'Cause I put her first." They had discussed alternating names on their coauthored publications, but Jim thought that arrangement would be confusing, and they both insisted several times that they "couldn't care less whose name goes first." Now they remain consistent and place Kathleen's name always in the lead "for ease of readers and for people using [their] work" (Strickland and Strickland). But most teams claim they are satisfied alternating names and believe at this point in their careers that a new problem arises. Stuart Brown identified a single struggle in his coauthorship with Duane Roen; often he cannot get Roen and another coauthor, Theresa Enos, to take the credit they deserve. When we asked Roen and Brown how they decide author order, they joked that they "have a big fight about it" and then added, "usually we end up drawing straws or flipping coins...or something" (Brown and Roen).

Coauthoring as Epistemic

Even more evident in our study than the issue of first author is the enthusiasm with which one co-author characterized the contributions of the other. The cognitive gains the coauthors identified come from sharing knowledge and experiences, as well as from learning and practicing strategies for improving the writing itself. One coauthor expressed a collective conviction when he said, "If I had written it on my own it wouldn't have been nearly as good as it was," and another coauthor exclaimed, "Doesn't your brain just think more?!" For all the coauthors, the cognitive advantages of their collaboration went beyond what they believe to be excellent products.

The coauthors we studied had come to realize that coauthoring is epistemic; some had sought out each other's expertise initially, while others were able to describe the learning experience only on reflection during their interviews with us. Susan Besemer and Karen O'Quin came together because Besemer, a librarian, needed O'Quin's expertise in analyzing quantitative data and then found that their skills complemented each other. They agreed they produce "more and better" than either of them could produce alone, and O'Quin credited Besemer with being the "brains of the gang because it's her theory initially....it's sort of like the kernel...Sue is the germinal one" (S. Besemer and K. O'Quin). Duane Roen also subscribes to the more and better theory. For him, "The important thing is that more than one mind is coming together," and Stuart Brown enjoys that another mind provides "a different critical perspective that gets you kick-started" (Brown and Roen). Another pair, an education professor and a psychology professor, told a story of a four-hour car trip during which they both "moved positions" on theories of constructivism and behaviorism, theories that were relevant to their teaching philosophies as well as to a current writing project. Many pairs echoed the power of talk in the coauthoring ethos; Matthew Oldman, an inveterate collaborator, thrives on being confronted with people who don't think he has all the answers, and his current writing partner says she welcomes "changing [her] ideas because of what someone else has said" (Kent and Oldman). And Kathleen Strickland insisted that Jim has taught her much about writing because he was a writing teacher before she was. She confessed to feeling "humble" when they began writing together, but she added, "We have both gotten better at what we do, and I'm just tickled pink I have somebody to work with that complements what I do" (Strickland and Strickland).

They recognize, as does Frank Walters in his interpretation of Isocrates' *Antidosis*, that "within the thematic scope of *ethos* a number of diverse issues adumbrate the relationship between individual and community...the private *episteme* is meaningless—it means nothing—if it is separated from the community which holds the power of granting epistemological validity" (9). Typically, scholars present their putatively individually generated work to the academic community, and the community acknowledges the scholar's contribution to their field's body of knowledge. Both writer and reader do learn from that experience but on different planes, perhaps separated from each other by space and time. But for coauthors, the experience of sharing and weaving together diverse knowledge begins during the writing, resulting in a richer, more complete product, partly because of a built-in, immediate, trusted audience, or even audiences. As Gere points out,

> the dominant concept of authorship serves to isolate (and therefore frequently alienate) writers from their readers...this alienation decreases writers' ability to visualize their audiences....One of the benefits continually attributed to the collaboration of writing groups is that they bring writers and readers closer together, thereby providing writers a direct experience with audiences. (67, 66)

In their article "Audience Addressed, Audience Invoked," Ede and Lunsford use the term *invoked audience* to describe the audience writers imagine as they create a text and the term *addressed audience* to characterize the concrete audience known to the author. We see that coauthors have an initial advantage in that they have, in each other, an immediate, addressed audience. Not only that, each coauthor, in addition to being an audience for the coauthored work, has their own experience with audiences involving themselves, colleagues, friends, critics, students, and so on. Consequently, writers working together increase exponentially the potential for invoking "a vision which they hope readers will actively come to share as they read the text—by using all the resources of language available to them to establish a broad, and ideally coherent, range of cues for the reader" (Ede and Lunsford 167). Writers working together multiply their audiences, both invoked and concrete, and their language resources. Ede and Lunsford maintain that coauthors' commitment to make knowledge with each other can "attest concretely to the power of a co-author's expectations and criticisms and also illustrate that one person can take on the role of several different audiences: friend, colleague, and critic" (168). If the community of the academy at large seems to value the private episteme, then coauthors are motivated to create a space that validates a more collaboratively generated epistemology. Respect and trust inhabit this coauthoring space and are requisite in allowing these cognitive gains to be realized.

Ownership

Just as respect and trust are involved in the issues of first author and cognitive gains, the issue of ownership also involves respect and trust. Individual writers must be willing to give up recognition of their unique contributions, respect the voices of their coauthors, relinquish possession of their own language, and trust that the collective voice will represent them well. For all writers, the idea of sharing texts with peers, getting feedback from readers and being willing to make changes, is based on trust, and this sharing is especially visible and explicit in coauthoring. Successful coauthors may be following Chaim Perelman and Lucie Olbrechts-Tyteca's advice to trust the audience, to imagine an audience that is receptive. In laying out *New Rhetoric* in 1969, Perelman and Olbrechts-Tyteca described an ideal audience, not ideal in the foundational sense but ideal in that the audience is willing to listen, think, and accept the words of the speaker or writer, at least for a while. As we mentioned previously, for the writing teams we studied, the first and ideal audience is each other, and they trust that audience. The good will extended in that mutual audience created by coauthoring demonstrates the dimension of respect and trust we claim is located in the ethos created by working with others.

The coauthors in our study described their collective writing processes in a way that indicates a lack of possessiveness about their individual contributions and respect for each other as audience. One math professor in our study admitted that she and her coauthor both like to get their own way, but sometimes one of them just says, "Okay, fine, it's a stupid quote but you can have it." When we asked why they would "give in," one of them answered, "Because I trust her judgment. She thinks it's good … she knows what she's doing" (Smith and Sebastian). And from the beginning of their coauthorship, C. Mark Hurlbert and Michael Blitz agreed that what they contributed would not be held sacred. They said:

> We have an unwritten rule that either one of us could change the other person's words completely. We could chuck it and the other person wasn't going to go, "Hey! What are you doing?" And it was clear early on that we wanted to say things that mattered in the best possible way we could say them.

One of them might have an idea and e-mail a draft to the other: "The other person can get rid of it down to a single syllable and send it back…and there's never been a moment when the other person has acted offended or defensive." (Blitz and Hurlbert). The Stricklands too were insistent about the level of respect and trust they maintain. Jim said, "When you're writing together you need to feel comfortable with changing somebody else's words," and Kathleen agreed: "And that person needs to be comfortable with your changing them. Anything that Jim would change would be a welcome change to me because there is such respect back and forth for the process and what we can each bring to it" (K. Strickland and J. Strickland, personal interview, January 1998).

Susan Besemer, in describing her coauthoring with Karen O'Quin, remarked, "Neither of us is possessive about our language. If she reads something that I write and she rewords it, I'm just so grateful...and when I've made a change, it's generally received well...it's not received with any question or hostility" (Besemer and O'Quin). Mark Bonacci, a social psychologist, and Katherine Johnson, a sociologist, described how they coauthored a cross-disciplinary textbook: they exchanged drafts, "messed up the other person's draft," and then discussed revisions as they worked on the book. Johnson claimed, "The big thing is that we respect each other and trust each other and know that what we're getting from the other person is real quality." In addition, both found the other's style a useful counterweight: Bonacci appreciates Johnson's ability to write in a more academic, less "over the top" style. He said, "I like the feedback because ever since I've been writing, people have argued that I am not subtle and I go a bit beyond the pale, so when Kate said, 'look Mark, try to make this a little more balanced,' it was fine with me" (Bonacei and Johnson). Through these stories, the writing teams we studied acknowledged what Lunsford calls "the largely collaborative and highly dispersed nature of most creative endeavors" (529). On their way to both producing texts and improving texts, they involve a trusted reader much earlier and more consistently throughout the process. These co-authors share responsibility and credit for the text which is jointly produced, moving the idea of co-authoring closer to Lunsford's vision of "alternative modes of ownership" (541).

Affective Benefits

Few studies of coauthoring have addressed the affective benefits of writing with another. In a study of female academic coauthors, Cynthia Sullivan Dickens and Mary Ann D. Sagaria point out that "affective qualities enmeshed in academic research relationships have not been captured by traditional quantitative research methods" (95). We mentioned earlier that the coauthors we studied seemed to honor the relationship around their work more than the text production. In fact, their talk about their relationships—and the trust, respect, and care they involve—revealed the most about their success as coauthors. They claimed that coauthoring led to significant friendships, fun, and the opportunity to better link what they do with what they value and who they are. None of the coauthors we studied were simply colleagues; most had begun their coauthoring as friends, and their work together had deepened their friendships. One of the best examples of a deep friendship is that of Michael Blitz and C. Mark Hurlbert. Although both could write (and have written) with others, their best coauthoring experiences have been with each other. Blitz explained, "There may be thousands of people I'd have great collaborations with but life is very limited … it's like when you have a family you want to make sure that family is sustained. Mark is my family and I intend to enjoy that as long as it is enjoyable." Hurlbert added, "Certainly I am a fuller human being for my relations to him [Blitz]—so the value is personal—or even spiritual…to put it simply, my life is more meaningful for Michael's presence in it" (M. (Blitz and Hurlbert). His words echo phrases Gere quotes in *Intimate Practices*, phrases such as "richer for having known and loved her," spoken by women whose "literacy practices embodied their love, liking, and care for one another" (39, 45).

Many of the coauthors told stories of generous emotional support their coauthors offered them during times of personal and professional challenge: job searching and moving, family tragedies, divorce, and health problems. Some vacation together, visit each other's families, help each other work on their homes, and care for each other's children. That they achieve a level of comfort with each other is illustrated in a story told by one pair, Gilbert Adams and Julie Knight. Adams remembered a time when he and Knight decided to go to Knight's apartment to work on a book chapter. He remembered thinking,

> I'm so tired…now if I were home I would just lie down and take a nap…[and] I forget who mentioned what but somehow we just got on the topic of we were really tired…and Julie said, "Well, let's just take a nap." So she gave me a clock and went to her bedroom, and I lay down on the couch and we set the clock, and a half hour later we woke up and we started writing again! And I was thinking, "I've never done that…that's what I would do if I were on my own!" (Adams and Knight).

Almost every team brought up the "F" word—FUN—an element sorely missing in most conversations about scholarly work. Hurlbert and Blitz admitted that a project sometimes has a "goofy start" and that they often "play around a little bit." In discussing her one singly authored book, Kathleen Strickland lamented, "I didn't have as much fun…I wouldn't look to do that again." When we asked Lunsford and Ede how writing together is different from writing alone, they agreed that alone they "don't have as much fun," and they wanted us to know that although they both have a sometimes punishing work ethic, they like to play too. Knight described her coauthoring with Adams as "a hoot," and Adams added, "It was a blast!" One team had a great deal of fun teasing and provoking each other during the interview, and, at one point, one of them said about their coauthoring, "Your time is gone, that's for sure…that [the loss of time] would be punishment, but the fact is you enjoy what you're doing so much more that it's not the pay…it's not any of that."

Perhaps these coauthoring relationships go beyond friendship that can develop during extended workplace interaction. These scholars were not just working together, they were writing together. In a telling comment, Knight defined collaborative writing as "an intimate process…and I think when you do it well and you get to that level of intimacy then you start to cross assumptions and values…and you can't help but develop a good relationship." This statement may sum up the relationships of the members of the teams more accurately and profoundly than any other in our interviews. When coauthoring is successful—when collaborators recognize and value each other's strengths, watch out for each other, and trust each other to nurture their professional and personal relationships—perhaps intimate relationships are a natural and beneficial outcome. Perhaps the ethos created by coauthoring involves the space where affective responses, rather than being suppressed, become integral to the work.

A Place of Caring

The term *ethics* is a cognate of the word *ethos*, meaning that *ethos* is the parent term. Ethics has come to be regarded idiomatically as having to do with integrity, fairness, honesty; however, as we pointed out earlier, *ethos* is a neutral term. It has to do with a set of customs, a "totality of characteristics," inherently neither good nor bad, that develop in "habitual gathering places": the family home, the classroom, the workplace. We acknowledge that all coauthoring is not successful; most of the coauthors in our study told stories of coauthoring derailed by issues of hierarchy, ego, and irresponsibility. However, as we have shown, in the "habitual gathering place"—the ethos—of successful coauthoring, ethics of respect, trust, and care are enacted. In addition, we also believe coauthoring has the power to construct, or engender, an ethic of care. Nel Noddings, in proposing an ethic of care, claims that the impulse to care "lies latent in each of us, awaiting gradual development in a succession of caring relations" (83). She describes the ethic of care as "relational," focusing "on the human beings involved in the situation under consideration and their relations to each other" (173). In an ethical relation, participants strive to maintain or transform the relationship into a caring one. For Noddings, for us, and for the coauthors we studied, collaboration has the potential to engender ethical acts of caring.

Furthermore, the "habitual gathering place" created by coauthoring puts down a welcome mat and keeps the light on. The late Jim Corder describes a "generative" ethos that "opens up the borders of the discourse" (32). For him, an "ethos is generative and fruitful when the time and space stewarded by a speaker [or writer] give free room for another to live in.... Generative ethos is commodious" (34). This ethos welcomes other writers' views, voices, ontologies, and experiences; everyone is invited. For example, Michele has recently coauthored two articles, one with five graduate students and one with a graduate student and her forty-three undergraduate fresh-man composition students. One of the coauthoring teams we studied con-sisted of two experienced faculty and one graduate student, and several of the coauthors told of writing with students and junior faculty. Coauthoring, as least in our findings, has a mentoring quality yet cuts across hierarchies.

Over the last few years, as we coauthored ourselves and became ac-quainted with other coauthors, we have often tried to visualize what the coauthoring ethos might look like. If ethos is a place, as we are asserting, then the metaphor of a group gathered around a pond illumines the term dramati-cally. When a number of people encircle a pond, coming to the water's edge as separate individuals, they are suddenly reflected as one entity in its sur-face; that collective reflection is their ethos. Without the pond, without hav-ing come together over something (a civic problem, a community issue, a classroom project, a scholarly endeavor), there is no ethos. The ethos, in this case coauthoring, appears productive, commodious place. Some academics search in vain for such hospitable places; it is rare to hear a singular author claim to have enjoyed the writing process, even if the product has been posi-tively received. But the successful coauthors we studied found a place to which they return time and again, knowing they will find deep satisfaction in the process due to the caring, respectful relationships they find there.[2]

Fox and Faver (1984) speak of the "costs" of collaborative work: exces-sive time, financial expenses, the "personal, socio-emotional cost of devel-oping and maintaining a good working relationship," and lack of commitment are termed "process costs" (352–53); "outcome costs" are de-lays caused by a "sluggish collaborator," deciding who gets credit, and pos-sible loss of quality (353–54). In a study of educators who collaborate, Joan P. Isenberg, Mary Renck Jalongo, and Karen D'Angelo Bromley (1987) re-port similar findings: fully 50% of the educators studied related negative ex-periences with collaboration. In addition, they found these drawbacks: inability to achieve consensus, the inability to resolve differences in writing styles, and a "clash of philosophies and interests," which includes decisions about "purpose, focus, audience, and outlet for the publication." But, for

---

[2]We realize that after one experience, many authors choose not to return to coauthoring.

the respondents to their questionnaire, the most "pervasive and difficult" problem was "failure to share a vision" (14).

As we considered the coauthors in our study in light of these reports, we found that none of the teams we studied brought up money, and although some wished they had more time, and all but one team admitted that coauthoring took more time than singly authoring, they did not see the extra time as a cost. In addition, all the interviewees saw the quality of their products as enhanced by collaboration. None of these successful coauthors saw maintenance of a good relationship, allocation of credit, or reaching a consensus as difficult or costly. Our work has been criticized for presenting an ideal or romantic version of coauthoring, one devoid of horror stories and negative cases. In reflecting on collaborative research, Kirsch states: "I have come to realize that the ideal scenario of successful collaboration is just that: an ideal…. It has become abundantly clear to me that collaboration rarely unfolds in all the ways we wish" (1999, 159). And though we don't disagree with her, we believe that this ideal is possible with the right mix of coauthors and approaches. Some of the writers in our study mentioned past negative coauthoring experiences, but the stories they told in the interviews revealed a positive and productive process. We studied successful writing groups to find out why they work—for those who may desire to write with others and for those who hope to teach students to write together.

The writers in our study choose to coauthor and to continue coauthoring; they write from a place of respect, trust, and care, creating an ethos or place where writers agree to share and accept each other's views while working toward a product that values and accommodates multiple voices and subject positions. In this way, a fresh environment is created, one that reflects the collective character and disposition of the community, dyad, or group. Moreover, we believe coauthoring possesses the power to engender an ethos of care; rather than attempting to represent an ethos split from his or her lived life, a coauthor forms an ethical character by "learning to speak to the interests of the community [or team]" (Jarrett and Reynolds 44) and coming to value the connections such a stance makes possible. And, consequently, we find ourselves more and more likely to respect the work of scholars who are in the habit of coauthoring; that they work successfully together suggests that they incorporate an ethos of care in their scholarship, in their interaction with colleagues, and in their pedagogy.

Acknowledgments

We thank the academic coauthors who took the time to become part of our research. In addition, C, Mark Hurlbert, Kirk Branch, and the reviewers of this essay provided thoughtful feedback, and working with this collection's three editors was a pleasure.

Works Cited

Adams, Gilbert, and Julie Knight. Personal interview. December, 1997.

Aristotle. *The "Art" of Rhetoric.* Trans. John Henry Freese. London: William Heinemann, 1927.

Austin, Anne E., and Roger G. Baldwin. *Faculty Collaboration: Enhancing the Quality of Scholarship and Teaching.* ASHE-ERIC Higher Education Report No. 7. Washington, DC: The George Washington University, School of Education and Human Development, 1991.

Barber, Benjamin. *A Place for Us: How to Make Society Civil and Democracy Strong.* New York: Hill and Wang, 1998.

Besemer, Sue, and Karen O'Quin. Personal interview. May, 1998.

Blitz, Michael, and C. Mark Hurlbert. Personal interview. March, 1998.

Bonacei, Mark and Kate Johnson. Personal interview. March, 1998

Brown, Stuart, and Duane Roen. Personal interview. March, 1998.

Corbett, Edward P. J. "The Ethical Dimensions of Rhetoric." *Selected Essays of Edward P. J. Corbett.* Ed. Robert J. Connors. Dallas: Southern Methodist UP, 1989. 253–66.

Corder, Jim W. "Studying Rhetoric and Teaching School." *Rhetoric Review* 1 (1982): 4–36.

Dickens, Cynthia Sullivan, and Mary Ann D. Sagaria. "Feminists at Work: Collaborative Relationships Among Women Faculty." *The Review of Higher Education* 21 (1997): 79–101.

Ede, Lisa, and Andrea Lunsford. "Audience Addressed/Audience Invoked: The Role of Audience in Composition Theory and Pedagogy." *College Composition and Communication* 35 (1984): 155–71.

Ede, Lisa, and Andrea Lunsford. Personal interview. March, 1998.

Fox, Mary Frank, and Catherine A. Faver. "Independence and Cooperation in Research: The Motivations and Costs of Collaboration." *Journal of Higher Education* 55 (1984): 347–59.

"Faculty Attitudes and Characteristics: Results of a 1998–99 Survey." *Chronicle of Higher Education* 3 Sept. 1999. http://chronicle.com/weekly/v46/i02/facts/4602facultysurvey.htm 23 May 2003

Gere, Anne R. *Writing Groups: History, Theory, and Implications.* Carbondale: Southern Illinois UP, 1987.

Gere, Anne R. *Intimate Practices: Literacy and Cultural Work in U.S. Women's Clubs, 1880–1920.* Urbana, IL: University of Illinois Press, 1997.

Halloran, Michael. "Aristotle's Concept of Ethos, or If Not His, Somebody Else's." *Rhetoric Review* 1 (1982): 58-63.

Harris, Muriel. "Collaboration Is Not Collaboration Is Not Collaboration: Writing Center Tutorials vs. Peer-response Groups." *College Composition and Communication* 43 (1992): 369–83.

Isenberg, Joan P., Mary Renck Jalongo, and Karen D'Angelo Bromley. *The Role of Collaboration in Scholarly Writing: A National Study.* Paper. Annual meeting of the American Educational Research Association, Washington, DC, 1987. ERIC Document Reproduction Service No. ED 287 873.

Jarrett, Susan C., and Nedra Reynolds. "The Splitting Image: Contemporary Feminisms and the Ethics of *êthos.*" *Ethos: New Essays in Rhetorical and Critical The-

ory. Eds. James S.Baumlin and Tita French Baumlin. *SMU Studies in Composition and Rhetoric*. Ed. Gary Tate. Dallas: Southern Methodist UP, 1994. 37–63.

Kent, Diane, and Matthew Oldman. Personal interview. November, 1997.

Kirsch, Gesa E. "Reflecting on Collaboration in Feminist Empirical Research: Some Cautions." *Feminist Empirical Research: Emerging Perspectives on Qualitative and Teacher Research*. Eds. Joanne Addison and Sharon James McGee. Portsmouth: Heinemann-Boynton/Cook, *1999. 158–62*.

LeFevre, Karen Burke. *Invention as a Social Act. Studies in Writing and Rhetoric*. Carbondale: Southern Illinois UP, 1987.

Liddell, H. G., and Robert Scott. *A Lexicon: Abridged from Liddell and Scott's Greek-English Lexicon*. New York: Oxford UP, 1984.

Lunsford, Andrea Abernethy. "Rhetoric, Feminism, and Textual Ownership." *College English* 61 (1999): 529–44.

Neel, Jasper. *Aristotle's Voice: Rhetoric, Theory, and Writing in America*. Carbondale: Southern Illinois UP, 1994

Noddings, Nel. *Caring: A Feminine Approach to Ethics and Moral Education*. Berkeley: U of California P, 1984.

Perelman, Chaim, and Lucie Olbrechts-Tyteca. *The New Rhetoric: A Treatise on Argumentation*. Trans. John Wilkensons and Purcell Weaver. Notre Dame: U of Notre Dame Press, 1969.

Reamer, Frederick G. "From the Editor: Publishing and Perishing in Social Work Education." *Journal of Social Work Education* 28 (1992): 129–31.

Roen, Duane. Personal interview. March, 1998.

Rogers, Priscilla, and Marjorie S. Horton. "Exploring the Value of Face-to-Face Collaborative Writing." New Visions of Collaborative Writing. Ed. Janis Forman. Portsmouth: Heinemann-Boynton/Cook, 1992. 120–46.

Sattler, William M. "Conceptions of *Ethos* in Ancient Rhetoric." *Speech Monographs* 14 (1947): 55–65.

Smith, Emily, and Roja Sebastian. Personal interview. January, 1998.

Strickland, Kathleen, and James Strickland. Personal interview. January, 1998.

Walters, Frank. "Isocrates and the Epistemic Return: Individual and Community in Classical and Modern Rhetoric." *Journal of Advanced Composition* 13 (1993): 155–71.

II

Writing Groups in the Extracurriculum: Broadening the Focus

CHAPTER NINE

ဢ

"Species" of Rhetoric: Deliberative and Epideictic Models in Writing Group Settings

Candace Spigelman
Pennsylvania State University at Berks-Lehigh Valley

Although we rarely think about it, writing group discourse is inherently persuasive. It isn't just student writers who resist peer advice; even the most experienced writers are, at times, reluctant revisors. As a result, writing group members must devise the best argument or case, choosing rhetorical forms that will move their listener—the writer—to make changes in his or her manuscript. Reader-responders cultivate active revision by proving that a particular textual decision will be expedient or effective, by demonstrating what works well, and by pointing out what does not work at all. Whether they know it or not, writing group members usually select among strategies that represent the "species," or persuasive genres, described in Aristotle's *Rhetoric*. In particular, deliberative and epideictic rhetoric have relevance to writing group theory and practice.

According to traditional definitions, deliberative rhetoric is forward looking; it is oriented toward finding the best solution or most reasonable course of action. Writing groups may be said to employ deliberative rhetoric when members interrogate the logic of an argument, suggest textual changes, or provide additional examples for helping a writer to make his or her case. Epideictic, in contrast, is set in the present; its central purpose is praise or blame. Writing group members invoke epideictic rhetoric when they express an emotional response to a peer's essay or story and when they explain what they found meaningful or dissatisfying, attractive or ugly. Ideally, both rhetorical models should guide writing group practice. In many situations, however, either an epideictic or deliberative orientation will dominate, and thus constrain, a group's process by diminishing the complexity of response and the potential for subsequent revision.

This is the situation Marvin Diogenes describes in "Creativity and Commonplaces: A Rhetoric for Fiction Writers." In general, he says, creative writing class workshops are grounded in an epideictic model, which often serves only to confirm or deny the value of the writer's existing draft. When that happens, students respond to peer feedback with defensiveness and resistance, and sessions can deteriorate to brutal, competitive attacks, where instructors' comments count as the only valid critique. Because an exclusively epideictic model may confound the purpose of writing group activity and stunt the potential for revision, Diogenes encourages creative writing workshops to imitate the deliberative process modeled in many first-year writing class groups. As Diogenes acknowledges, however, composition class writing groups are not models of perfection. Although peer readers are taught to provide "more forward-looking responses," he notes that "composition classes often have the problem of focusing that deliberative energy" (correspondence). Peer group discourse can easily shift off task, or readers may suggest changes that are ultimately inconsistent with the writer's intentions. Moreover, without the counterweight of epideictic rhetoric, response groups run the risk of becoming too coercive or appropriative.

In my research, I found that practicing creative writers who meet voluntarily outside of the academy actually alternate between these genres or engage them simultaneously. Their workshops invoke a version of deliberative rhetoric found in many composition class response groups; at the same time, epideictic features of group discourse acknowledge a writer's skill, intentions, and authority and thus allow writers to explore alternatives while retaining ownership of their manuscripts. This essay focuses on the dynamic practices of the Franklin Writing Group, five writers who gathered monthly in a downtown Philadelphia café to share and critique their writing. My research shows that the Franklin Writing Group relied on both deliberative and epideictic discourses, through a process that enabled readers to provide productive, action-oriented response and simultaneously allowed writers to resist appropriation by their expert peers.

When I began my study, Fay, Stephanie, Brenda, Doug, and Ellen, had been together for close to a year. They first met in a noncredit creative writing class at Temple University Center City, where, during class workshops, they discovered that they worked well together. At the professor's suggestion, they began meeting outside of class, and the Franklin Writing Group was formed. All of the members were college graduates; several had graduate degrees. Fay was a professional fiction writer, and Doug, Ellen, and Brenda wrote nonfiction prose in their professional lives. Writing in different genres, from science fiction to psychological thrillers to young adult romance, the Franklin members composed novels, short stories, and news articles and shared these at their meetings. Although they had different expectations for publishing their creative work, all were equally committed to contributing and responding to their peers on a monthly basis, and all took their writing very seriously.

In the discussion that follows, I trace the deliberative and epideictic features of the Franklin Writing Group's discourse. By examining their methods, arguments, and goals, I show how these two "species" of Aristotelian rhetoric operated in tandem as well as interdependently so that, in many instances, the discourses could not be separated. Finally, I argue that both models of response are necessary for productive collaboration in writing groups at all levels and in all settings.

Balancing Methods: Deliberative and Epideictic Practices

In most voluntary creative writing groups, rhetorical choices are intrinsic to the workshop processes. Members do not consciously decide to use one approach or another: invoking deliberative or epideictic rhetoric depends entirely on the discursive needs of the moment. Thus, in any given session—indeed, within any given verbal exchange—reader-responders will select among genres to accomplish particular ends.

Writing group members use deliberative rhetoric to persuade a peer writer to make changes in his or her manuscript or to revise in a particular way. Often translated as "political oratory," deliberative rhetoric "urges us either to do or not to do something" on the grounds that the proposed course of action will be most expedient and least harmful (Aristotle, "Rhetorica" I.3.5). It focuses on issues that warrant a change or decision, including policies, procedures, and intellectual products, and it seeks to encourage an active response. Aristotle notes that although his central concerns in *Rhetoric* are with public forms of persuasion, rhetorical strategies have equal import when guiding individuals in their personal decisions. He explains that "deliberative advice is either protreptic ['exhortation'] or apotreptic ['dissuasion']; for both those advising in private and those speaking in public always do one or the other of these" (*Rhetoric* I.3.3). Members of writing groups can thus be understood as rhetors operating in a private domain, using the same strategies as public speakers to urge a writer to revise. While Aristotle holds that "true judges" are those who decide issues of public concern, he allows that persuasive speech is always intended "to lead to decisions ... even if one is addressing a single person and urging him to do or not to do something, ... the single person is as much your 'judge' as if he were one of many; we may say, without qualification, that any one is your judge whom you have to persuade" ("Rhetorica" II.18.1). In writing groups, the writer whose text is under examination becomes the "judge," determining which suggestions for revision are most helpful or expedient.

Deliberative rhetoric was a significant feature of every creative writing group I observed for my research and was a sustaining characteristic of the Franklin Writing Group's monthly transactions. In its written form, it appeared on drafts as margin notes with brief suggestions for revising. For example, Stephanie's experimental epistolary short story garnered written comments like the following: "Maybe make a bigger show of the fact that the dates go backward"; "Put in more reminiscences about 'when we did such and such'"; "Instead of dates, put 'X days earlier.'" Group members usually supplemented their marginalia at the meetings, and these oral comments represented the most productive and persuasive features of their deliberative responses. Augmenting their written comments to Stephanie's story, group members fashioned a variety of alternatives to her narrative chronology.

Fay:	You need more red flags .... Maybe she's talking to a good friend. There is lots of fear running through the letters. It could be revealed. In the letters, she is afraid to reveal who she really was. She is afraid—she is who, what she thinks he wants her to be. "Remember when" should be revealed in dialogue.
Ellen:	You could use New Years, Christmas, Valentine's Day instead of the dates.
Doug	... Maybe that's the problem: there is no dramatic tension. Either you need more tension—bad feelings played out—in your face tension ... Or you can take this as experimental: she goes back and re-edits. She goes back and rewrites. We get several versions of the scenes. You can play with reality. Use the frame of the letter device.
Ellen:	You can make the title "Palindrome."

These dynamic coinventing, cocomposing activities encouraged writers to reconceptualize their work and to revise accordingly. Presenting alternative revising options, like the "alternative possibilities" into which deliberative rhetoric inquires ("Rhetorica" I.1.12), helped to prompt action by easing the creative burden. Writers had suggestions "in hand" to incorporate in their stories or to serve as models for the kinds of changes they might later want to make.

In contrast to the active orientation of deliberative rhetoric, epideictic speeches are defined as those that "do not call for any immediate action by the audience but that characteristically praise or blame some person or thing, often on a ceremonial occasion such as a public funeral of holiday"

(Kennedy 7). Often glossed as "demonstration" or "display," epideictic rhetoric is grounded in the present, for, as Aristotle explains, "all speakers praise or blame in regard to existing qualities," although they "often also make use of other things, both reminding [the audience] of the past and projecting the course of the future" (*Rhetoric* I.3.4). As Aristotle describes it, epideictic address concerns itself with what is morally honorable, fine, or good. Even in Aristotle's time, however, ceremonial rhetoric was also applied to objects and concepts, not just to individuals; in recent years it has been understood to assume a literary critical function, emphasizing aesthetic merit, rather than moral virtue (Fahnestock and Secor; Oravec; Sullivan, "Epideictic").

Dale L. Sullivan's emphasis on the epideictic character of literary criticism (that it is grounded in the present and that it is centrally concerned with aesthetic judgments of value) links it to writing group discourse. Sullivan explains, "When I respond to a paper under review for publication by recommending that it not be published and go on to give reasons for my opinion, I engage in censure" ("Epideictic" 343). Sullivan describes critical discourse as "a rhetoric of unveilment" ("Epideictic" 341–42), suggesting that something immanent in a written work is revealed to the critic and expressed in the criticism. From the perspective of writing group theory, however, we might say that during workshops reader-responders engage the epideictic rhetoric of literary criticism when they expose the values in, or assert the value of, their peers' texts. When Diogenes labels classroom-based creative writing groups as "predominantly epideictic" ("Creativity"), he is noting their literary critical emphasis.

In the Franklin Writing Group, ceremonial rhetoric included praise for literary merit as well as negative criticism. As margin notes, written epideictic responses tended to be quite brief: there were negative assertions, such as "Don't like this opening line," and positive comments, such as "good" or "yes," alongside a marked passage, or "I can see all this—very real," noting a successful scene. Positive comments were not simply niceties intended to smooth the way for harsher criticism. They were starting points for lengthy oral expositions on the strengths and merits of a piece, and they enabled writers to see the impact of their work on their readers.

In workshops, group members often used the Aristotelian strategy of amplification, which is intended to heighten the effect of praise by means of superlatives and contrasts. In *Rhetoric*, amplification demonstrates an individual's superiority compared to others, but in the Franklin Group, greater emphasis was placed on improvements and innovations in a single text. Stephanie's comments about Doug's novel, for instance, emphasized successful features of his newer sections, in contrast to earlier chapters, which he would ultimately need to revise:

I have to say to my surprise, Doug, I'm getting into this the story. Because I'm not into science fiction, it confuses me at times, but I'm much more into these chapters. They were long, but they read much faster than the others, so I liked it a lot better. One thing these chapters have that the other chapters didn't have is dialogue. It makes it read faster, and it takes away some of the wordiness. I liked the way the characters played off of each other. It's very clever. Also, some of the things you explained were really clear, where they could have been confusing.

Stephanie continued by applauding the clarity of one specific scene, then went on to praise Doug's handling of technological elements, characterizing his effort as "really interesting." She then identified a particularly strong piece of dialogue, and, finally, complimented his handling of a crucial fight scene:

I liked how J [the protagonist] observed the first part of the struggle through his phone. I thought that was really interesting and a good way to do that. The other thing I liked was your imagery of the fight scene. I thought you described that well. You didn't get out of hand with description. It was to the point.

Although group members were extremely tactful, they did not shy away from negative critique. Reacting to Fay's murder mystery, Doug said:

The explanatory comments are still hitting us on the head. There are too many snap decisions, and they're too abrupt. Take Jane's decision to kill herself, for example. I know you're trying to consolidate it, but everything falls into place for Jane too easily .... There are too many coincidences. It needs to become more subtle.

In their approach, readers often couched their negative comments in a rhetoric of reader response, indicating their emotional and cognitive reactions to the piece rather than directly faulting the writing: "I feel like I am watching from the outside. I need to feel closer to her [a particular character], to know why I am sweating"; "I got confused in this scene. I thought you meant the kids were arguing when now I see that they were supposed to be friends."

Balancing Evidence: Logical Reasons and Reader Response

Both deliberative and epideictic are genres of persuasion, and, therefore, both employ strategies that will bring listeners into agreement. Characteristically, deliberative rhetoric persuades by providing logical and compelling reasons for accepting a particular course of action. To this end, the Franklin writers sometimes invoked fiction-writing principles as logical evidence. Discussing a scene in Doug's novel, Stephanie argued that the climax "needed to be more clearly stated." She explained that crucial character insights "got lost

in the scientific window of what was going on [because] the science information was very strong technically" yet didn't actually inform the narrative.
When Ellen intervened, asserting that the technical information could be
skimmed, Stephanie countered with the literary commonplace, "If it's good
enough writing, everything should be important. I shouldn't be able to skim
through a whole paragraph and not need to read it." Likewise, Doug invoked
the principle of reader knowledge when he suggested that Ellen abbreviate
her exposition for a popular news article she was writing.

Evidence was also grounded in the necessary confluence between actual and fictional life. When Doug's twenty-first century super-hero asserted, "She's a bonafide human fruit of her mother's womb yata, yata,"
Ellen exclaimed, "No way! No way would that phrase survive into the future! Zap that one and fast." Following up on Fay's advice that Stephanie's
teen protagonist be more introspective about her parents' separation,
other group members offered logical reasons for the revision: that children often feel responsible when their parents divorce and that the character's adolescent status would contribute to excessive contemplation or
self-examination.

This form of deliberative response immersed readers in the "life" of the
stories they were reading, and in their persuasive arguments they often embraced characters as living beings, speculating on characters' cultural and
social contexts, motivations, and histories and investing texts with a kind of
"living space," or extratextual reality. This "reality test," as Ellen called it, encouraged readers to question characters' motives, interrogate the writer's
intentions, demand clarification, and, most important, pose solutions to
writing problems.

At one point in his novel, for example, Doug's futuristic government
agents, R and J, appeared to reverse roles, and Stephanie argued for a logical explanation, which would compel Doug to augment his narrative.

Stephanie: I thought R and J were partners, but in the scene in the op-
            erating room, R seemed like he really didn't know what he
            was doing. He didn't seem to know anything about the
            medical end of it. Yet in the field, they seemed equal ....
            Then I remembered that J was a medical student so I
            thought maybe that's why he can examine patients, and
            R's not usually in there with him.
Doug: Right, Right. Usually—
Stephanie: So J does both the field stuff and the operating room stuff?
            R only does the field stuff. He's never in the operating
            room?
Doug: Yeah, yeah or else he can't. Maybe he goes back out on the
            street. The other two [characters] who know about the

> medical procedure are both hospitalized or in jail, which
> is why J is doing it by himself.
>
> Stephanie: Okay, that was my question. It was kind of weird with J tell-
> ing R what to do, without maybe a statement from R like,
> "Well, I'm never in here, so where's that instrument kept?
> I don't know where that is."

By questioning and verifying the characters' assumed knowledge, Stephanie could determine whether the scene had successfully negotiated the
delicate blending of real and fictive worlds. At the same time, she showed
Doug where he needed to make his characterization more explicit.

While the Franklin Group's deliberative rhetoric focused on logical response, in their epideictic discourse they provided evidence of a text's wor-
thiness or inadequacy. But group members' comments generally went
beyond isolated statements of praise and blame, for as Aristotle explains,
"Those who praise or attack a man aim at *proving* him worthy of honour or
the reverse, and they too *treat all other considerations with reference to
this one*" ("Rhetorica" I.3.5, my emphasis). To further illustrate, Stephanie
did not simply applaud Brenda's handling of her character; she also gave
reasons for her response:

> I liked the dialogue with Raymond. That was probably the best dialogue in
> the whole chapter. He was really funny. He was this lonely drug dealer guy,
> who wanted to play his CD player for his drug clients. He was disappointed
> that they were going to leave him alone. It was a really good picture you cre-
> ated with him.

Likewise, to condemn Stephanie's depiction of teenage characters,
Brenda described her reading experience and her readerly agitation:
"About the kids being scared of the city, I found it believable, though slightly
annoying. I thought,'Oh, get over it already.'"

In Sullivan's view, the critic functions in two simultaneous roles: as the audience for the text being reviewed and as the rhetor for those who will read (or
hear) the criticism. Noting the antifoundational, interpretive nature of both
roles, Sullivan reminds, "The critic can be said to be judging the text's depiction of reality and to be presenting a depiction of reality as well" ("Epideictic"
343). By subjecting a work to multiple "reality tests" and at the same time expressing their own reader-responses, members of the Franklin Writing Group
continually fulfilled both critical functions as Sullivan defines them.

Balancing Goals: Coauthorship and Authorial Control

Willingness to offer specific suggestions, in effect, to co-write excerpts of
their colleagues' stories, was a hallmark of the Franklin Group. Readers not

only encouraged narrative and stylistic changes, but they also furnished specific suggestions and alternatives for the revision that would follow the workshop session. Thus, Stephanie supplied actual dialogue for an important love scene in Brenda's novel:

> I thought that there should be a little better lead into all this foreplay and romance that goes on in the apartment, like more dialogue. So on page 38, you describe Jesse's apartment with the [bed]sheets on the furniture .... They could have some good dialogue about it, like "Oh, have you had this couch since you were nine years old?" or something like "Does your mom know you have this picture?"

Then other members joined in, offering Brenda additional snippits of conversation that she might include in her story. From the synergy of workshop sessions like this one, new ideas were created and new literary strategies developed.

Such deliberative, action-oriented discourse is present in all productive writing groups, of course. Likewise, the attendant danger of reader appropriation poses a threat to voluntary groupings, just as it does to composition class writing groups (see Spear; Leverenz). However, it seems more pronounced in response groups composed of serious and, often, professional writers, who may intrude upon or even take over a manuscript, divesting writers of their claims and purposes. Because it is easy for invested peers to appropriate the texts they are responding to, deliberative discourse must be balanced by judgments of quality that acknowledge the writer's skill, intentions, and authority.

For the members of the Franklin Writing Group, epideictic rhetoric acted as a counterweight to secure for writers ultimate control of and authority for their stories and essays. In their comments, readers focused on the strengths and weaknesses of the text rather than on the writer. Furthermore, they tried to honor writers' intentions and to acknowledge that writers had their own strategies, purposes, or effects in mind as they composed. To illustrate, while discussing one of Stephanie's chapters, Ellen said, "I liked the ending, when he kissed her—Did he mean it or was he just manipulating her? I am really getting suspicious of him. If that's your intention, good job." In another session, Stephanie told Fay that her character, Jim, "seemed kind of *Bridges of Madison County*, if that's what you intended." Epideictic comments like these helped to reinforce a writer's central authority and to mitigate the effects of deliberative appropriation.

In the writing group setting, praise rhetoric also provided ego satisfaction and encouragement to writers, helped them to cope with external rejection from editors, and gave them a sense of genuine readership and support. As Doug explained in a private interview, "It's sort of a confidence booster to have people [discussing your work] .... Mostly they are just reaffirming what I'm doing, and I think that's the best confidence booster I can have to keep writing and to keep on a schedule." Similarly, Ellen stated:

> I wrote [an article] and thought it was terrible, and I brought it in and they really liked it. I mean, actually the group has made me believe .... They said where it was strong and where it wasn't. But I always felt it was not strong at all .... I feel like my writing has gotten better and the group has been part of it.

Negative epideictic comments served myriad functions for the writers, but all of the members acknowledged the importance of negative critique. According to Fay,

> Writers have a tendency to fall in love with their stuff. They fall in love with certain passages, and it's usually their strong point—the thing that they do well. They'll throw it in, but they don't realize they are throwing it in, and they think it makes sense until they get an outside pair of eyes that says, "You know, this is stopping the story."

Reflecting on the balance between deliberative and epideictic aspects of the group's process, Stephanie explained, "It's almost like we are not making a judgment on the quality of it [the text], but we are saying how we think the writer could make it better."

Balancing Community: Consensus and Dissensus

Writing group response activities are persuasive; they are designed to promote changes in a text by convincing the writer to revise in particular ways. Thus, both consensus and dissensus are significant features of writing group communities. Like all rhetorical situations calling for deliberative rhetoric, writing group deliberations begin in a state of dissensus. Among the members there will be several different points of view, reflecting different values and beliefs within the group. As deliberative speakers, reader-responders know that their audience—here the writer—will need to be convinced of both the need for change and the superiority of the suggested course of action. They also know that if they can create arguments that establish a common ground between the speaker and audience, they will move the group as a whole toward a consensus that will sway resistant members.

In the Franklin Writing Group, a majority viewpoint often affected a writer's decision to make changes in his or her draft. All of the writers said that if several readers had the same reaction, their criticism was probably valid, and, as a result, they would likely reconsider and revise. In one case, while discussing an important scene in Brenda's novel, several group members described her protagonist as "a nag." Brenda explained that "because there were several of them saying the same thing, I thought that they were probably right. I think I'll tone it down as far as [the main character's] questioning [her date] .... I wanted him to be mysterious ... and I guess I didn't get that across." Likewise, because everyone found Stephanie's experimental story confusing, she conceded that she would need to revise it. She said, "I recognize that if four people read it and tell me that they couldn't understand it basically, ... I'll definitely make some changes," although she asserted that she would determine for herself the exact nature of those alterations.

But writers often revealed a vigorous and healthy defensiveness about their work, and, at times, they adamantly rejected comments, staunchly asserting their authorial intentions or explaining their dramatic purposes. For instance, Doug's science fiction story elaborately depicted a shopping mall, where his protagonist sought refuge from the pressures of his job and personal life. Although futuristic icons colored the scene, Ellen opposed its similarities to contemporary culture. In response to Ellen's assertion that "malls are not that long for this world," Doug argued, "There was something I was trying to bring out here: that people go there to see other people and commodities." Unwilling to relinquish the mall scene, Doug took special pains to explain his perspective on the future of retail shopping, asserting that "there's something fundamentally human about the desire to go to a store where you are surrounded by objects." The writer's defensive stance, in the face of readers' objections, served two significant functions: it helped to sustain the writer's authority and ownership in the face of expert readers' appropriative gestures, and often it encouraged readers to clarify and to reconstruct their feedback, which led to significant group-generated revision.

Epideictic rhetoric's community-building feature serves as a countermeasure to deliberative dissensus and resistance and appears to be vital to long-term writing group engagements. Epideictic rhetoric offers the reader-responder, as central speaker, the "relative freedom to state opinion without grounding it with detail" (Sullivan, "Ethos" 123). Specifics are unnecessary since the reader seems to be articulating the group's shared set of assumptions. Most theorists agree that this shared set of values tends to be conservative and contributes to the maintenance of the group or community (Perelman and Olbrechts-Tyteca; Beale; Sullivan, "Ethos"; Carter). This was true for the Franklin Group, where epideictic rhetoric helped to sustain the group. When asked whether group members tended to "tread cautiously" on each other's writing, Doug acknowledged,

> There has to be some sort of compromise somewhere in the group. If you just go out there and you just rail on each other ..., the group is going to fall apart. People's feeling are going to be hurt, and there's going to be a lot of discomfort. I think it's a pretty comfortable group, as we've seen so far, and maybe it comes at the expense of full disclosure.

Although other members disagreed about the extent of critical withholding, they all saw in their workshop talk a group-maintenance function.

Notably, Diogenes's critique of school-sponsored, creative writing workshops concerns the relationship between epideictic rhetoric and consensus
building, since neither praise nor blame necessarily leads to changes in the
draft ("Creativity"). Scholarly work in the field, however, has extended a
longer view to epideictic outcomes, a view supported by the discourse of
the Franklin Writing Group. In Christine Oravec's account, Aristotle's use of
"theoria" to describe the "spectator" function of the epideictic audience
suggests two acts of observation: contemplation and theorization. Like listeners at a formal speech or presentation, the Franklin writers did not simply receive compliments or criticism; in the construction of meaning
between reader-responders and the writer, both cognitive and perceptual
processes were at work, fostering both learning and judgment. Through
these active processes of intellection, in contrast to the passive process of
sense response alone, the writer hears the epideictic speech of his or her
peers and "understands or theorizes as a preparation for learning and ultimately for practical action" (166).

Writing group members can thus be said to use epideictic discourse to
"invite or engender continued thought and discussion as a prelude to decision and action" (Sheard 788). According to Cynthia Miecznikowski
Sheard, "By bringing together images of both the real—what *is* or at least
appears to be—and the fictive or imaginary—what *might be*—epideictic
discourse allows speaker and audience to envision possible, new, or at
least different worlds" (770, emphasis in original). Although Sheard re-
gards epideictic as an invocation for changing the real-world order, from a
slightly different vantage point it also enables creative writers to work together to invent alternative fictive worlds. By securing the writer's authority and primary textual ownership while preparing the way for
deliberative means and methods, epideictic discourse seems uniquely
suited for the work of writing groups.

Bridging Rhetorics: Praise as Action

The so-called educative function of epideictic brings to view the ways in
which deliberative and ceremonial discourses of writing groups intersect
and complement each other in actual practice, making it difficult at times to
distinguish one type of response from the other. According to theorists, the
epideictic rhetor "educates" by expounding on particular institutional, social, political, cultural, or personal qualities that the audience is expected to
adhere to and emulate, by fostering "a vision that inspires, even compels an
audience to act" (Sheard 787; see also Sullivan, "Ethos," 126–7; Vickers 503;
Oravec 169–70). Indeed, Aristotle is quite specific: "To praise a man is in

one respect akin to urging a course of action" ("Rhetorica" I.9.35). For most writers and readers in writing groups neither praise nor negative criticism is an end in itself. Reader-responders enact Aristotle's advice for encouraging both action and intellection: "Thus, when you want to praise, see what would be the underlying proposition; and when you want to set out proposals in deliberation, see what you would praise" (*Rhetoric* 85; for the application of this point by Aristotle's successors, see Vickers 504).

The Franklin writers often came to the sessions with questions about the effect of a scene or character they had created—that is, seeking epideictic response—but they fully expected to revise, to act, as the criticism necessitated. For example, hoping her readers would respond negatively to a mysterious but unappealing character-turned-murder-victim," Fay asked, "Did you sympathize with Dubrowski?" An affirmative response from the group would have compelled Fay to sharpen her characterization of the evil Dubrowski. Even more productive exchanges occurred when readers criticized a scene and the writer pressed for suggestions about how the problem might be remedied. To give one brief instance, Stephanie said that she had trouble distinguishing among Doug's futuristic corporations, an epideictic response. Spanning rhetorics, she advised him to use "reminders" to help readers to keep track of the differences. When Doug asked, "How would you suggest including that sort of reminder?" Stephanie provided concrete, deliberative directions, explaining, "Not every time you talk about it [the company], but maybe the first time you talk about it in a chapter, say something about the content. You don't have to say 'Xenocorp does this,' but maybe 'the guy from Xenocorp said blah, blah, blah,' just kind of revealing a little bit about what he does." In this manner, potential epideictic rhetorical situations turned into deliberative events, with the writer providing a bridge from praise or blame to concrete revising suggestions.

Epideictic and deliberative rhetorics also combined when group members raised penetrating questions about a character's motivation or about events that occurred prior to the unfolding plot. This additional background, which would not necessarily appear in the written text, helped members (as cowriters) to evaluate the coherence and consistency of the story. At the same time, the exercise forced writers to work through the unseen, unwritten parts of the text, which often led to significant changes. Speculating on the whereabouts of the male protagonist in Stephanie's young adult novel, Doug questioned, "Where is Taylor hanging out when he's in the city? Is he one of the skate punks in Love Park? He's not a people person. Is he just skulking around by himself?" Stephanie's reply brought new insights for fleshing out her character and, perhaps in the future, adding to the plot. "He takes the train in most of the time, so he hangs out in Suburban Station, especially the coffee place in Suburban Station. Also, he takes his soccer ball to Rittenhouse Square and plays around with it. He doesn't want to get picked up by cops. He cuts school a lot." As other group members continued to co-create along with Stephanie, they uncovered issues that she would need to address as she revised her text:

Doug: Okay, and it's easier not to be picked up by the truant offi-
           cer when you are in Philadelphia, where there are all
           kinds of kids running around.

Stephanie: And he just likes the city. I guess I should have written
           more about that.

Ellen: I was under the assumption that he was into some kind of
           underhanded dealings in the city.

Stephanie: I kind of thought he was. I keep changing what's going on,
           so I have little pieces left in parts of it, and I know I've got
           to take that part out.

Peer response in the Franklin Writing Group continually confirmed Oravec's observation that "judgment is incomplete without deliberative action" (167). For the Franklin writers, the purpose for joining a group was to solicit from fellow members both criticism and suggestions for textual changes. At every turn, they assumed that members' comments would lead them to revise, and hence they embraced both positive and negative response as guideposts for future revising activity.

Balancing Instructional Models: Deliberative and Epideictic Rhetoric in Classroom Writing Groups

Because they are mandated, neither creative nor composition classroom writing groups are, as a rule, motivated by the desires that dominate voluntary groups, where, as Anne Ruggles Gere explains, members' discourse and actions are predicated on mutual respect and individual autonomy. Gere points out that voluntary writing groups form because writers want to share their writing with others. Inherent in their decision to join a group is an appreciation of community and collaboration, a regard for reader feedback, and a willingness to revise based on suggestions they receive. Moreover, Gere notes, "Because authority originates in individual members rather than in something or someone outside themselves, it always returns to them. They retain the right to leave the group, or to disregard the comments or advice of others" (50).

Particularly at the beginning of the semester, students in classroom groups do not know each other, do not know whether they can trust each other, may not trust themselves as writers, or may not be emotionally ready to place their texts in a public arena. However, as members of classrooms configured around workshops or collaborative response groups, they will find themselves compelled to engage in such activities and, likewise, to respond to the writing of their peers. As Diogenes observes, in creative writing classes, these conditions can result in excessively epideictic discourse, with little praise and much blame but with few deliberative suggestions for change. Often student comments remain too grounded in personal preference; positive response is pro forma and negative response is degraded to questions of taste ("Creativity"). Also, competition among writers, a common feature of creative writing classes, may stifle genuine critique or limit productive feedback. (For a discussion of competition in process writing classrooms, see Tobin 93–113.) Unlike their counterparts outside the academy, creative writing students may judge their texts as finished and complete when they bring them to workshops, assuming that inadequacies lie in the reader rather than in the writing. They may thus be disinclined to offer or accept peer comments for further revisions and invest the writing instructor with exclusive authority. Potentially more expressive than constructive, more present centered than forward looking, epideictic discourse always runs the risk of spinning its own wheels. At times, it may be viewed as, if not impeding the development of writers and texts, certainly not contributing actively to their progress.

In many composition classes, in contrast, students are working with a deliberative textual model, writing persuasive texts and seeking reasons or rational arguments. Allowing for variation in the orchestration of composition class writing groups, the same model pertains when instructors encourage groups to offer concrete reasons and suggestions (Diogenes, "Creativity"). In contrast to epideictic, an exclusively deliberative approach may, however, contribute to wholesale reader appropriation with little concern for writer's intentions or motives (see Spear 36–37). When groups believe that their primary function is to change the existing text, they may fail to notice and therefore to positively reinforce successful literary or rhetorical elements in their peers' essays. Because beginning writers often feel that they have no authority to evaluate each other's writing or because they are impelled by deeper commitments to social (goodwill) discourse (Spear 23–26,34–36; Brooke, Mirtz, and Evans 31–51; Goodburn and Ina), they may be reluctant to reaffirm or question textual attributes in the context of a writer's own plans or intentions. Furthermore, if group members perceive literary judgment as opinion, and therefore arbitrary and relative, they will not view themselves as a community with shared values appropriate to epideictic discourse. In this context, deliberative response may seem strategically safer because of its purported rationality.

As the Franklin Writing Group demonstrated, successful writing group practice involves a fusion of these rhetorics. A combined epideictic and deliberative process enables readers to provide productive, action-oriented comments and, at the same time, allows writers to resist appropriation by their peers. Helping students to recognize the intrinsically persuasive dynamics of writing group response can contribute to more productive collaboration and more genuine writing practices for developing writers. When students learn to appreciate and to apply deliberative and epideictic rhetoric in their peer groups, they begin to understand that response is a persuasive construct quite apart from authority or taste.

Since deliberative rhetoric is more common to writing group pedagogy, composition instructors can augment their modeling of and instruction in deliberative response with both traditional and contemporary samples of epideictic rhetoric, including Gorgias' *Encomium of Helen*, Lincoln's *Gettysburg Address*, selected samples of *New York Times* literary reviews, or even essays like Phillip Lopate's "Portrait of My Body." (For additional examples and topics, see Corbett and Connors; Crowley and Hawhee.) In writing group role play, student readers might learn to identify and explain their reading experiences in response to peers' essays. (Peter Elbow's "movie in the mind" exercise is one of many techniques for practicing reader response). Simultaneously, students might learn how to use logical arguments to persuade their peers to enact textual change. Instructors can also introduce discussions of judgment and opinion, distinguishing between questions of taste and the productive, educative force of reader critique. Significantly, student responders must be encouraged to consider writers' intentions, to ask questions about writers' plans and purposes and about the effects the writer is trying to achieve. By the same token, student writers must be taught to take a more aggressive stance with their work and its possible meanings, to examine closely and critically the worlds they are creating and to be willing to defend those constructs or to reconsider them.

Most important, however, students need to be aware that discourse in productive writing groups is unequivocally persuasive. To provide meaningful response and to foster fruitful revision, writing group participants must learn to choose the best "available means" (*Rhetoric* I.2.1), by invoking in their workshops, as the situation demands, both deliberative and epideictic species of classical rhetoric.

Works Cited

Aristotle. *On Rhetoric*. Trans. George A. Kennedy. New York: Oxford UP, 1991.

Aristotle. "Rhetorica." Trans. W. Rhys Roberts. *The Basic Works of Aristotle*. Ed. Richard McKeon. New York: Random House, 1941. 1317–451.

Beale, Walter H. "Rhetorical Performative Discourse: A New Theory of Epideictic." *Philosophy and Rhetoric* 11 (1978): 221–46.

Brooke, Robert, Ruth Mirtz, and Rick Evans. *Small Groups in Writing Workshops: Invitations to a Writer's Life*. Urbana: NCTE, 1994.

Carter, Michael. "Scholarship as Rhetoric of Display: Or, Why Is Everybody Saying All Those Terrible Things About Us?" *College English* 54 (1992): 303–13.

Corbett, Edward P. J., and Robert J. Connors. *Classical Rhetoric for the Modern Student*. 4th ed. New York, Oxford UP, 1999.

Crowley, Sharon, and Debra Hawhee. *Ancient Rhetorics for Contemporary Students*. 2nd ed. Boston: Allyn and Bacon, 1999.

Diogenes, Marvin. "Creativity and Commonplaces: A Rhetoric for Fiction Writers." Conference on Fundamental Controversies in Rhetoric and Composition. Tucson. 13 November 1998.

————. Personal correspondence. April 24, 1999.

Elbow, Peter. *Writing Without Teachers*. 2nd ed. New York: Oxford UP, 1998.

Fahnestock, Jeanne, and Marie Secor. "The Stases in Scientific and Literary Argument." *Written Communication* 5 (1988): 427–43.

Gere, Anne Ruggles. *Writing Groups: History, Theory, and Implications*. Carbondale: Southern Illinois UP, 1987.

Goodburn, Amy, and Beth Ina. "Collaboration, Critical Pedagogy, and Struggles Over Difference." *Journal of Advanced Composition* 14.1 (1994): 131–47.

Kennedy, George A., trans. "Introduction." Aristotle On Rhetoric. New York: Oxford UP, 1991. 3–22.

Leverenz, Carrie Shively. "Peer Response in a Multicultural Composition Classroom: Dissensus—A Dream (Deferred)." *Journal of Advanced Composition* 14.1 (1994): 167–86.

Oravec, Christine. "'Observation' in Aristotle's Theory of Epideictic." *Philosophy and Rhetoric* 9 (1976): 162–74.

Perelman, Chaim, and Lucie Olbrechts-Tyteca. *The New Rhetoric*. Trans. John Wilkinson and Purcell Weaver. Notre Dame: U of Notre Dame, 1969.

Sheard, Cynthia Miecznikowski. "The Public Value of Epideictic Rhetoric." *College English* 58 (1996): 756–94.

Spear, Karen. *Sharing Writing: Peer Response Groups in English Classes*. Portsmouth: Heinemann-Boynton/Cook, 1988.

Sullivan, Dale L. "The Epideictic Character of Rhetorical Criticism." *Rhetoric Review* 11 (1993): 339–49.

————. "The Ethos of Epideictic Encounter." *Philosophy and Rhetoric* 26 (1993): 113–33.

Tobin, Lad. *Writing Relationships: What Really Happens in the Composition Class*. Portsmouth: Heinemann-Boynton/Cook, 1993.

Vickers, Brian. "Epideictic and Epic in the Renaissance." *New Literary History: A Journal of Theory and Interpretation* 14 (1983): 497–537.

CHAPTER TEN

ろつひ

Questions of Time: Publishing and Group Identity in the StreetWise Writers Group

Paula Mathieu

Karen Westmoreland

Michael Ibrahem

William Plowman

Curly Cohen

We hope this writing group will be a place where you can work on whatever is important to you now: some poetry, an article for the paper, a scholarship application essay, some rap lyrics, or your own life story .... A place where we all see ourselves as writers, philosophers, and social critics, with important things to say to a world that desperately needs to listen.

The *StreetWise* Writers Group first met in Chicago's south loop on a snowy night in March 1998. Five homeless or formerly homeless vendors of *Street-Wise* newspaper[1] joined two editors to share their interests, ideas, and stories. The opening quotation is taken from the make shift mission statement that Paula, founder and facilitator of the group, drafted for that first meeting. Looking back at these words now, we see that the current tensions of

---

[1] Street newspapers run in most major cities around the world, and these unusual hybrids of newspapers and social-service-advocacy organizations are affiliated through two cooperative networks, the North American Street Newspaper Association (NASNA) and the International Network of Street Papers (INSP). NASNA defines a street paper as a publication that meets at least one of the following criteria: "1. to inform the public and shape perceptions about social issues, poverty and homelessness, and 2. to empower homeless people through employment." NASNA has roughly fifty *(continued on next page)*

our group have been present since its beginning. The first sentence fore-grounds "work that is important to you now"—thus dedicating the group to flexibility based on the needs and desires of individual participants. The second sentence, however, focuses on publication—articulating stories, ideas, and criticism "to a world that desperately needs to listen." At our best moments in this group, personally important work and work that the world should hear have been one in the same. At other times, however, we have struggled to set priorities and experience these dual agendas as competing demands, competing most acutely for our time.

In this article, we—the group's founder and facilitator, a teaching assis-tant who works with the group, and various members[2]—discuss some of the issues that have challenged us as we seek to maintain our dual focus on writing for personal fulfillment and group-oriented publishing projects. We have found that establishing a writing group involves an ongoing pro-cess of negotiation and struggle to define (and redefine) a collective iden-tity that works for the individual writers. A tension between a writing group's overall mission and the desires of individual participants is faced by any group of writers, especially those who set out to publicly share their work. We feel the tensions most at those moments when our personal am-bitions as writers conflict with or make unclear our desires for group cohe-sion and a collective voice. Because the writers in our group are poor and politically marginalized in this city, and because so many of us have mes-sages of injustice we are "burning to tell the world,"[3] our tensions between group visions and individual ones are often urgent and readily visible. What we present in this article, then, is a medley of voices that looks at why we write and publish and reflects on key moments in our history when setting agendas has been of central concern. At some points, such as during the Gregory Becker trial (see later section), we have benefited from being a col-lective of writers with varying writing styles. At others time, however, some members have worried about the public exposure of publishing or how a group project might take energy away from us as individuals. We hope ac-

---

[1] (*continued*)   members across the United States and Canada, and the INSP has another forty members across Europe, Asia, Africa, and South America. Writing groups similar to the one described in this article are common at many of these papers. A survey Paula conducted at the 2000 INSP conference revealed more than a dozen active writing groups at papers in Europe, Af-rica, South America, and Asia. In North America, writing groups and discussion of vendor writing have been part of the conference proceedings since its inaugural conference in 1995.

[2] This article is the work of the entire *StreetWise* Writers Group. We spent several meeting sessions discussing these issues and framing the questions. We are especially indebted to Rayford Allen, Joe Harding, Charles Lee, Greg Prichett, and Charrisse Smith Or-Sabe, whose words and ideas appear within this work. William Plowman, Michael Ibrahem, and Curly Co-hen agreed to read drafts of the article and provide feedback to receive a writing credit. This option was open to any member of the group.

[3] For a pedagogy based on "what you are burning to tell the world," see Michael Blitz and C. Mark Hurlbert. *Letters for the Living: Teaching Writing in a Violent Age*. (Urbana: NCTE, 1999).

counting this history of constructing an identity for a publishing writing group will help other writers and group leaders find ways to negotiate this complicated terrain of desires.

History Of The *Streetwise* Writing Group

Vendors of *StreetWise* newspaper have contributed to the publication since its inception in 1992. This Chicago "street" newspaper, which provides an income source to individuals who are homeless or at risk of becoming so, regularly publishes articles, columns, and poetry by the men and women who sell the paper for income.[4] Prior to the Writers Group's forming, however, any vendor wanting to write for the paper had to do so on his or her own, with little or no support from the already thinly stretched editorial staff who put the paper together. Paula remembers this time:

> In 1997, I was a volunteer copy editor at *StreetWise* and often typed and edited articles handwritten and turned in by vendors. If I couldn't read the handwriting or if useful information was missing, questions remained unanswered. I made changes using best guesses that weren't always very good. Reasons for the changes were only communicated to the writers in chance encounters. Oftentimes, writers were understandably angry or hurt because they felt their work had been changed to reflect ideas with which they didn't agree. The newspaper's editor and I talked often about setting up a group for interested writers to engage the entire writing process, where changes would be made with them, not to their work without their knowledge. It was from these conversations that the StreetWise Writers Group was born.

Our group began meeting weekly on Monday nights but frequently had to change days and times because of space demands and editorial schedules. The number of writers varied, as new participants came and went. A small core (of about eight) came to the group most weeks. The question of who could make it to meetings each week, was and remains an issue of serious concern. Nearly all of the group members have been homeless at some point in their life, many are currently housed in unstable situations (staying with friends or relatives or in a shelter), and a few are currently homeless. Two former members of the Writers Group have not been seen in more than a year. They have either left Chicago or died (serious medical concerns cause us to fear the latter). One member has rarely attended this year because she is caring for her grandchildren while her daughter

---

[4] Interested men and women attend an orientation meeting to become vendors of *StreetWise* and are given ten free papers. Vendors purchase subsequent papers for thirty-five cents each and sell it to the public for a dollar, making sixty-five cents on each issue sold. Writing in the newspaper also exists outside of the Writers Group. As of May, 2000, for example, *StreetWise* has vendors working as the sports columnist, editorial columnist, restaurant reviewer, and horoscope writer. These writers are occasional participants in the writing group but are not regulars.

works. Another must miss or bring her small children to the group. Two others are in drug detoxification programs, which keep them out of the city. For every member who does make it to a meeting, the time spent together represents a financial cost, since it is time not spent selling *StreetWise*. Will describes it this way:

> I make certain sacrifices to be at these Writers Group meetings .... I sacrifice time and money. I've even been known to sacrifice my sanity for this group .... I sacrifice at least three hours of selling time (which can yield an income of $9–$20) to come to these meetings. I also spend $0.85 for a commuter train ticket to assure punctuality.

Since time is precious and attendance voluntary, the group tries to meet the expectations and desires of current attendees. The focus of the group changes and has ranged from a news-writing workshop to a meeting place for camaraderie and support where people share personal writing or poetry just because they want or need to do so. Our affiliation with a non-profit, advocacy-based street news organization gives our group a regular publishing outlet, and many writers thus come to our group expecting to publish in *StreetWise*. "Vendor Voices" is a one-page regular section of the weekly newspaper that is devoted to the writing of the group. Since the newspaper sells more than eighty thousand copies monthly, this access to publication represents a significant public platform for our work. At times, as the following section shows, the "Vendor Voices" page has become a site for working together for a common aim of social justice.

Writing and the Struggle for Justice:
The Gregory Becker Case

> The Becker case was very personal. *StreetWise* and the Writers Group made it a personal issue. (Charrisse)

In 1995, on a hot July evening, after leaving a nightclub with a date, an off-duty Chicago policemen named Gregory Becker encountered *StreetWise* vendor Joseph Gould, who asked to wash Becker's car windshield. An argument ensued, allegedly because Joseph spilled some water from his wash bucket near the feet of Becker's date. Becker removed a 9 mm Beretta handgun from his trunk, struck and then shot Joseph in the head. Becker and his date then fled the scene, leaving Joseph to die in the street, still clutching his washrag and bucket. Initially, Becker was charged only with official misconduct for leaving a civilian in distress and for failing to report the discharge of his weapon. *StreetWise* vendors and staff were outraged, and the organization held a series of protests, wrote articles and editorials, and held rallies seeking to have murder charges levied against Becker. This struggle took many months and faced many setbacks. In 1997, however, Becker was found guilty of armed violence with a handgun and sentenced to fifteen years in prison under the 1995 Illinois Safe Neighborhoods Act. Though not a conviction of murder, this sentence meant that Becker would spend at least seven years behind bars.

In early 2000, however, the Illinois Supreme Court overturned the Safe Neighborhoods Act on procedural grounds, and Becker's attorneys were in court immediately seeking to have his sentence cut from fifteen to six years. With time off for good behavior, this would have meant Becker's immediate release from prison. Although the original events around this trial occurred before our Writers Group had formed (between 1995 and 1997), this new development became an immediate concern and focus of attention within our group. Hearing the names Gregory Becker and Joseph Gould on everyone's lips in 2000 seemed like reliving a bad dream. The future of this case remained in question for roughly a seven-week period between Becker's first court appearance and the resentencing date.

Several members came to group that first week discussing the Becker case, a few had not heard the news, and others were not affiliated with *StreetWise* in 1997 and did not know the story. We discussed the case and decided that we needed to do something to try to intervene in its outcome. We discussed how our writing might do that.

First, we decided that the *StreetWise* "Vendor Voices" page would highlight the Becker case each week until the resentencing hearing was over. Although some grumbled this would mean the publication of other writing would be delayed, all agreed in the end that this case was important enough to warrant this focus. The challenge then became finding ways to keep the case fresh in *StreetWise* and in the public's mind for nearly two months. In other words, how could we use this time to raise public awareness about the events surrounding Joseph Gould's death without losing readers by telling the same story repeatedly?

We decided that the "Vendor Voices" page had to be different each week while maintaining a consistent focus on the Becker case. We wanted to write for two audiences: the judge in the case and other readers whom we wanted to get involved with this issue. We used half of the "Vendor Voices" page to print an open letter to the judge in this case, asking that he maintain Becker's fifteen-year sentence. Paula wrote this letter and showed it to the group for revision. The first week, it ran in the paper signed by "Vendors and Staff of *StreetWise*." We planned to run the letter each week, encouraging others to sign on, and adding names to the list. We invited readers to send in comments about the case, and we circulated a copy of the letter by e-mail to the street-newspaper community worldwide.[5] In the subsequent weeks, we received more than ninety endorsements worldwide, from street papers, nonprofit organizations, and supportive individuals. We also received nearly a dozen letters from readers—some written as letters to the editor and some as direct appeals to the judge. The page ran new letters each week alongside our open letter, signed by a growing list of supporters.

The remaining quarter of the "Vendor Voices" page featured new writing by group members in various genres and styles, all about the Becker case. Rather than remind readers repeatedly about Joseph Gould's death, we decided it would be more effective to discuss it in the context of broader social trends, such as police brutality, both city- and nationwide. Individual writers took up this group objective in different ways. One writer did research for the following editorial and chose to publish it anonymously.

Who Should Be Fearful?

Some civilians present a definite threat to the safety of police officers, however, in my opinion there is a greater threat to the safety of civilians from some police officers. More often than not when an unarmed civilian is killed by a police officer, the statement, "I was in fear for my life" is recited. Granted being a police officer is a dangerous job; none the less, every police officer should know this before they sign on. Police officers wear bullet-proof body armor and carry semi-automatic weapons, which puts them at a distinct advantage over the general populace. Yet this seems not to have any effect on the level of fear present among some officers on the police force.

Statistics provided by the Chicago Police Department show that for the period 1990 through March 23, 2000 there were 154 fatal shootings of civilians by police officers, 26 self-inflicted fatal shootings by police officers, while 15 police officers were fatally shot in the line of duty. It is a tragedy to lose even one police officer in the line of duty, but these statistics indicate that it is we the civilians who have a just cause to fear for our lives when confronted by the police. Using the jargon of the military, the police have a kill ratio of 10 to 1. In other words, for every police officer killed in the line of duty, they have killed 10 civilians .... [And] police officers are killing themselves at a rate of almost two officers for every officer killed in the line of duty. To me this indicates that police officers are more of a threat to themselves than the bad guys are. And I do know that there are bad guys out there.

Another chilling fact is that that 170 civilians were shot by off-duty police officers. The general perception is that if anyone is shot by a police officer they did something wrong, and the officer was probably justified in his actions. That is

---

[5]We consulted legal counsel about the risks of seeking to influence a judge through an open letter. Also, we did not want to explicitly ask readers to write to the judge because we were cautioned that a direct appeal to a member of the judiciary could work against us. As part of the open letter, however, we printed the name of the judge presiding in the case and his court address. Several readers sent letters directly to him and forwarded copies to *StreetWise*.

not always true. Greg Becker while off duty shot and killed Joseph Gould. He did it with malice and forethought. He is a murderer, and a threat to society.[6]

This writer addressed this case through a reasoned appeal to statistics in a direct effort to alter general perceptions about police shootings. The title implies that we should all be fearful because the police pose a greater threat to civilians than the reverse. In attempting to debunk commonplace notions about police and public safety, this writer arrived at a discussion of the Becker case through the context of statistics on police violence. Two other writers confronted this issue through indirect references to the case:

Cop Slop

By Curly Cohen

Cop slop
Ain't Chop Suey
It's blood
And it's red
It's entrails
And lead
And the hollow point
Through the head
Of another life wasted
Shot dead.[7]

Enough

By Joe Harding

After daily reports of criminal acts by police and prosecutors and judgments devoid of justice, what does your conscience tell you? A person of good conscience will speak up and say, "This is enough!" Or will your silence speak volumes? Others are speaking and their messages will be heard.

If I ask you, are you a racist, what will you say? Before you answer, do me a favor. Pick up a pencil. Tap your leg with that pencil … 41 times. Do it! This is how many shots were fired at an unarmed man. Is this your message to my children? If you are not a racist, we await your voice. It says, "Enough is enough, no more!"

If your position, privilege, opportunities or prejudice allow your conscience to excuse forty-one shots, SO BE IT! But in the end, when that power you held with a death grip slips away, whose voice, "in good conscience" will be there to speak for you?

Others voices will be heard, they say, "No justice, no peace!"[8]

---

[6]Anonymous. "Who Should Be Fearful?" *StreetWise* 8.13 14 April 2000: 17.
[7]Cohen, Curly. "Cop Slop." *StreetWise* 8.13 14 April 2000: 17.
[8]Harding, Joe. "Enough." *StreetWise* 8.13 14 April 2000: 17.

Curly and Joe here do not employ journalistic style but instead seek to persuade their audience through poetry and creative prose. Neither piece makes
specific reference to the Becker case, but by running on the "Vendor Voices"
page alongside the open letter to the judge, the connections were clear.
These writers suggest connections between the Becker case and other violent incidents, such as the New York Police Department's infamous shooting
of unarmed immigrant Amadou Diallo, the target of forty-one bullets. At the
same time as generalizing, though, these pieces make the issue of violence
deeply personal, through use of graphic details in one instance and direct
second-person address to the readers in the other.

Through these and other pieces of writing, our group kept the Gould
murder case alive on its pages for the full seven-week period and even beyond the Becker resentencing hearing. In the end, Becker's prison sentence was reduced from fifteen years to ten. Although this was not the
outcome the group had hoped for, it was also not as drastic a time reduc-
tion as we had feared. This period in the Writers Group was significant because our focus was singular and clear. Our members were personally
invested in the same issue, which was also pressing for *StreetWise* to cover.
Not every member wrote about the Becker case, but all agreed on its importance, even as other writing and issues were discussed at our weekly meetings. During this time, we realized some of the advantages of writing and
publishing as a group: our various writing styles and approaches helped
keep the story of Joseph's murder fresh in the news. Looking back some
months later, most of us feel that this time was well spent and that writing as
a group with a shared focus, though not revolutionary, was worth the effort.

Inventing the Writers Group:
Views on Writing and Publishing

Because our group was founded on the notion of "work that is important" to
our members, desires other than providing weekly editorial content can and
do steer the direction of the group. More often than not, we do not face an issue as urgent as the Becker case, and thus we need to continually invent and
reinvent our group identity and agenda. The occasion of writing this article
has allowed us to reflect explicitly on the directions our group has taken in
the past and where we want to be in the future. We started this process by recording members' various reasons for coming to the group. What we found is
that our understandings of the group and its purpose are often different, in
part because members join the group at different moments in the group's
history and for varying personal reasons, and they join with a range of ideas
about what writing and writing groups should be. Karen, a teaching assistant
from a graduate program at a local university who works with the group, reflects on how the group did not conform with her initial expectations:

> I wasn't sure what to expect during my first few meetings. I thought it would be like writing groups I had participated in as a writing major—lots of talk about the writing, process, form, drafting, criticizing, scrutinizing each other's work. I was excited to see if I could use what I knew to help other writers hone their craft a bit. Since I have been a part of the writing group, however, there has been less talk about writing as there has been about the issues that affect members' lives. Talking over issues of the Gregory Becker case, police violence, redlining, racial profiling, housing, shelters, reparations, and genreal ideas of humanity. The group's focus is much more on what the writing will be about and how that writing can make a difference in the world than on things like schemes of arrangement or the rhetorical effect of asyndeton .... But we still try to blend talk of form and content to get that message out in an effective way. The writing seems very urgent. Instead of me teaching anyone much about writing, I am learning so much about life.

Several writers articulated their relationship to the group in terms of their own personal needs as writers, some in terms of emotional or spiritual needs, and some largely stressed the political possibilities of creating editorial content. Charles states:

> I'm writing because I am addicted to writing, you know, that is my whole form of communication. I'm not accustomed to orally communicating with people, I'm more accustomed to writing literary communication .... [This] happened as a direct result of my being penalized for being a bad boy. I was always carted off into the wilderness and isolated from my family and friends. I could never visit. I could only communicate by correspondence. I always did communicate because I couldn't live within the confines of the penitentiary or reform school. So I always reached out to the outside world .... I had a lot of good ideas come to me, expressed some ideas, so I feel alive when I write and when I don't write I just go within myself.

Michael's reasons for writing also tend toward the personal: "I feel I must write or risk not being able to fulfill my dreams .... It is in writing and the achievement of certain goals, perhaps the least of which is success as a writer, that I find fulfillment—which in old age is of immense importance to me." Ray, a group member and freelance reporter for the newspaper, has said on many occasions, "I write to keep myself sane." Jackie, a newer member of our group, wants to share the poetry she has been writing, a collection detailing her eight-year drug addiction and recovery. Another group member, Patricia, is just beginning to explore writing as a form of communication. She defines a writers group in rather general terms as "a place to develop writing skills." Another new member to the group, Greg, says the group is a setting where he can share a part of himself:

> I came to the writers group to read my poems and get a response from people. When you write poems or stories and keep it to yourself is one thing, but to be

able to get a response is very interesting to me as a writer. I have been in a shell for a long time, and now is the time to come out of my shell. Being in the writers group gives me that chance. Plus, I get a chance to interact with other writers and inhale their feelings.

For these writers, the personal or interpersonal dimensions of the group are very important. In contrast, other members articulate more explicitly their beliefs that we should remain primarily an editorial group and a platform for social and political change. Joe describes his writing in explicitly political terms: "Things that make you go hmmm … that's what I want my writing to do. Make you question your preconceived notions and examine your prejudices. Make you want to get involved. Getting recognition is nice. Getting paid to write is nicer, but getting people to realize we are all here to help each other would be the greatest outcome of any writing I do."

Curly expresses his beliefs in writing groups as an act of group political identity:

If you can tell your story, you can see other stories, and that's politically urgent enough to transform society. The need is no different here than in Cuba or China, or for anyone else for whom hatred of circumstances is acknowledged …. At our group meetings, we alternate chairs to have an agenda that sometimes is followed. And a key to the agenda is the public reading of those who write. Sometimes it's breathtaking or madness. Just under the surface, and many times on top, our writing discusses class, color, and gender madness, warfare. That must keep us relatively sane.

Ray and Charrisse see the group as a potential way to strategize and take on issues in a scope broader than what an individual can consider. Ray writes: "As an individual, the scope of my writing is limited to my own insights, style, and talent. A writers group in my opinion should be able to engage in projects that an individual writer would find difficult." Charrisse talked about it this way:

The Writers Group is a place to gather other opinions about certain current and contemporary news issues, so that maybe we can get together as a group and put some ideas out into the public through the medium of the newspaper …. We have the chance to gather a bunch of opinions—some people want to tiptoe around and not deal with [an issue], and some people want to directly attack it. The Writers Group should be about asking what is the best approach to addressing a particular problem, to develop personally. Whether you want to write poetically or journalistically, the group helps you get it into print. You may see what you wrote in print some day, a poem, community news, whatever you believe to be important. You can take any personal issue and make it important.

Although many personal and political reasons encourage members to write, getting published is cited as a key reason that writers join our group.

Finding a public voice often takes on more importance than issues of prestige or even money, as the following two writers describe:

> When I die, I'd like to leave something behind for other people. As a Street-Wise vendor I am trying to open up people's minds about things that are happening, what they might not see or hear on TV ... I never dreamed of being writer, it just happened .... I thought writing would be a fun chance to express, I don't write to be well known, or lights, camera, action, that thing, you know. What I'm saying is that I don't write to be a famous writer and all that, I just want to know I did something for other people, or other writers. (Robert)

William writes, "The advantage of having what you write published is that everyone has a chance to hear what you have to say. Even if only one person reads what you write and takes it seriously, you've still accomplished something. At least, one person might have learned something from you .... A journey of one thousand miles begins with a single step. Hey, we all have to start somewhere."

One of the trickiest issues with regard to our group identity is how high a priority publishing or otherwise publicly circulating the work of our writers should be. Publishing is a de facto privilege and reality for our group. At the same time, the push to publish can be experienced as a burden as much as a pleasure. Charles states:

> You might have a national or international audience but when I have one person that I communicate with and I'm writing a correspondence back [and forth], a pen pal, I value that ... a comfortable audience is okay. But as soon a I'm [publishing] and am controversial, then I have these sick people who are coming and saying well "you're not really all that." I'm not saying I'm all that, you know. It's really great for me to be writing on a very simplified level where it's a small audience but unfortunately it expands to a greater audience any way.

Here Charles articulates the risks that publishing his writing entails: loss of control over his audience, airing opinions that may be contrary to popular opinions, and in turn making the self vulnerable to public attacks in whatever form.

On a similar note, Ray writes:

> Writers are by necessity observers; by choice, interpreters; by nature, artists. I am comfortable when I look at actuality and create a reality based on my interpretation and my ability to convey it to others. Lately, though, it seems as if the roles are reversed: actuality is looking at me and creating a reality in which I am interpreted. This is extraordinary and stressful to me. Attention to my writing is welcomed and appreciated. To attract attention to myself, however, is not why I write. I write because I write. It is difficult to explain sometimes, but the closest I can get is to say that the writing has a life of its own. It writes itself and I just try to keep up with it.

Ray describes his attempts to negotiate between the reasons he writes and the attention he has begun to receive as a writing group member and a published writer.[9] These are tensions that all writers contend with in different ways, especially when making the choice to share their work, within a writing group or by publishing. For Ray, writing is integral and necessary to his life, and the attention his writing receives is "welcomed and appreciated." And though he is drawn to public writing, he is nervous about the world "looking at [him] and creating a reality in which [he is] interpreted." According to Stella Fitzpatrick, who works with adult basic education publishing groups in England, feelings of attraction and apprehension are inherent to writing and publishing groups, especially when the writers are in vulnerable social situations. Writing and publishing, she describes, is a constant negotiation between safety and risk: "Making ... entertainment out of the struggle to capture and express thought ... encourages appraisal, shared or unshared, of message and writer." Fitzpatrick characterizes this experience as simultaneously "liberating and alarming, a mixture of apprehension and pleasure."[10]

This mixture of pleasure and apprehension can be especially acute for homeless writers, who struggle between social invisibility and being seen in stereotyped ways. Claiming a public space in print means claiming a right to respond to issues, yet claiming that space might bring unwanted attention. This is especially the case as our Writers Group has begun to receive some attention in other media outlets for our writing. For example, while planning a public reading and press conference for the release of a writing collection, one writer said that he did not want to be on camera, because the news station is carried by cable outlets in his family's hometown. He said, "I don't want them to know I sell this paper." The issue of affiliation has also arisen as we planned a book release of our writing. Several members said they did not want the word *StreetWise* to appear on the book's cover, or if it does, they request the print to be small. Most gave as a reason that they feel that potential readers might be turned off by the "homeless angle" and would not want to buy it. For many in our group, to claim an identity as a published homeless writer is a conflicted one to say the least. Ironically, by writing and publishing, members try to claim an identity other than that of a homeless person, but this avenue of publication comes by affiliating with a street newspaper and to some extent, the image of homelessness.

---

[9]Members of the *StreetWise* Writers Group have been profiled and photographed within s of *StreetWise,* have appeared on local cable television shows, have participated at adings, and have been invited to speak at schools and universities.

la Fitzpatrick. "Sailing Out from Safe Harbours: Writing for Publishing in Adult Basic 1." *Literacy, Language & Community Publishing*. Ed. Jane Mace. (Clevedon, Phila-Multilingual Matters, 1995) 1–22.

Sometimes the risks of publishing go beyond issues of personal identity and extend to concerns about personal safety, as a recent conversation shows:

Atilla: So you gotta tell the truth all the way right?

Paula: No.

Ray: No, I lie constantly ...

Joe: That's the beautiful thing about writing, you can lie, you can lie like a rug .... It's called fiction.

Atilla: I'm just saying because I feel that if you tell the truth ... and some of the wrong people hear the truth, they know it's the truth ... you can be tried.

Ray: That's why I lie.

Joe: People have died from the truth, for writing the truth.

Atilla: All the time, I know, but I'm saying ...

Jackie: Look at Martin Luther King ...

Atilla: But see, what I want to talk about is none of this nice stuff.

Joe: If I write something about what the police do ... and then they come and get me, I ain't going no where ...

Later in this conversation, Atilla says he's afraid to publish a story about his experiences in Chinatown because, he says, "you never know who could be reading it and who might not want to read it." Because some members realize that the "truths" they want to write about might not be what other groups—like the police or gangs—want to hear, they are apprehensive. Ray expressed this concern after covering a news story about a police shooting of a homeless man who was shot for carrying a fork.[11] After this story was published, Ray felt the police approached him differently on the street, watching him more and starting conversations with him at the regular corner where he sells his papers. Regardless of whether the behavior of the police was related to his story, Ray felt more vulnerable out in public for choosing to publish writing that raised questions about police conduct. Similarly, one founding member of the Writers Group fled her abusive husband in another state several years ago, and publishing a story with her photo or name might make her identifiable to him. We try to use group time to discuss these difficult issues. We also honor the wishes of those who have concerns about using their real name or having photos printed.

In framing this discussion of writing and publishing, we are reluctant to set up an opposition between members who come to the group simply to

---

[11]Rayford Allen. "Homeless Man Shot and Killed by Police." *StreetWise* 8.13 28 March 2000: 1.

get published versus those who do not wish to be published or between members who come for political reasons versus those who seek personal fulfillment. The truth is that most writers share varying degrees of all these impulses. The bigger issue is that this very range of views shapes our individual beliefs about how strong the core agenda of our group should be. Put another way, we often ask ourselves, how much should our group delay collective projects to allow our individual members to pursue individual writing interests? (Or, conversely, how much power should group projects have in deciding or forestalling individual projects?) Two members recently expressed diverging positions about this issue:

Ray:	Over the months that I've been here, I've noticed that there is a [political] agenda going on here ... I think that there should be an agenda like that so we have an avenue on which to put these views forth .... When I came down to the writer's group the only thing I was interested in was getting that short story out and I wasn't too much focused on using StreetWise as a political platform or a social platform .... I think that as a group if we make that one of our priorities in the writing that eventually that it will happen.
Michael:	What [will happen]?
Ray:	Social change and economic change, you know.
Michael:	Well, why do you have to have an agenda? I don't think that's really appropriate. You can have that as an individual but why as a group? It's so narrowing.
Paula:	Well, what do you think the writers group should be, Michael?
Ray:	Yeah, what is the purpose of having a group if you don't have group dynamics or group perspectives or group objectives? Why not just have the writers?
Michael:	Usually a writers group is for people who are going to do some creative writing ... if you're gonna say I want people to come down here and I want to have a group that's going to be responsible for social change, for social criticism, politics or whatever it is, ... then maybe they should get paid because that's sort of like ... what people do together and they move as a single unit for a specific task towards specific goals .... But a group of people, a writer's group, is usually something more ... what?
Ray:	Anarchic? Chaotic?
Michael:	Artistic and creative.
Ray:	Without purpose or direction.

Michael:	That's your mind …
Ray:	If [this group is] just for creative writing then I can do that out on the corner while I'm selling my papers …
Michael:	I think you are trivializing the advantage of being in a group like this, I mean, in a creative writing group as such …
Ray:	It's like a ship without water. Where are we going in this group?
Michael:	We're not all in the military. You have a ship. As a man you're supposed to know where you're going for God's sake …

What this type of discussion shows is that the very idea of our writing group and its goals is an imaginary construct, one that we each create in our minds somewhat differently. How we construct our individual ideas of the group determines our expectations and concerns. Our challenge is to find ways to use our members' differing agendas and expectations in productive ways and not let them undermine the group or upcoming projects. What we have experienced is, in some ways, a double bind. The individual energy and creative interests of our writers make our group and its writing special. Yet at the same time it is through publishing and larger group projects that we have built our public identity, attracted funding, and gained a measure of credibility within the community. To take on a public voice through writing, our group needs some shared public identity. Our lingering task is how to find group projects that harness our viable energy in good ways without overburdening the individual creative process.

"Let's Put on a Play": One Past and Future Struggle Over Group Identity

In January, 1999, one of our members said, "Let's write a play." She had just completed a drama writing class at a local university and wanted to connect her college world with her world at *StreetWise,* selling the paper and working with the Writers Group. This idea excited many of us. Almost all at once, scene ideas, titles, formats, and even performance venues started circulating at our meetings. For about five months, our weekly meetings were large and full of energy. New members came because they heard about the play and were interested in being involved. *The Real Deal*, our working title, would be a series of real-life vignettes from our writers' lives, dramatically staged. We decided to string the separate scenes together by using a narrative device of setting our play within the writers group itself and around its weekly discussions.

_al months, this play was a vital group project. Scenes were writ-
_and read—with great delight. Writers showed talents not previously
seen in the group, such as singing, drumming, and illustrating. Over time,
however, problems began to creep in. Most significantly, our focus on producing the "Vendor Voices" page got lost in the shuffle, and we risked losing
the space in the newspaper we had worked so hard to get. Dissension between individuals arose. Some of the more journalistic writers, for example, did not appreciate the more creative aspects of the project. They
worried that it took too much time away from our group's normal publishing outlet in _StreetWise_. Other writers felt the group project was too demanding of the group's energy and wanted time to share other individual
projects, like poetry or news stories.

Finally, we decided to jettison this project from the main group. Those
still interested in a play formed a separate committee that met for another
month or two at a different time. Eventually, they gave up that extra meeting, and the theater project ended, at least for the time being. Curly first
came to the group during the time of the play's discussion and describes his
experience:

> I began coming to writers group in the spring of 1999 and as a whole have
> stayed and contributed as best I can, which is not very much. The first serious is-
> sue on the table was a play that would be written, produced and acted by _Street-
> Wise_ vendors, taking some inspiration from a play written by gay and lesbian
> teenagers that was taking place in Chicago. Our play died a natural death, I
> guess, with six months discussing of it. But some good things were brought to
> the fore because of it. The Writers Group had developed a solid core group, and
> the meetings themselves could produce at least volumes of laughter. But more
> so, the group began to formulate lines, positions, reflect political positions.

Although the play did not occur at that time,[12] we reflect on it not as a failure but as an important learning point for our group. The six months of
work and discussion about this proposed play led to more structure and co-
hesion in our group. As a result of this project, our meetings are now run by
group members, who take turns serving as chair. We write an agenda, and
anyone with announcements or work to share gets a space on the agenda.
The structure is loose. Sometimes we follow our script, and sometimes we
get lost in digressions, storytelling, or a good debate. Also during this time
we made the commitment to devote between five minutes to half an hour of

---

[12]Our theatrical project was reborn in 2000 as a much more ambitious project: a bus tour
around Chicago with writers performing scenes on the locations that they really occurred. It
hit the streets with a successful three-week run in August, 2000 and has continued for three
summers. For a discussion of this theatrical bus tour, see Paula Mathieu, "Not Your Mama's Bus
Tour: A Case for Radically Insufficient Writing." _City Comp: Teaching Writing in Urban Spaces_.
Eds. Cynthia Ryan and Bruce Mc Comiskey. SUNY P, 2003.

each meeting to actual writing, which we then read aloud. As our project aims grew bigger and more ambitious, we found the writing getting too easily lost in discussions of writing. Setting aside time just to write was our effort not to lose what brought us together in the first place. This process also helped us not to lose sight of our primary publishing outlet—the pages of *StreetWise*—even if and when we pursue other projects.

Group in Progress: Lingering Questions

We expect the tensions of our group regarding its focus to continue rather than calm anytime soon. This is not a statement of despair but one of optimism, acknowledging the many possibilities before us, including public performances and alternative sites of publishing. In May, 2000, the Writers Group saw into print "This Is My Job," an issue of the *Journal of Ordinary Thought,*[13] featuring the work of our group. This new publishing source opens up new reading and performance possibilities. In deciding how to divide our already-pressed time among the options for circulating our work, personal agendas and expectations of group members will of course appear and conflict. Time spent preparing for a public poetry reading, for example, is time not spent getting new content into *StreetWise.* As we go forward, questions of how to best spend our time and energies will remain open and open to debate.[14]

---

[13]The *Journal of Ordinary Thought* is the publication of the Chicago-based Neighborhood Writing Alliance, a nonprofit organization running writing groups in libraries and schools in low- and no-income areas in Chicago. The Alliance has been a source of support and information since the *StreetWise* Writers Group's inception. But in 1999 we mutually decided to formally affiliate, and the May 2000 issue was our first effort from this collaboration. The Writing Alliance sponsors poetry readings and other city-wide events in which many of our writers participate <http://www.jot.org>.

[14]This article was composed in 2000, and therefore the present tense refers to events that occurred between 1998 and 2000. Although in 2003 the group no longer meets in the form described here, several contributors continue to write, either for a street paper or other public venues.

CHAPTER ELEVEN

ฅ๛

Making Space for Collaboration: Physical Context and Role Taking in Two Singing and Songwriting Groups

Rebecca Schoenike Nowacek
Marquette University

Kenna del Sol
VoiceArts Studio

The power of space to facilitate or constrain collaboration in a writing group has been demonstrated to us by our experiences writing songs together in two ensembles of singers and songwriters. An in-depth, retrospective analysis has led us to conclude that there are some important and commonly overlooked aspects of facilitating writing groups: namely, the effect of both physical space and timespace on the collaboration and role taking that can occur in writing groups. To this essay we each bring our histories in a variety of roles. A legislative drafting attorney in her first career, Kenna is now a vocal coach and group facilitator, a published poet, and a member of several vocal ensembles. Rebecca brings years of experience in musical performance and the teaching of writing as well as a doctoral degree in composition and rhetoric. We combine these legacies of writing and of learning (both formal and informal) with our shared musical ensemble experiences to propose some specific guidelines for developing environments that facilitate productive writing groups.

Buckets of Noise was a seven-member group that performed several times during a two-year period; Woven was an eighteen-member group formed later for a single performance.[1] Both ensembles were in essence

---

[1]These group names are fictitious, and we have used pseudonyms for all group members but ourselves.

writing groups: women assembled to scrutinize and develop texts together. However, as a cappella singing and songwriting groups, Buckets of Noise and Woven differ from traditional writing groups in several obvious and potentially significant ways. Unlike participants in many traditional writing groups, the members of these musical ensembles had to negotiate not only the words of a text but also the harmonies and melodies of these songs. And although many writing groups produce texts for public consumption, the efforts of these musical ensembles culminated in live public performances of the sung product of each group's collaboration.

Despite the musical orientation of Buckets of Noise and Woven, we believe our experiences in these writing groups are significant for other writing groups as well. Although the musical dimension of our groups added an important complication to the collaborative process, Buckets of Noise and Woven were fundamentally more similar to than different from traditional writing groups. Both Buckets and Woven are easily identifiable as the type of self-sponsored (rather than academically sponsored) writing group for which Ann Ruggles Gere has provided a rich historical context. Further, although many researchers have focused on writing groups in which writers compose texts individually (e.g., Spigelman or Bruffee), our writing groups are very much like the groups that Ede and Lunsford, Locker, and others have described: groups in which authorship itself is collaborative.

The question of how the members of Buckets of Noise and Woven negotiated this process of collaborative authorship—negotiating who would play what role in the process of joint authorship—is one of the central questions of this chapter. As will become clear, the mode of collaboration in our two singing and songwriting groups frequently varied. Sometimes one member would draft a text and bring it to the group to be refined. Other times a member would bring a stanza of lyrics or several measures of melody or a rhythmic bass line and ask the group to develop it. And other times songs would emerge entirely from an improvised collaboration. In this regard as well, our musically oriented writing groups were very much like traditional writing groups found in institutionally and self-sponsored contexts. And if, as Gere and many others have suggested, the members of self-sponsored groups proceed with greater commitment, respect, and motivation, then examining Buckets and Woven should allow us to observe with greater ease the factors that make difficult the processes of collaborative authorship—observations that have implications for self-sponsored and institutionally sponsored writing groups alike.

In *Writing Without Teachers*, Peter Elbow presents an inspiring vision of writing groups operating outside the university. For Elbow, these writing groups—which he calls teacherless classrooms—are a way to make the writing process less painful: "The teacherless class comes as close as possible to taking you out of the dark about how your words are experienced, and thus making it easier to produce meaningful words on paper" (125). Although Elbow certainly acknowledges the potential difficulties facing writing groups and provides some helpful advice for participants in such groups, he does not look in detail at the difficult process of how individuals negotiate their authority—over their own writing and over collective group writing—in such writing groups. This is an important omission, particularly in light of Spigelman's persuasive argument that authors' attitudes toward textual ownership profoundly influence both the workings of writing groups and the revisions that authors undertake on their individual texts.

In addition to a focus on attitudes toward textual ownership, current research on collaborative writing has recognized the importance of looking at individuals' role taking in writing groups. Ede and Lunsford as well as Condon and Clyde, for instance, have proposed taxonomies of collaboration—taxonomies based on identifying the roles various individuals play in the composing process. Furthermore, Kitty Locker has argued that one of the characteristics of successful collaboration is a willingness on the part of each writing group member to take on different roles. Locker quotes a member of a successful collaborative group who describes the group thus: "Throughout this whole process, there has usually been someone who's taken a lead. And it's never been the same person" (47). These studies of group collaborations suggest that when group members become more aware of the roles they play in the collaborative effort, the group is better able to overcome the obstacles that inevitably arise in collaboration.

These studies have not, however, closely examined contexts that may influence individuals' ability to take on certain roles. Scholars have by and large assumed that individuals are able to take on the roles they wish, an assumption that Elaine Chin's study of graduate-level journalism students demonstrates is questionable. Chin argues that the material context of composing exerts a subtle but powerful force on the work of writers. In particular, Chin argues that the students' location (their workspaces were isolated from professors, visiting faculty, and other graduate students) and their scanty resources (they had carrels rather than offices, inadequate phone access, and limited computer facilities) influenced not only their ability to do journalistic work but also their sense of how they were valued in the department. As a result, these students "came to believe that their activities were less valuable to the Department than those required for doing research" (468)—a conclusion that influenced the writing they produced. In essence, Chin argues that "material environment can constrain writers' activities in important ways ... [and] forms the basis of a social 'text' writers read in making sense of their position within the situation for writing" (472). Although Chin focuses on individual writers rather than writing groups, her argument is relevant for understanding collaboration within writing groups because it demonstrates the need for increased attention to the influence of physical context on the composing processes of individuals and groups.

The power of space to influence collaboration became increasingly clear to us as we analyzed our compositions in Buckets of Noise and Woven. Buckets of Noise began its formation process in January of 1994. Initially, membership ebbed and flowed; eventually the group consisted of seven women, ranging in age from nineteen to fifty years. Four members, including Rebecca, were studying at the graduate or undergraduate level at a Big Ten University in the area; three members, including Kenna, were college graduates. The group wrote together on a weekly basis and performed occasionally during a two-year period, disbanding in December of 1996. Woven was formed in December of 1998 for the purpose of writing the text for an upcoming performance art event scheduled for a single performance in mid-January. Woven consisted of eighteen women, three of whom (Kenna, Rebecca, and Cecilia) were original members of Buckets of Noise. Woven disbanded after the January performance.

As the coauthors of this essay, our primary source of data is our own retrospective accounts of collaboration in Buckets of Noise and Woven. Because we came to these collaborative endeavors to compose music rather than to write an academic essay, we did not methodically take field notes and we only occasionally saved drafts of lyrics or audiotaped the melodies that were sometimes produced. So, although we looked back at and drew from the records we do have, we relied largely on our retrospective accounts, making every effort to identify differences in perception. In fact, a key element in our collaboration on this chapter was conversations in which we sorted out our personal recollections and divergent understandings of those shared experiences. We also invited the members of both groups to reflect on the issues we are writing about in this chapter, and we gratefully acknowledge the four members who responded for their contributions, some of which are quoted directly in this essay. Ultimately, we acknowledge the subjective nature of our account and do not claim to speak for all the group members. What we can and do offer in this essay is an extended analysis—motivated by each of our long-standing commitments to collaboration and based on our shared collaborative experiences—of what kind of space writing groups require for collaboration.

In essence, our argument is this: the influence of physical space on collaboration in writing groups is often overlooked, but we found that its influence is significant. Specifically, three aspects of a space—its material characteristics, its dedication, and its ownership—can influence the collaborations that take place there by opening up or closing a range of role-taking options to the participants. In addition to these physical characteristics of space, we also look at the effect of what we call timespace on collaboration and discuss how the convergence of physical space and timespace affected collaboration within Buckets of Noise and Woven. We conclude by offering three specific suggestions for more effectively making space for collaboration.

Three Characteristics of Physical Space

Through our collaborations, we came to recognize three aspects of physical space that can influence collaboration. The first aspect is its material characteristics. By material characteristics we mean the size, qualities, and content of the space, specifically such things as design, location, outside views, building materials, furnishings, lighting, and temperature and humidity control. Such characteristics affect the occupants' ability to carry out their purpose. For example, Buckets of Noise—especially before Kenna joined the group—sometimes met in the living rooms of group members, living rooms that were shared with people not in the group. These living rooms could generally seat two to four people but were cramped when the seven or so member of Buckets tried to work in them. Group members were forced to sit at different levels, some on the floor, some on available seating. As a result, some members were more comfortable than others. Furthermore, these living rooms absorbed sound, and the dining rooms and halls to the bedrooms were visible. Because of the material conditions of these spaces, it was difficult to collaborate effectively.

When Kenna joined Buckets of Noise, we moved our meetings to a large room located in the back of her home. It is primarily used for voice lessons and music making by individuals and groups. This space—which Kenna named the VoiceArts Studio—features a fifteen square-foot wooden floor, a high ceiling, walls of windows to the south and west, scant furnishings, and high resonance. It is attached to the back of Kenna's home with doors that separate it visually from the rest of the house. In addition, it is well equipped for recording and listening to the group's recorded product. Kenna has been living in her home for more than 20 years and has developed extensive perennial gardens around her home. Julia, another member of Buckets, wrote to us that she felt supported by "[a]ll the plants around us, the windows streaked with the sunset, the wooden floors, the songs of the birds that would seep through the screens from the backyard, our animal friends greeting us with affection whenever we arrived, the aromas of various tea mingling in the air." Rose concurred with Julia on this point: "[T]he physical space provided by Kenna was ... large enough, private enough, and a lovely 'homey' atmosphere." The material qualities of VoiceArts—in particular the acoustics, the presence of enough personal space, and the feeling of seclusion—facilitated group collaboration in a way that other members' living rooms did not.

After one crowded meeting at VoiceArts Studio, Woven met for collaborations, rehearsal, and performance at the Gates of Heaven—an historic landmark owned by the city and maintained and leased to the public by the city. Originally a synagogue, it is a small stone building located in a city park with a stunning lake view. Its ground floor measures twenty-five feet by forty-two feet, it includes a small balcony and a full basement, and it holds about one hundred people. Because it features a wooden floor and a high ceiling with no furniture except a piano and folding chairs, it is a very open and acoustically alive space; vocal sounds reverberate easily and resonantly without the need for electronic amplification or enhancement. Thus, the more spacious Gates provided appropriate support for the collaboration of Woven's eighteen members in the same ways that the smaller VoiceArts studio supported the seven-member Buckets of Noise.

The activities of Buckets and Woven required enough space so that all members could feel included in the group's formal structure (a circle) while also being able to negotiate for personal space comfortable enough to be fully present for the work. To illustrate this common need, consider the way many of us negotiate personal space in a movie theater, choosing to sit closer or further from the screen, choosing more or less densely occupied areas, moving away from loud talkers, and avoiding seats behind tall people to really take in the movie. In these two groups, the material qualities of VoiceArts Studio and Gates of Heaven enabled members to satisfy their personal space needs in relation to each other and to the writing process.

A second important quality of physical space is the degree to which its use is dedicated to collaborative writing or another use that complements collaborative writing. We contend that a space's dedication—or, more specifically, individuals' *perceptions* of the space's dedication—affects the ability of group members to settle into their writing, to take creative risks, and to try out new roles. To make this point, we offer the following accounts of our own very different experiences of collaboration in three different spaces, beginning with an account by Rebecca:

> When Buckets of Noise met in the living rooms of members, I was extremely reluctant to take risks as a writer in these spaces. From the beginning, our collaboration process involved experimenting with uninhibited, unstructured vocalizing that would sound more like noise than music to anyone within earshot. These living rooms were not acoustically discrete spaces. There were sounds of other house members going about their business, reminding me that there were other people in these houses who might feel ousted from their space. Furthermore, because the two host members expressed their own concerns about interrupting the patterns of their housemates, I could not experience either space as dedicated to song writing. These were spaces for which many people and many purposes competed, and as a result I was much less willing to take the risks necessary for our collaboration.

As we mentioned, the material characteristics of the VoiceArts Studio in Kenna's home provided Buckets of Noise with a procollaborative meeting space. However, those material characteristics were not in and of themselves enough. Rebecca says:

> When we first began to meet in Kenna's studio, I worried about distracting Kenna's husband. It was only in the writing of this essay that I learned that Kenna had a name—the VoiceArts Studio—for this part of her home and that she and her husband had designed and built that space to be both an integral part of their home and a discrete, community-oriented space dedicated to facilitating vocal expression and collaboration. But even without that explicit knowledge, I eventually came to trust that our group's activity really belonged in this space, thanks to repeated assurances from Kenna and—importantly—from her husband.

Though the material characteristics of the space did in fact facilitate the group's collaboration, Rebecca wasn't able to take full advantage of the space until she understood that it was truly dedicated to unlimited vocal expression. Experiencing that space as dedicated to the group's activity made a significant difference in the collaborative process for other members as well. Julia, for example, describes the VoiceArts Studio as follows:

> [It was] a space where we felt safe—one that respected boundaries and honored life. The space we used soaked up sound and hopes and dreams of others doing similar things with self-expression all day long. We were reminded of them .... We built a relationship with one another as we collaborated, but we also built a relationship with the world around us. We benefited from returning to that space every week; its gentle security and steady presence gave us encouragement to explore possibilities we didn't know were there. The environment we shared in was natural and simple—our thoughts settled and our hearts were able to sing.

The Gates of Heaven (where Woven wrote, rehearsed, and performed) is rented out to the public for multiple purposes, the most common of which are small weddings and other celebrations, workshops, and intimate performances. When the members of Woven were in that space to rehearse and perform, they were the sole occupants of the space; there were no competing purposes. Having never been in the space before, Rebecca could experience the space as dedicated to the group's purpose. Kenna had been part of many different events at the Gates in the past and rented it for the Woven project because she knew it would support her project's purposes. There is no question that its dedication supported the creative writing of Woven as well as its material characteristics did.

A third aspect of physical space that can influence role-taking and thus collaboration in writing groups is the degree of ownership of the space assumed by the various members of the group. Kenna speaks to how being an actual owner of the space where Buckets of Noise wrote influenced in several different ways her role taking in that group and how assuming almost no ownership in the space where Woven wrote influenced her to take on a different set of roles:

> As host of the Buckets of Noise meetings, I felt responsible for maintaining the space and providing hospitality to the group: serving tea and picking up after everyone had left. And despite my conscious intent not to play the voice teacher and facilitator role in the group, still I found myself attending to the other group members as if I were in the professional role I normally play in the studio space where we met. Since I am the mother of an adult child and the other members of the group were at least 20 years younger than me and unmarried, I sometimes also fell into a mothering role in the group. Playing the various roles that I've just described—host, facilitator, and mom—separated me from exercising the role for which I'd joined the group: singer and songwriter. In sharp contrast to the degree of ownership I felt in the writing space of Buckets of Noise, my sense of ownership at the Gates of Heaven, where Woven wrote, is limited to being a member of the general public entitled to rent it and to having participated in a variety of group meetings there over a twenty-year period. Because the city manages and maintains the Gates, I naturally do not feel the same sense of obligation there that I feel in my own home. Thus, I felt much freer to write with the other members of Woven.

As Kenna's experiences suggest, the degree of ownership group members feel can significantly, if subtly, influence their participation in group collaboration.

Perceptions of Timespace and Purposes of Collaboration

Taken together, these three aspects of physical space—its material characteristics, its dedication, and its ownership—can significantly influence individual role-taking in writing groups. But it is not solely physical space that influences the collaborative process of writing groups. We contend there is a temporal dimension of space as well: although time is not usually thought of as space, we would argue that time is an intangible form of space and for this reason we here introduce the term *timespace*. We use the term timespace rather than time to stress that the time available for collaboration can facilitate or impede the work of a group just as surely as physical space can. As with physical space, it is not simply the space's qualities in an absolute sense but individuals' perceptions of the timespace available to the group that influence collaboration. And indeed, those perceptions of timespace often spring directly from the goals and agendas members bring to the group. Throughout this section we argue that if group members' perceptions of timespace are disparate, collaboration will be challenging, if not impossible. In particular, we focus on how the question of public performance became a point of often unarticulated contention in Buckets of Noise. Because the members of Buckets never had a clear or unified agenda, we had very different perceptions of the timespace available to us. In the context of our singing and songwriting group, these perceptions of timespace manifested most clearly in attitudes toward public performance, and these differences impeded our collaboration.[2]

Buckets of Noise was originally convened by two friends who placed advertisements in local music-scene papers and signs in the university's music school. One sign advertised that "two funky sopranos" were looking to start an a cappella women's singing group, to perform original and cover pieces. Another ad proposed a musical ensemble modeled after Zap Mamma and Sweet Honey in the Rock, two internationally acclaimed women's a cappella groups; this ad noted that strong harmonizing and improv skills were a must and that the goals were to have fun and perform locally. Not all members saw both ads, and not all members joined with a deep commitment to performing publicly. Though the goal of public performance was made clear to and accepted by all members, because members' motivations for being in the group were still fundamentally different, their perceptions of timespace remained different. And those differences strained the collaborative process.

Three members who knew each other prior to forming Buckets of Noise shared the goal of using the group as an opportunity to develop their individual songwriting and performance skills and to develop a name in the musical community. This particular agenda influenced their perceptions of timespace. Because they were committed to showcasing their own texts to develop a public following, their priority was preparation for performance: the sooner the group performed, the better. Their perception of timespace as limited consequently influenced the roles they played in the group. Most notably, these three members most often booked shows and took on the role of musical director.

The other four members came to the group with very different agendas and therefore had very different perceptions of timespace, which led them to take on very different roles. Rebecca recalls:

> I joined Buckets of Noise for recreational purposes and in order to develop my musical improvisation skills, rather than to perform out or become known as a songwriter. In fact, I remember (as does Kenna) stating very clearly to the group that I did not wish to take on the role of lyric writer in this group. Instead, I found myself taking on the role of vocal percussionist.

---

[2]Although public performance was a somewhat idiosyncratic factor that significantly influenced perceptions of timespace in our musically oriented groups, other groups may be similarly influenced by questions of long-term commitment to a work environment, ability to prioritize a class that assigns group work, worries about grades, and so on.

Two other members—Julia and Cecilia—shared this recreational, non-performance agenda. As Julia wrote: "Deadlines, those ugly lurking monsters ... I felt like they dammed up our creative juices." We are not suggesting that the recreational motivation was somehow more appropriate or procollaborative than the motivation to perform. The different motivations, though, resulted in very different perceptions of timespace. In that vein, Kenna recalls:

> Although I shared with some group members the goal of performing songs publicly, I had a very different vision of how those songs would be composed. I had experienced group songwriting via improvisation many times; that type of collaborative songwriting was what I wanted with Buckets of Noise. Furthermore, I was operating with a very different sense of timespace. I had been participating in songwriting groups for over ten years and envisioned Buckets of Noise as an ongoing group that would develop over many years.

In this description of her hopes for the group, Kenna conveys not only her broader sense of timespace but also her reason for joining the group: a particular vision of the collaborative process that would mean all members contributing to the writing and arranging of songs. We see no reason to suggest that Kenna's specific collaborative vision and her perception of timespace are inextricably linked: that is, we can easily imagine that a commitment to this type of collaboration could coexist even with a far more restricted sense of timespace. However, we found that there is, in general, a connection between perceptions of timespace and models of collaboration: when group members do not agree on what model of collaboration they are using, they may develop conflicts over timespace, or vice versa. To be more specific about our experiences with Buckets of Noise, each member of the group had her own tacit vision of the model of collaboration on which the group would operate, but the group never discussed these visions, how they differed, or how they might be reconciled. Instead we alternated between several different modes of collaboration, unreflectively. On this variation, Rose observed:

> I agree [that certain members seemed to use the group as a means to perform their songs], and I think, in many cases, that is perfectly acceptable. I don't think it's necessary for all songs to be collaborative ... Some of them can be brought from individuals within the group. The important thing is to remember that every individual has the capacity to create songs and contribute them at different times. And some people might not enjoy the creation aspect as much as the learning and singing along aspects.

We agree with Rose's observation that these differing approaches to collaboration are perfectly acceptable; however, our lack of consensus on exactly how we were going to collaborate (and for the members of Buckets the mode of collaboration was closely tied to their purposes for being in the group) resulted in seven different perceptions of our timespace, and that in turn created conflicts that affected the roles we played and ultimately affected our ability to collaborate.

For example, on one occasion, the group wrote a chant to an original tune Kenna had offered, hoping that it would lead to a collaborative arrangement. Kenna thought things were going well when Julia, who had been staying in the background, brought some new lyrics to be added to what Kenna had brought. However, the timespace for continued collaboration collapsed when one member booked the group a performance date and two members who had frequently brought original songs to the group stepped into the role of directors, even going so far as to assign solo parts for this song on which Kenna and Julia had been primary authors. In retrospect, it appears that under the pressure of a looming deadline, these three members' desire to set a song for performance, combined with the ease with which they could take on the roles of director and musical expert, which they habitually played, overwhelmed the group's incipient collaboration. We do not see this as an example of some group members intentionally defeating the efforts of others. From the perspective of members who joined the group to publicly perform songs they had individually written, taking on the role of director was the most appropriate way to meet their goals and occupy timespace effectively. Only from the perspective of other members, who placed a higher priority on songwriting by the whole group than on public performance of individually written songs, would this be seen as diminishing the collaborative process. The disparate agendas that were linked to the different modes of collaboration and resulted in the divergent sense of timespace led to this conflict in the group's writing process.

Similarly, another song called "Rainforest" began as a group songwriting collaboration when we recorded a free-for-all jam session, liked what we heard, and decided to set it into a wordless song. In this process, Cecilia stepped forward and contributed, another good sign that we were making progress as a group writing together, since she had been among the most reticent. It was during the process of working on "Rainforest" that Kenna began to experience with the group the improvisatory, collaborative songwriting she'd hoped for when she joined. However, the differences in individuals' goals for the group again intervened when Patricia booked a performance date and, under that timespace deadline, stepped in to arrange and direct the song—interrupting the other mode of collaboration the group was discovering.

We wish to be very clear here. We are not suggesting that public performance is an unworthy goal or that performance deadlines are inherently negative. As Julia stated,

There are some aspects of deadlines that are good—one I think is most important is the idea of sharing with others what we are learning and discovering. It
gives everyone (persons sharing and persons listening) a chance to see new
possibilities in themselves. It also helps us all develop new relationships and
discover new insights.

Julia further notes:

The problem didn't really lie in the "performances" or "deadlines," but maybe
more in how seven different people were interpreting these things. To some
the quality of the sound was most important, or maybe a technique or style; to
others the spirit of the piece is what mattered most, to another getting the
message to the audience was key, or having one's own part go well. All these
things are important and have a place, but sometimes, in our group, they did-
n't always feel balanced or agreed upon.

In other words, the perceptions of timespace mattered very much, and
they were closely tied with people's agendas for the group. When agendas
conflicted, collaboration faltered.

Writing Groups and Role Shifting

As our examples suggest, like Kitty Locker, we believe that an essential in-
gredient for successful collaboration—along with physical space and
timespace—is the space for group members to shift roles during the writing
process. Without the provision of that kind of space, groups are prone to
develop "role ruts"—the tendency of group members to unconsciously fall
into unchanging roles within a group. Both physical space and timespace
encourage people to take on certain roles—for example, Kenna taking on
the role of nurturer in her home, Patricia taking on the role of director under public performance time pressures—and can make it difficult to break
out of these roles. However, just as inhibiting physical space and constrained timespace can contribute to the rutting of certain roles, adequate
amounts of either, or both, can lead to fluidity and expansion of roles,
thereby enhancing collaboration.[3]

---

[3]Although we focus in this paper on the relationship between timespace and role shifting,
there is also a connection between physical space and role shifting. To illustrate the relationship of physical space and roles, we refer again to the seating in a movie theater. Most people
do not feel as free to be themselves (perhaps the most ideal role) when the theater is almost
empty or so crowded that they are forced to separate from their companion and sit alone,
closely surrounded by strangers. On the other hand, there can be an optimal seating experience, sometimes even with a packed house and one or more companions seated next to us,
that makes a good movie even better because of the crowd energy, combined with our own
sense of personal comfort. We offer this illustration to suggest that there is a "just right" physical space for each of us to develop and to share new roles in writing groups and other collaborative situations.

It is natural for people to fall into certain roles in the early stages of a group's process, often based on their role in their family of origin, how they define themselves as adults, and the dynamics and needs of the group. Despite the initial stability that well-defined roles can bring to a group, role ruts ultimately impede collaboration, making it difficult to negotiate the conflicts in agendas and roles that will almost inevitably occur. For example, in an effort to avoid any one member playing director, the members of Buckets of Noise tried several times to find a way of passing that role around. None of these efforts were successful, primarily due to the limited timespace we've already discussed. As suggested earlier, Kenna's attempts to move away from the roles of host, facilitator, and group mom were frustrated by both the physical space and the lack of timespace within which she and the other members could better define and practice the roles they needed to play to really write together.

Rebecca recalls another example that illustrates the implications of a failed effort to shift roles:

> I wanted to cover a song that would push the members of Buckets of Noise to sing with a tighter rhythmic and harmonic structure. In essence, I was asking members to take on new musical roles. When I brought the song to the group, I hoped that Cecilia would sing lead. However, based on our previous patterns of collaboration, other members seemed to expect that I would sing lead on "my" song. The situation was made more complicated by the fact that no other group member wanted to take on the role of singing the complex bass line, a role that was usually mine. Rose, who generally sang lead and was often primary author or musical director of the songs, didn't want to sing bass; instead she proposed an unstructured improv based only loosely on the song. Because I had brought the song to the group with a particular vision, I grew frustrated by Rose's resistance. I am still uncertain what exactly caused the conflict—perhaps Rose mistrusted her considerable talents and felt unable to carry the rhythm, perhaps I was violating an unspoken contract by proposing a cover song and asking people to shift roles. However, at some level I recognized that if we were to do the song the way I wanted I would have to take on a very new role, not only musically, but within the group: I would have to push Rose to take on a new role. Recognizing that I would either have to challenge Rose or release my investment in the song altogether, I chose the latter and the group dropped the song without ever confronting these issues.

This example suggests the need for a writing group to have methods to identify role ruts and to use physical space and timespace in ways that can help members break out of those ruts.

When perceptions of space are better defined and shared by group members, allowing people to become more conscious of their roles, the possibility of successful collaboration increases. Woven was organized after Kenna had the experience of mentoring Delia, a gifted vocalist with a background in classical music who was unfamiliar with improvisational singing. Her progress as an improviser and songwriter over a two-year period was very exciting to both Kenna and Delia and taught Kenna a lot about facilitating improvisational singing. Since Kenna and Delia had already collaborated together on another performance art piece, they decided to produce a new work together celebrating collaboration and improvisation. In their written invitation to other women, selected for their openness to the creative process and community, they were careful to spell out a number of boundaries, including a main theme, the artistic elements they expected to use, the dates of rehearsals and of the performance, and what they expected of participants regarding time commitment and financial support. Their communication to prospective members stated clearly that "as we create together, our focus will be as much on how we create ... as on what we create. In other words, we hope to balance process and product and to demonstrate at the performance the unique nature of art that is created collaboratively and flavored with improvisation."

In response to the invitation, eighteen women chose to participate, including Rebecca and Cecilia from Buckets of Noise. And in three meetings this group together created an original piece, which it performed once. Kenna recalls that she consciously assumed the role of space-maker and facilitator for improvisation:

> I watched each participant stretch out, take risks, and discover new texts within herself. I watched the group blend those texts into a beautiful and moving work of art. I watched my coproducer negotiate between her music-major persona and her newly found let-it-flow side. Despite very strict timespace constraints, I watched all the members of Woven, including two members under age ten, contribute something authentic to the final piece, much of it improvised during the performance.

That Woven was able to work so well together under a performance deadline confirms our earlier point that it was not the public performance deadlines that negatively affected collaboration in Buckets of Noise, but the very different ways in which the seven members perceived those deadlines. Unlike the members of Buckets, every member of Woven understood the timespace involved and recognized that Kenna and Delia were playing lead roles in the production.

Rebecca recalls how the clarity regarding timespace and leadership roles in Woven affected the roles she was able to take on in that group:

> Though it was difficult to shift roles in Buckets, I was able to shift roles with ease in Woven. I feel strongly this was possible because it was clear to me who I should approach about my various levels of comfort and discomfort. At one point in the performance I sang a melodic solo, playing a role I'd never found space for in the Buckets group. In Woven Kenna deliberately carved out a place for my solo and three others, by working out a system so that each one of

us indicated when it was time for the next person to perform. Since the roles were clear and we were very explicit, I didn't have to worry about trespassing on another person's solo space and was able to fully enjoy spontaneously composing my own solo.

A similar experience in Buckets of Noise suggests that this clarity about roles and about timespace boundaries can have positive impacts even in situations—like Buckets of Noise—where roles have become habitual and therefore difficult to break out of. Rebecca remembers:

> Throughout the entire existence of Buckets of Noise, I never once took on the role of lyric writer. However, there was one experience in which the group used physical context and structured timespace in a way that invited me to take on the role of lyric writer. During a final meeting, Rose proposed an exercise in which the seven members sat on the floor in a circle, holding hands. One member started, improvising the words and melody of a song. When that member felt done, she squeezed the hand of the person next to her, who then picked up the melody—altering it and composing new words. In this way the solo lyric-writing and melody-making role was passed to every member. For the first time I contributed song lyrics to Buckets of Noise.

Based on these experiences, we contend that unless there is a clearly structured opportunity for people to experiment with roles that are unfamiliar to them but essential to the group process, collaboration can be inhibited by the unchanging roles various members of the group assume.

In retrospect, we both recognize the value of the lessons we learned in the collaboration processes of Buckets of Noise and Woven. That Buckets of Noise, despite its unresolved conflicts, continued for several years, was the birthplace for perhaps a dozen original songs, and made real progress toward the type of improvisatory, collaborative songwriting Kenna initially envisioned is reflected in a letter that Cecilia wrote to Kenna after leaving the group to travel abroad:

> There have been a lot of times where I REALLY miss the freedom, creativity, outlet, spontaneity, friendship, aura of women, spiritual, craziness of our practices/get togethers. I yearn for it and wonder what has happened to our group.

This perspective is echoed by Julia:

> Rehearsal was always a treasured retreat. It was quite a contrast from the constant buzz of campus life. It was two hours a week, where seven very different people from seven very different worlds could come together and share in something, together, that meant so much to them all. Kenna's back room became a sacred place where dedicated voices and souls were able to create music in a positive, non-stifling environment.

We conclude by offering three suggestions for nurturing collaboration in writing groups. Paradoxically, we have found that to effectively collaborate, it is frequently necessary to operate within highly structured, seemingly artificial contexts. These concluding suggestions grow out of our experiences with Woven and Buckets of Noise, but we also include examples and illustrations from other collaborative experiences.

1.   Develop a group statement of purpose. To avoid the conflicts arising from unarticulated agendas, like those that occurred in Buckets of Noise, have each member of the group write a personal statement of purpose and then have the group write collaboratively a collective statement of purpose. This helps individual members identify their personal timespace perceptions and helps the group negotiate timespace perceptions common to all the members. In this way the group knows, for example, how much time is available for each member to receive attention from the group and what each member's time commitment to the group is expected to be. We also recommend establishing a procedure for refining or redefining the statement of purpose if necessary, a procedure for the group to hold itself to its statement of purpose, and a procedure for resolving conflicts and building consensus.

2.   Leave room for role shifting. As we saw in this essay there are any number of ways to do this, most of which involve a very careful structuring of timespace and physical space. When Rose and Kenna opened up the timespace for authorship, Rebecca finally took on that role. Rebecca, in turn, regularly requires her students to work in writing groups throughout the semester. At midterm, she audiotapes each group, then asks them to listen to themselves collaborating, paying attention for both the topics of conversation (is it on topic and appropriately focused?) and the dynamics of participation (who talks when and for how long?). Then she asks the group members to write a contract reflecting on what they are doing well, what they need to improve on, and how they will go about improving. These activities are examples of ways to intervene in what can otherwise become reified and unconscious patterns of interaction and role taking.

3.   Be attentive to material space. Realizing the limitations inherent in institutional contexts, we nevertheless offer the following list for consideration. Provide a work space with "just right" dimensions so that all members fit without feeling crowded or lost. Allow enough room for each member to negotiate comfortable personal space. Create a feeling of relaxed roundness; a set of institutional chairs in a perfect circle can feel confining to some people. Round off the corners of a square space with furniture, use furniture that is easily moved into arrangements that feel natural to the group as it evolves. Rather than forcing a circle, leave space in the process for the group to form its own circle. Add some elements that soften the space and lend it character (e.g., a large plant, an

area rug, a banner). Provide lighting that can be brightened or dimmed, preferably incandescent lighting, even if you have to bring in a few lamps. There is a world of difference between the type of mood created by incandescent lighting and that created by fluorescent lighting. Consider the views from the space. If they are distracting and uninspiring, they might be better covered. Also consider the view of the members by passersby and do whatever is possible to create a sense of privacy for the group. Create a way for the group to share tea, snacks, and so on in its meeting space. Ensure that no other activities compete for the space (including sound space) while the group is meeting. Provide the group with a sense of genuinely occupying its work space (e.g., it doesn't have to move the possessions of other occupants out of the way or clean up another group's mess).

To conclude, we reiterate our belief that although the self-selected and deeply committed members of these two a cappella songwriting groups differ from many participants in traditional academic and workplace writing groups, studies of such nontraditional writing groups offer valuable insights for scholars of composition and rhetoric. The members of Buckets of Noise and Woven brought to the group a variety of passions and agendas, and our challenges and successes shed light on the ways in which space can both facilitate and constrain collaboration. Although it is not certain that our experiences in this nontraditional context will translate unproblematically to more traditional contexts, nevertheless our analyses suggest ways in which facilitators of and participants in writing groups might attend to the influence of space on their collaboration. In short, studies of nontraditional writing groups, such as the songwriting ensembles discussed in this chapter, provide valuable data for theoretical work that can lead to innovations for greater success in academic group writing programs and, hopefully, someday, to much more space for the kind of collaborative writing the coauthors of this essay enjoyed in its creation.

Works Cited

Bruffee, K. A. "Collaborative Learning and 'the Conversation of Mankind.'" *College English* 46 (1984): 635–52.

Chin, Elaine. "Redefining 'Context' in Research on Writing." *Written Communication* 11 (1994): 445–82.

Condon, Mark W. F., and Jean Anne Clyde. "Co-authoring: Composing through Conversation." *Language Arts* 73.8 (1996): 587–96.

Ede, Lisa, and Andrea Lunsford. *Singular Texts/Plural Authors: Perspectives on Collaborative Writing*. Carbondale: Southern Illinois UP, 1990.

Elbow, Peter. *Writing Without Teachers*. New York: Oxford UP, 1973.

Gere, Anne Ruggles. *Writing Groups: History, Theory, and Implications*. Carbondale: Southern Illinois UP, 1987.

Locker, Kitty O. "What Makes a Collaborative Writing Team Successful? A Case Study of Lawyers and Social Workers in a State Agency." *New Visions of Collaborative Writing*. Ed. Janis Forman. Portsmouth: Heinemann-Boynton/Cook, 1992.

Spigelman, Candace. *Across Property Lines: Textual Ownership in Writing Groups*. Carbondale: Southern Illinois UP, 2000.

CHAPTER TWELVE

ภาณ

The Thursday Night Writing Group: Crossing Institutional Lines

Linda Beckstead
Bellevue Public Schools

Kate Brooke
Opossum Track Press

Robert Brooke
University of Nebraska-Lincoln

Kathryn Christensen
Lincoln Public Schools

Dale Jacobs
University of Windsor

Heidi LM Jacobs
University of Windsor

Carol MacDaniels
University of Nebraska-Lincoln

Joan Ratliff
Unaffiliated

Introduction

Thursday night: 6 p.m. The Mill coffeehouse in Lincoln, Nebraska. We have our favorite corner where the wooden bench hugs the rough-sided wall. We push together square, mismatched tables and gather up creaky spindle-backed chairs.

Thursday night has been our most common meeting night, although at different times we've met on other days to accommodate individual schedules. Robert, walking over from the university campus, sometimes arrives as early as 5:30 p.m., bringing a book to read while waiting for other group members. The rest of us arrive sporadically as our commute and parking allow. When we first started to meet in the Haymarket, the restored agricultural warehouse district, parking wasn't a problem, but others besides ourselves discovered the restaurants, antique shops, and specialty boutiques, so we have to park farther and farther away from the Mill, which has become one of the "in" spots of the Haymarket.

Last year, the owners of the Mill expanded to provide more space for tables and (thankfully) modern bathrooms. The walls are original brick, more than one hundred years old and rough, but with the soft red that comes with age. The decor is eclectic, posters announcing poetry readings, a velvet painting of a horse, greeting cards for sale depicting dogs wearing tennis shoes and old ladies in curlers smoking cigarettes in eight-inch holders, and fifty-pound sacks of coffee beans piled in the center of the room. The menu is handwritten in chalk, and new additions are added in the margins at random. Favorites are the sandwiches with the dill bread, Gouda cheese, and turkey, and there is a killer chocolate caramel cookie to look forward to on days we're especially tired. There is no service at the Mill. We each queue up to the counter to order coffee or food and appreciate the lack of interruptions from waiters or waitresses.

The group brings together eight of us, including two married couples, Kate and Robert and Dale and Heidi. We originally came together following a Nebraska Writing Project Summer Institute in 1993, so most of us are educators: Linda teaches high school journalism; Kathy teaches middle school English; Dale, Heidi, and Robert teach at the college level; and Carol is a graduate student. Joan works as a subrogation specialist for an insurance company, and Kate is a visual artist. Despite our professions, we are not easily defined. Marriage. Children. Health issues. Religious beliefs. Income. Our circumstances are not only diverse but are also often in a state of flux, for better or worse. The membership of our group flows and ebbs over time, too, although a hearty loyal core perseveres through the inevitable writing droughts. This is the Thursday Night Writing Group.

While waiting for everyone to arrive, we talk about our lives—after many years little preliminary context is necessary. Our papers lie beside our drinks and snacks, the variety as different as the people who create and consume them.

As we get down to work, we become absorbed in the task, tuning out the background jazz, clinking of glasses, tapping of spoons on thick pottery mugs. We share. Listen. Respond. Support. Beneath the seeming simplicity is a subtle myriad of relationships. Everything and everyone in the group is in a state of progress or evolution: growth and frustration, beginning and ending, hot spots and final revisions. Because we are human, it is not always easy. As with anything vital and valuable, the price and sacrifice is worthwhile.

We spend about thirty minutes on each paper, but that varies depending on the length of the piece, and before we start we always find out who has writing to share, so we can divide the time equally. There are no limits stated, but we each respect one another's time and if the piece is especially long, we'll ask the others to take it home to read and bring the response back the next week. After everyone has had a chance to read and hear response, we finish up pretty quickly, agreeing to our meeting time for the next week, saying our goodbyes, and then heading to our cars for the trip home.

This chapter includes maxims and stories that illustrate how the Thursday Night Writing Group has affected us as writers, responders, and teachers inside and outside of the group. As we were writing and talking about this chapter, we found our essays naturally grouped around certain themes. Some of us found ourselves exploring issues of becoming readers and responders to our own and others' writing. These pieces became the focus of the first section. Several of us chose to write about how the group influenced us in other contexts. These pieces make up the core of the second section. In the third section, Heidi and Carol write about how the group (and leaving the group) challenges them as writers.

Section One: Individual Writers and the Complicated Issues of Response

By Carol MacDaniels

> Sometimes response is about the craft of writing, sometimes it's about the content, and sometimes it's about the writer.

I remember arriving at group one night, exhausted from teaching full time, taking graduate courses, and trying to survive as the single parent of two teenagers. Frustrated because I hadn't brought writing to share for weeks, I asked group members to tell me what they saw good in my writing, needing to hear others tell me that I should keep writing, that no matter how busy my days, writing should not be the thing I gave up. Group members responded just right, talking about appreciating honesty in my writing and about my ability to get at the heart of an issue, and yes, I absolutely should keep writing. On that evening, the important response for me was about myself as a writer, not how I wrote or even what I wrote, and the Thursday Night Writing Group recognized and responded to my needs. We've come to know one another well during our years together, so the group becomes a safe place to receive help from others whether about writing or about ourselves as writers.

Learning to know the nature of the response I most need has taken years to develop, and most of what I have learned has come from interaction with other writing group members. In the early days of the group, most of my writing centered around my divorce. After reading an emotional essay one night, I remember Robert asking whether I wanted response to the content or to the style. His question made me pause. I'd always assumed that responding to writing is about technique rather than content, but Robert's question made me realize that I did want to talk about the story, not about how I'd written the piece. I just needed to talk about what had happened.

In contrast to the positive response and support for my writing that I receive from group members, I remember another painful lesson I learned about response, which came from outside the group. In a writing class years ago, I had included several emotional entries about divorce in a portfolio that I submitted to the instructor for comments. I didn't know enough about myself as a writer then to tell the instructor what kind of response I wanted from her, so reading her notes later I was hurt and disappointed when she essentially said, "You'll get over it." Only then did I realize I had expected and wanted to hear about how I portrayed feelings and described details of my divorce. I did not want comments addressing the feelings themselves. As a result of this misunderstanding, I put the writing away and haven't gone back to that particular piece since.

A long time later, after several years with the writing group, I tried writing about divorce again. I didn't go back to my first emotional writing, but I did attempt to convey the anger, fear, and frustration I experienced during that time of my life. By now I was learning more about response through group experience, both as an author and as a responder to others' writing. Knowing group members would take their cues as responders from what I said as the author challenged me to reflect on what I really wanted to hear about a piece of writing, and though I often struggled to articulate my thinking, group members supported me by asking questions that helped me understand what kind of response I needed most. As a responder to other group members, I learned to listen carefully to their authors' notes and to their talk about what they wrote, knowing that my responses could make a difference in keeping them writing. With my new divorce stories, the group offered positive and constructive response, and I went on to write several chapters of what I imagine to be a self-help book for newly divorced women.

The group also helps me with the techniques of writing—most recently with my efforts on nature writing. Several members of the group often share wonderful, detailed descriptions of places, inspiring me to improve my own descriptive passages. On long drives to and from school, I watch the seasonal color changes on the Plains. As I drive I play with words, trying to recreate images of the landscape. One morning, seventeen miles south of Nebraska City, I rounded a sweeping curve, and directly ahead of me a red combine harvested soybeans in the adjacent field, throwing up that choking grey cloud of chaff and dust that is a constant with fall harvest. I worked on that image for weeks, and, deciding that I needed to see a soybean plant close up, I stopped on the side of the road to pick a soybean pod. I worried that a passing motorist would stop to see if I needed help, but no one did, and I ended up with an entire plant resting on the car seat beside me. That moment—the nervousness, the fibrous plant itself, the rich smell of dirt— all became part of an essay on soybean harvest. Group members watched that descriptive essay evolve over months, contributing to its evolution by helping me find places in the description that resonated with the reader as well as those places where the piece became too wordy or abstract. I am currently getting ready to submit the essay for publication, something that would never have happened without the inspiration and input of my Thursday Night Writing Group.

After years as part of a writing group, I've learned from group members both about writing and about myself as an author, and I am better at recognizing what kind of response I need or want on a particular piece of writing. However, whether I need to talk about myself, to explore more about content, or to talk about technique, I know the group will invariably respond with positive support, and that what they say will keep me writing.

Joan Ratliff

A writing group can energize and educate the stubborn writer.

A writer can't afford instant gratification. But usually I am so pleased with the first draft of anything I write that, by the time I read it for the group, I have my Oscar or Pulitzer acceptance speech already planned. The group wakes me from this daydream to see a first draft for what it is: merely the opening of a door.

Some years I enter a short story contest that I don't have a snowball's chance of winning (three prizes are awarded out of three thousand entries) but that provides me with the comfort of a deadline and parameters for theme and length. The last time I entered this contest, I was influenced by a recent visit to the Joslyn Art Museum in Omaha, Nebraska, where I had seen a Degas exhibit centered around his sculpture *Little Dancer Aged Fourteen Years*.

I wrote a story about Edgar Degas and the young girl who posed for the sculpture. When I read it for the group, they were encouraging as always, pointing out both moments they really liked ("hot spots") and ones for which they could suggest improvement. Before reading the piece I'd made a statement, an "author's note," to focus response where I felt it would be most helpful. In early drafts, my author's notes were vague, but over time the group came to sense the type of responses I needed throughout the process. For this story's first draft, the responses appropriately focused on general structure and language. But maybe because I didn't hear anyone say, "Wow! This is a shoo-in for the O. Henry!" I began to reconsider that structure and language.

So I tried again. This time the young model narrated the story. Again the group pointed out hot spots and made useful suggestions, but the pattern of responses was similar to the time before, which made me suspect that I hadn't gained any ground with the second draft.

Then something happened that the group cannot influence, except slightly: I suddenly "got it." The focus of my story wasn't the making of the *Little Dancer* sculpture but rather the impact that the sculpture has today. I started over, framing my story within a high school field trip and using as my narrator a modern teenaged girl. I reverted to my most natural written voice, which is contemporary and colloquial, and created an original character in the narrator.

I must stress that this epiphany *had* to come outside of group. In any creative process lurks that "Eureka!" moment, the part of the equation that can only be worked out deep in the mind of the solitary artist. Sparks cannot fire in a vacuum, so I believe that the group's influence, though immeasurable, contributed to my epiphany. But their suggestions could only point the way; no group can ensure that the individual writer is ever going to get it.

The new version of my story went through several drafts before the group. They suggested that I increase the narrator's slang quotient, turn her attention to certain aspects of the sculpture, take historical information away from the narrator and put it in the mouth of her art teacher. I weighed all these suggestions and realized that many of them would improve the next draft. Eventually my story was "ready for the box," meaning the mailbox and the irrevocable act of submission. I sent off "Field Trip With *Little Dancer*" before the contest deadline, and, as usual, didn't win.

But by then I had fallen in love with the voice of my narrator. One night I wrote down the facts of her life and gave her a name. Immediately I began writing what I've come to call "The Christa Monologues." After four or five pieces, I found myself struggling for momentum.

Then Robert brought to group the results of an experiment: a monologue *about* Christa as told by a character he had created. Robert's spin-off reflected Christa back to me through two new pairs of eyes: those of a fictional secret admirer and those of Robert the Author (who is quite different from Robert the Responder).

I wish I could say that I finished the monologues, shopped them around as juvenile fiction, was published, and appeared on the talk show circuit. But I'm still working at my usual crawl to realize the daydream. A writing group cannot guarantee any writer the required daily amount of industry and discipline, but the Thursday Night Writing Group continues to shore up my flagging enthusiasm through fellowship and friendship. Over time, the group has taught me patience, analytical thinking, and the ability to recognize and use that rare "Eureka!" moment.

Dale Jacobs

Writing groups are about human relationships.

Writing is a social process that can only be achieved through interaction within a supportive community. As a group, we are there to provide supportive yet critical feedback as directed by each writer, a structured environment for writing, and continual exposure to each other's writing. Each week, we are in dialogue with one another not only about our writing but also about our lives; we see each other's texts as situated within lived experience, the products of each of our unique positions within the world. Because we met each week during the three years I was a member, this dialogue became as much a part of our lives as our lives became a part of the dialogue. For such a dialogue to be sustained, I argue that love and trust must be present; I discuss these concepts in relation to feedback to and revision of not only our writing but also our lives.

Love and trust are words not usually associated with writing groups but ones that I see as essential to the functioning of a successful group. A successful writing group should be constituted as a sustained dialogue between people who not only care about writing but also about each other as human beings; it should be arranged around the concept of love, a profound caring for each other that helps us move beyond a response to texts and toward a concern for the way in which we can all help each other become more fully human. When Carol wrote about her divorce, Robert about his father, Kathy about her brother, or Kate about her mother, we were not only concerned with the craft of the writing and the effect on readers, but also and more importantly, we were concerned with the individual writers and how the process of writing was helping them to write and make sense of their worlds. Whether I brought poems about my relationship to the prairies or proposals for conference presentations, the group helped me to see how my experiences had led me to this writing and how the writing could be used to understand and intervene in my life. When I brought in one of the many poems I wrote about my father, our dialogue helped me not only to revise the work but also to revise and think through my relationship with him. I wasn't alone in the kind of response I received; the feedback we all received went beyond the usual emphasis on craft, straying instead into the intersections between writing and living. And it is love—caring for and respecting each other—that allowed us to give the kind of feedback that made revisions, in both our writing and our lives, possible.

I don't mean to imply that there were never disagreements or irritations within our group; such a picture is patently false because any relationship involves a wide range of emotions and thoughts. However, if there is an underlying love for each other that is continually nurtured, those disagreements will eventually be surmounted and transformed into ways of thinking about each other and the shared dialogue. As Carol points out in the final section of this essay, the process of undertaking this group project has been stressful and, at times, frustrating, but the underlying care and respect we have for one another fostered the trust in each other that enabled us to talk through those tensions in such a manner that all members were granted voice. In a group arranged democratically, disagreements become discussion fodder and help to strengthen the group as a whole. Trust, which itself grows out of love, arises as a result of constant interaction and willingness to engage with each other on many levels. We met every week and relied on each other to not only be prepared but also to listen with empathy and full attention to the text (and life) at hand. When I brought in material about my father, for example, I trusted that the other group members would take both the work and my life seriously and respond accordingly. In our particular group, it took a lot of time for us to begin to understand each other as individuals so that we could become more democratic and thereby stronger as a group. As in any relationship, trust in a writing group arises from love that is extended over a period of time.

A writing group, especially one sustained over a number of years, requires intense trust in the other members and their powers of creativity, not only as writers but also as human beings. Dialogue within a writing group provides each of us with the chance to open up to the ideas of others, but such an opportunity is only valuable if we have trust that the contributions of the other group members are important. As other group members point out, if writers have trust in the feedback provided by their respondents, their revision processes will be positively affected. I want to push it further and argue that if love and trust are present, then we will be able to work through the process of revising not only our writing, but also our lives. My involvement in the Thursday Night Writing Group has convinced me that, at their best, writing groups offer the kind of sustained dialogue that can allow each of us to learn to read and write our words and our worlds, becoming, in the process, more fully human.

Section Two: Extending Learning Beyond the Writing Group

Kathryn J. Christensen

Nurture the writer and the writing will emerge.

When I joined the Thursday Night Writing Group during the summer of 1993, my older brother Mike was in the final stages of AIDS. To my school colleagues, I often joked that I wrote because "it was cheaper than paying $75 an hour for a therapist." In those early days, my writing was prolific as I struggled to cope with the complex issues surrounding my brother's illness. For well over a year, I poured out every detail of the situation—from T-helper cell counts to my brother's struggle with being gay in a small Catholic Midwestern community.

Considering the emotionally charged nature of my work, I realize now my trust in the group was nearly immediate. I believed in the ground rules that directed our most basic procedures of asking for and receiving response. Authors always maintained control and ownership of their work and were expected to direct the group's focus and nature of response. Moreover, every week I witnessed our group members in action and saw the careful reflection and compassion that preceded any comment.

It soon became apparent to me that the group, consciously or not, nurtured the writer as much as the writing. Whatever the topic, form, or purpose of the writing, the group affirmed the writer to be a writer and allowed him or her their own path of evolution. This was quite liberating for me. In the past, I had always written with a definite plan and model of the finished product.

In my seventh-grade classroom, I try to nurture the students as writers regardless of their current level of written expression or communication. It is important to me to create a safe environment for the students to write. A student I had a few years ago illustrates this well. His mother had died of AIDS-related complications, but he was very reluctant to share this with peers. He did write about it in his journal, and I responded with encouragement and understanding in light of my own experiences. As I shared a poem about my brother in class during a poetry unit, he listened intently and asked if I had others he could take home and read. Eventually, he chose to write a poignant poem about his mother and not only shared it with his English class but also elected to publish it in the class poetry booklet that is distributed to all seventh graders. Moments like this inspire me to believe that as a writer and teacher of writing I can make a difference.

The first time I personally considered publishing my work was with a poem I wrote immediately after my brother's death called, "Blood Brother." It was both exciting and intimidating to consider sending my work to strangers in a public forum, but in many ways it was a natural progression. The camaraderie of our writing group extends to the submission of work for publication. At times, members make suggestions of publications that seem to match an author's text. Sending material out to be considered is an individual's choice, but the comfort and support of the group remain consistent in the cold face of rejection form letters. There is also undeniable gratification in seeing other group members' work receive recognition or publication, and there is satisfaction and motivation in being part of the process that contributes to others' success.

Like many experiences in life, finishing a piece of work is bittersweet for me. The poem "Blood Brother" remains one of my favorite pieces because it reflects this dichotomy. Despite the loss of my brother, I found the experience to be quite intimate and beautiful. I felt my brother was being gently guided to death—"a delicate passage to unbirth"—with his family of women by his side. But the poem also symbolizes my evolution as a writer. The group affirmed that in this work I went beyond the obvious pain and ugliness of my brother's fate. Although I still wrote about my brother, it was soon afterward that I began to expand the topic, tone, and form of my writing. Eventually, I began to write pieces based on experiences other than my own. As the end of the poem implies, it was a real turning point for me:

> I didn't cry, not then, like the others
> In my embrace, you were warm
> not much more still, smelling sweet
> and tender
> But then the blood began to pool
> pulled by the forces of gravity
> making ugly spots, like bruises
> so I let go

So with my writing group I continue my development as a writer and teacher of writing. I have learned that the writing process is not linear but is more a spectrum of strategies contingent on the desires and needs of the author and a particular text. As my internal paradigm of a writer changed so followed my beliefs and expectations for my students. Under the group's care, encouragement, and direction I have become more bold and independent as a writer. Yet I will always need their focus, structure, response, and reassurance to continue this growth. And, thus, whether for yourself or your students, or ideally both, if you nurture the writer, limitless writing will emerge.

Linda Beckstead

Empathy for student writers is discovered through the writing group experience.

I originally joined the Thursday Night Writing Group for the selfish reason of nurturing my own writing. I also wanted to observe the process of writing. I wanted to learn how to knead words to recreate the images that are so clear to me, the writer, so that they are equally vivid to the audience. My experiences in the Thursday Night Group have exceeded my expectations. Not only have I become more confident to experiment and share early drafts, but also I've discovered that my experiences from the group are applicable to my classroom.

One goal each fall is to teach students to become both writer and responder. It makes sense to me to get students to talk about their writing. By allowing predictable meetings with consistent small groups, students begin to trust each other and often write for their members. I establish the pattern for small groups by beginning the year with a mini-lesson on response. Two strategies used successfully by the Thursday Night Writing Group are author's notes and hot spots. These devices have provided my students a common vocabulary to discuss writing.

I also use informal author's notes in my daily classroom activities. Students often need encouragement when they begin an assignment. After writing for only a short time, I usually find several hands up as students stare at the few lines they've generated. They say they want to know if what they've written is good, but I think they are actually asking permission to continue. They need affirmation. Before I answer, I ask for an author's note, "What do you want to know," and return the ownership of the writing to the student.

I have not always used author's notes. Several years ago, Robert asked me to participate in a writing exchange between my sophomore students and his preservice teachers. Our students exchanged weekly writings and provided written responses back to the authors.

Initially, the exchange went poorly. My students had been using writing workshop to revise and shape their writings. They met weekly with consistent writing groups, met one on one with self-selected classmates, and received written response from me. The goal in each setting was to provide encouraging comments to the writer. So when my students excitedly opened the first batch of responses from Robert's students, disappointment was clear. The preservice teachers had *graded* the papers. My students responded with vengeance and searched for errors on the second exchange. They worked earnestly with dictionaries and consulted the class grammarian to catch all the mistakes of these soon-to-be teachers.

Because Robert and I reviewed our students' comments to evaluate the success of the exchange, we immediately saw the need to try a new strategy and advised our students about author's notes. As an observer of the exchange, I discovered that my students were able to increase ownership of their work through author's notes. Not only did they create their writing, but they also evaluated its place in the process of that creation. And, ultimately, author's notes allowed students to dictate the type of response needed from their responders.

One type of response is hot spots. In what turned out to be a failed attempt to model hot spots, I brought a poem to share with my students. I wrote it from the perspective of a noncustodial father who sees his ten-year-old son only two hours a week. During their visit, the father reads a chapter of a novel to the child. In my author's note, I asked for hot spots and suggestions for the ending of the poem. Despite my prompts, students could not offer insight.

The silence in the room that morning was a humbling and confusing experience. In retrospect, my advanced sophomore students from two years ago offered many areas that they found descriptive in the same poem. As I stood before my current student group, I considered the differences. Many students in my class two years ago were avid readers; since then I started teaching juniors who qualified for our school's at-risk program. Several of these students were in the court system, and more than half had failed English and other classes, which demoted them to a sophomore standing.

I sought advice from my Thursday Night colleagues. As I described the awkward silence after reading the poem to my class, it occurred to me that the at-risk students might not have related to my poem because many were not readers. They may not have appreciated the father's attempt, albeit superficial, to connect to the son through a novel. The following week, I brought a poem that I wrote to my son about the death of his pet rabbit. Student conversation flowed this time. Comments about hot spots were provided without prompts and students shared memories about their own pets. This was my ah-ha moment. I had forgotten about my audience. The junior at-risk students needed to connect to writing differently than the advanced sophomores from two years before.

As I continue my membership in the Thursday Night Writing Group, I am fortunate to discover ideas to take back to my students. The process of creating, responding to, and receiving response to my writing has allowed me not only to grow as a writer but also to become a compassionate teacher. I empathize with my students as they struggle to find their voice in their writing and to gain courage to share their work. I know what it's like to have a dry spell or to write badly. But by sharing some of my drafts, and by promoting ownership of response through author's notes, my students gain skills to make writing a lifelong activity.

Robert Brooke

Response and a writer's self-conception develop together.

My colleagues described how the Thursday Night Writing Group helped them emerge as writers. Their descriptions resonate with my own experience. I would like to extend their comments by examining one way my group experience has enriched my teaching of writing.

In our group, I've been intrigued with how most of us moved through a progression in our writing. Much of our early writing circled around centers of pain, as if we just had to work through the deaths of loved ones or divorces or abandonments, as if those writing tasks are a kind of litmus test for both writer and group: can the group work out ways to respond so that the writer can get on? After this, many of us moved through periods of open experimentation, searching for genres through which to come to voice, to which the necessary response is consideration of options and their possible effects. Still later many of us settled in to larger projects, such as a series of sports poems or a young adult novel. At this point, we read voraciously in the genre and about the subject, and our responses served to connect our projects to the textual conversations that might surround them. I have seen myself and enough other writers move through this progression to think it might be central to the process of coming to authorship.

Because of this experience, I learned to watch students' writing for where they are in this progression of moments. I learned to give them different response at each moment. A few years ago, for example, I was lucky enough to work for two semesters with a student I'll call Cheryl, one of our transfer athletes, a track star from the center of Philadelphia. My experience with our group helped me to understand her work. She began as a fearful writer, much afraid of being corrected, and asked if she couldn't just keep a journal for the whole first semester. I negotiated compromise with her about the polished prose requirements in the class, and introduced her to a couple of books on writing as life practice. She chose to ignore the polished prose requirements and continued journaling straight through the semester, clearly enjoying the small group discussion of her journal topics (race issues on campus, in society at large, in relationships, and some private pages about her family and boyfriend, which she may have shared with her small group but asked me not to read). She described herself as growing tremendously in class, as writing far more and far better than she ever had before.

The next semester I was surprised to see her in my next-level writing class, along with one of her track teammates. She continued journaling. I remember the shock on her teammate's face when, three weeks into the course, Cheryl showed the green spiral notebook she had already filled. But about a month into the course, Cheryl began a new project. The journal entries suddenly stopped, and she began bringing in letters to the editorial page of the student newspaper, a poem for her mother, an expression of outrage at something in her anthropology class. She began experimenting with rhetorical forms she saw around her. I began responding by pointing out options: she could develop a certain idea in such-and-such a way for a more effective editorial or this-and-such a way for a personal essay. Around midterms, she focused her experimenting and announced in her goals conference that she wanted to complete a radio drama from a four-page draft she'd started featuring an African American woman detective. We worked out a set of readings to support this, and by the end of the semester she had completed three radio scripts (two creative, with her detective, and one informational about the real situation of urban youth). Looking back on these semesters, I am aware of how closely Cheryl's progression matches the progression I've seen in my group's writing. I was pleased to have that background to enable my work with her.

As this example implies, my experience with the Thursday Night Writing Group taught me to be on the lookout for patterns of long-term progressions in writing and response. It's taught me that people's behavior with texts comes from the understandings they hold of what texts are, where their meanings reside, and how they are shaped. Often the most productive responses I can give are aimed at those understandings and the practices that shape them.

Kate Brooke

Response and revision help author and text become independent.

When I feel close to and protective of an early idea, at that stage it usually needs protection. Through revision it is weaned. Given the right kind of response, the idea develops from an incomplete stage which needs a caretaker to defend and explain it, to an entity that stands on its own. Over the years of participation in our Thursday Night Writing Group, I have grown to experience response and revision as valuable tools. This is a welcome change from how I once understood group critiques.

As a fine art printmaker, early stages of my images often amount to a folder containing a collection of paper scraps that I feel work together: small sheets of Arches paper, each with sumi washes making an amorphous background; a corner torn from a relief print where a crisp blue line contrasts with pale green inks; my animal stamps; two computer printouts of text, one formatted as a column, the other as a horizontal pair of lines. When my turn arrives, we clear empty spritzer cans from the table, move cups, check for spills, and I try to locate my "draft" in a spot where everyone will be able to see. Sometimes I wonder if I should feel silly arranging these bits of paper on a coffeehouse table. Maybe it's premature to show anything. But I want to find out how the others perceive this assortment of scraps. So I carefully assemble the pieces as they were when I saw the spark of an idea back in my studio. The idea cannot exist without my being there to explain and say what it might become. Yet dialogue at this stage is a time-proven part of my creative process. My colleagues know this. I ask for hot spots, movies of the mind, encouragement.

Ten years ago I dreaded group critiques, feeling they too easily became a public forum for finding fault with my work. I rarely offered much about my ideas—the less information I volunteered, the less there would be to cut down. Had I understood how to give an author's note, I could have approached a critique as a context where I got to ask for responses more useful to my process than static evaluation. But I didn't. As group critiques neared, I lost motivation to create.

Dialogue with the Thursday Night Writing Group taught me to be greedy for response instead of feeling afraid of it. Joan finds a hot spot in the way the calm of the sumi washes balances the energy of the blue line piece and says it mirrors what's going on in the text. Robert sees a visual pun in the version with the ewe, a play that is absent with the figure of a giraffe. Carol wonders if handwritten text might convey the tone I want better than using letterpress text. Everyone agrees the horizontal collage has a visual energy that is lost when I change to a vertical format. By the time I collect all my pieces and close my folder, I have tested and confirmed several theories about what will be effective, and I've discarded others. Response and revision now represent opportunity instead of evaluation and correction.

Our processes allow me the confidence to step back from an image and treat it as a project with its own requirements for successful completion. To my delight, many of the writing response tools translated extremely well into tools for responding to images. A movie of the mind, for instance, given by someone unused to analyzing an image, can offer me a wealth of information. What viewers look at first, what next, and what associations and assumptions they make in the process of taking in the whole image and reading its text, all this can tell me a great deal about my work. In addition, learning to respond to another person's work helps me figure out how to describe what I want to have happen in my own.

When I first joined the Thursday Night Writing Group, I was composing short texts to include in my images, and I was confident I would receive help with my writing. But I was unsure what to expect in the way of responses to my visual work. Too often, nonartists refrain from making comments because they feel they lack the authority to do so. I wondered what would happen with this group of writers. I wondered, too, would they be easily fooled by superficial technique and not be able to help me negotiate more complicated issues of content and completion in an image.

I need not have been concerned. My colleagues easily find parallels to my work in their writing genres and are quick to pick up on visual puns and poems. The crossovers are exciting to me. Kathy's use of line breaks in her poems changes the meaning of a word, just as I might shift meaning by using green where purple is the anticipated color. Linda's writing about a barefoot childhood elicits memories of my own to draw upon. Some evenings, I get so excited about some spark of insight offered in someone else's work that I feel like a grade-school kid with my hand in the air (the ones who squirm and wiggle and say "Oh! Oh! Oh!" in hopes they'll be called on)—except what I'll want is to scurry back to my studio to see if I can't make happen in an image what my colleague did in writing.

The next time I bring my folder, no longer are all the pieces loose and liable to slip out like litter onto the street. I've glued and printed and now have a fuller draft ready. I'm still tinkering, but the next steps are so final: when I print onto this collage, there is no going back. Unlike my writing, I cannot in this case select "undo" or open a saved file of an earlier draft. But by now the piece has assumed its own identity, and though it may not yet be strong, I don't feel compelled to hover and protect it. If, in printing, it doesn't turn out quite right, the image will just have to rally. I'll figure out what to do next based on what is there.

Secure in my identity as an author of images, I can now take what I've learned about revision and response and use these tools in situations where the people are less familiar to me. Not long ago Robert and I were at the home of new friends, one of whom is an artist. Just before we left, our artist friend invited me to his basement studio. I was eager to accept but felt anxious because I didn't want to say the wrong thing. But as I looked at his images I was reminded of my own work in a similar stage, so I offered responses that I would have appreciated: hot spots (there were many), movie of the mind, encouragement to continue. My colleague's project was well beyond the bare beginnings, but this was the first time he had asked me to talk with him about it. In a sense our dialogue was itself in the beginning stages, so the early responses were appropriate. By using the group response patterns, our talk proved highly successful. Some forty minutes after our "quick visit" began, Robert had to interrupt us to remind me we had been about to leave when I made the detour to the studio.

Through participation in our writing group I have learned to claim ownership of and responsibility for my creative processes. I have a better sense of what kind of response I need at various stages of my work and of how to ask for what I need. The tools I've gained from writing group help me understand how to use response successfully in a creative community.

Section Three: New Challenges

Heidi LM Jacobs

A good writing group is hard to find.

In *A Room of One's Own*, Virginia Woolf declared that "a woman must have money and a room of her own if she is to write fiction" (4). Since I left Nebraska and moved to North Carolina, I have had money and a room of my own, yet I have written very little. In the past two years, I have struggled with one essay about being a Canadian hockey fan in the South. My journal writing is sporadic, and each entry begins with a lament about not writing more. While I could explain my lack of writing with a reference to the pressures of being a young professional, I find this explanation too easy. In my journal, I don't make excuses but instead try to discover the reasons why I haven't written. When I lament my lack of writing, I draw lines between academic writing and what I call "my writing" (journaling, creative nonfiction, fiction). For example, in some of the weeks where I lament "I've written nothing in two weeks," I also record that I'd written thirty pages on my dissertation. Rather than time or circumstance, my journal suggests that inspiration is the missing component in my writing life.

In my East Carolina University teaching notebooks, I have lots of ideas for writing, starts to essays that suggest that I did not lack subject matter to write about. Often I developed my writings in class to discuss with my students, but I rarely took them farther than a first or second draft. What I realize has been missing from my writing life is an audience who would be interested in my writing, who would help me with it, and who would, each week, expect me to have some progress. Ironically, the very things I insist my writing students have—community, goals, support, feedback, and expectation—I do not give myself.

It is not a coincidence that I wrote a lot while I lived in Nebraska. I had a strong community of writers who met weekly and who had unspoken yet firm expectations of its members. Simply put, I knew that most Thursdays I should have writing to bring. This pressure inspired me to take ideas and scribblings past the first draft stage. Once the group had commented on my piece, it seemed like a waste of their time not to make their suggested revisions. Although the group didn't expect all of us to have writing each week, there was peer pressure to be productive.

Expectation and structure are not specific to this group nor are they difficult to replicate. Inspiration, on the other hand, is a rarer commodity and one more difficult to find. What my writing process lacks at present are the individual members and what they brought to each meeting. On the weeks when Kate brought her artwork, I was inspired to get out of my word-bound world and think about ideas from a different perspective. Other weeks, Robert's commitment to writing his family's story made me aware of the way I flitted from piece to piece. Joan's cool and quirky writing made me want to try new things. Carol's woman-centered writing appealed to me very much as both a women's studies scholar and as a woman. Kathy blew me away with poems or images that have stayed with me for years. Linda joined in my last year and, at that time, brought writing sporadically. Her response to my work made me think I was on to something; her wanting more offered a much needed inspiration.

Each week, the group inspired me in different ways. Sometimes, it was the members' collective commitment to writing that inspired me to want to be a better or more productive writer. Other times, it was their enthusiasm or lack of enthusiasm over my writing that made me want to go back and revise it. Sometimes, when we were all in a writing rut, we'd come up with writing prompts or assignments for the next week.

After struggling for a year and a half with my hockey essay, I recently found another like-minded writer who, after one session, helped me get the essay "ready for the box," as we used to say. My writing life, I find, is not hopeless. I have found ways to piece together elements of the Thursday night group and get my writing life back on track. Virginia Woolf is correct that a writer needs money and a room of one's own, but a writer also needs inspiration and community.

Carol MacDaniels

A good group can get through anything.

When Dale first proposed the idea about us writing a book chapter on our writing group, we all jumped at the chance, thinking that it would be fun, that it would be a good exercise for us to tackle as a group, and that since we had been meeting successfully for years, maybe we had something to tell others. Now that we're at the end of the process, we're closer to "Let's get the damn thing in the mail" and wondering if the struggle was worth the effort. I don't know that any of us expected the tension, hard feelings, and frustration we've experienced in trying to come to consensus on twenty pages of writing.

Collaborating on writing posed a challenge for us. Over the years we'd been together as a group, we had all matured as writers and responders, but ultimately we went home to revise, complete, or abandon our writing on our own. As Joan points out in her story "Little Dancer," she came to her epiphanies on her own. Kate and Kathy also talk about how their writing evolves through the sharing and response process, which helps them shape their thinking and develop the piece. As a group we offer hot spots and movies of the mind, but each of us, on our own, must decide how to change the writing.

Our collective writing violated all the conventions, norms, expectations, and patterns we had established as a group over time. Suddenly, instead of having sole authorship over our writing, others had a vested interest in what was said and how it was said. When group members responded to one another's writing for this chapter and made suggestions ("If this were my house, I would …"), we listened with a different awareness. Now everyone had a stake in revision and the decisions made about a piece. That loss of sole ownership proved difficult for us to deal with as experienced, independent writers who have our own styles, strengths, and purposes in writing. These same characteristics interfered with how we each conceptualized the entire article, the introduction and the ending. The fact that there are eight of us didn't make the process any easier.

We had a lot going for us, though, which ultimately pulled the group through. In their writing, Linda and Robert both talk about how they take what they learn in writing group into their classrooms, and Kate mentions using writing group processes when she works with other artists. This ability to learn from what works in writing group and to transfer that insight into other situations helped us, individually and collectively, understand and work through the frustrations we all felt as we tried to finish our chapter. During the last week before deadline, e-mails got lengthier and more frequent, infringing into our already busy days, as we tried to negotiate our way through frustrations and proposing ways we could move the piece forward. Dale and Heidi, being 1,200 miles away, created new problems in addition to sheer distance. Those of us in Lincoln, Nebraska, would get together and discuss writing, procedures, and issues that they couldn't hear, and even though we sent drafts and e-mails and made several conference calls, the necessary intimacy and immediacy were missing. Dale and Heidi's contributions to the chapter emphasize the strength of our relationships and the love that we share as group members. That ultimately helped us get through this experience. We want to support one another, and we've become more than colleagues over the past years. We share our lives with one another. We feel love and trust toward one another, are in awe of one another's talents, are respectful of each individual's commitment to our group, and are aware that we are connected by our need to be artists—whether with words or with images.

I don't think any one of us would deny that we were glad to see the end of this project. I also don't think any one of us would respond so readily if asked to do it a second time. On the other hand, we've all grown through this process, learning more about ourselves as writers, about one another as friends and colleagues, and about group dynamics and processes. Maybe we could do it again.

WORKS CITED

Woolf, Virginia. *A Room of One's Own*. San Diego, New York, and London: Harcourt Brace Jovanovich, 1929.

CHAPTER THIRTEEN

ᔪᐢᐩ

A Group of Our Own: Women and Writing Groups: A Reconsideration

Terri Trupiano Barry
Michigan State University

Julie Galvin Bevins
Maryann K. Crawford
Central Michigan University

Elizabeth Demers
University of Nebraska at Lincoln

Jami Blaauw Hara
North Central Michigan College

M. Rini Hughes
Mary Ann K. Sherby
Michigan State University

To be a successful writer, Virginia Woolf asserts that a woman needs "money and a room of her own" (4). Although Woolf was specifically speaking of the link between the artistic and economic oppression of women, she revealed a principal dilemma in the personal and professional development of female scholars—that of maintaining the delicate balance between established gender roles and academic expectations. Poets, novelists, and critics have long struggled against entrenched patriarchal structures that saw women as objects rather than as subjects. Creating women's space, a "room of one's own," in a graduate women's writing group, like the one we discuss in this chapter, can help bridge the gap between the personal intellectual process and the competitive marketplace of academe.

The Group

In the fall of 1996, under the auspices of the university writing center, we formed a writing group of six women graduate students in fields ranging from linguistics, composition theory, and rhetoric to American studies and history. Five were in the PhD program; one was working on her MA. A seventh member, who is pursuing a PhD in history, joined the group in 1998. We are all white and from lower- to upper-middle class backgrounds; our ages range from mid twenties to mid fifties. The writing center offered us a quiet place to meet, and one of the directors provided us with some initial guidelines: making commitments to each other, being positive as well as critical in our comments, identifying our individual needs, and helping the group understand and meet them. Most of us were quite comfortable with the idea of collaborative writing and peer workshops, but none of us had ever participated in a writing group ourselves. Nor could we have predicted how important this group would become to us or how useful it would be in preparing us as professionals.

Throughout the fall semester, our awareness of the group's influence grew. To capture this increasing consciousness, we conducted an interview session in the spring of 1997, in which members reflected on the value of the writing group. The interview session revealed benefits common to most such groups—intellectual stimulation, real audiences for our writing, motivation to complete writing tasks, and the extension of literacy practices beyond the classroom. However, we also came to see gender as an integral part of the group's identity and success, creating a community of women scholars with a "group of our own."

In a follow-up reflection, conducted in 1999, we revisited the themes voiced in that first year of our group work and discussed, now via e-mail and electronic chatrooms, our memories of the group and the way the group helped us shape our lives. In the following sections, which include the voices of the group's members, we discuss and expand the themes that emerged. As we reflected on our work in the group, we found significant areas of commonality that we believe are more generally part of women's experience in academe. These areas include our increasing consciousness about the checkered history of women as writers and as academics, the importance of blending our public and private lives, a growing understanding and acceptance of ourselves as intellectuals and as professionals, and the role of the group in expanding our scholarship and in mentoring each other to achieve our individual academic and educational goals. Through our participation in an all-women's writing group, and by thinking, talking, and writing about the group's influence, we have gained a greater understanding of ourselves as scholars, as writers, and as women.

Women Writers

MRH: Although [the group was] decidedly "critical" about our
         writing, we were not forced to defend either the content
         or style we employed against charges of "writing like
         women" that is so often used to silence women. (1999)

For women, writing has long been contested terrain, in part because, as
Miriam Brody points out, "[t]o write well in Western Culture is to write like
a man" (3). Claiming the right to the written word has too often necessitated a bifurcation of the woman doing the writing—into the gendered des-
ignation of woman as against the male-identified role of author. Furthermore, historically, women have been both literally and figuratively locked
out of academic space, such as libraries, museums, and student unions
(Woolf 11). As the Brontës and other female writers of the past discovered,
entry into the intellectual world often carried a heavy price, including the
loss of personal and gendered identity from having to write under male
pseudonyms. This alienation from one's self as well as from the wider intellectual community created feelings of loneliness and isolation within female artists and led them to seek out a "sisterhood" of female audiences,
other women (both writers and readers) whose real or perceived presence
gave women the power to write in the face of patriarchal disapproval
(Gilbert and Gubar 50).

The alienation that women experience is detrimental either to true "art"
or to a professional, polished product, both of which benefit from the author's immersion in a creative or academic community. Cixous tells the
woman writer, "you've written a little, but in secret. And it wasn't good because it was in secret" (246). And, as if in response, Woolf asserts, "Master-
pieces are not single and solitary births; they are the outcome of many years
of thinking in common, of thinking by the body of the people, so that the experience of the mass is behind the single voice" (113). Writing, in other
words, cannot occur in isolation.

For women writers, having other female models is of paramount importance. We learn from our (metaphorical as well as real) mothers how to be
women as well as how to be writers—words flow as freely as mother's milk;
we "write in white ink" (Cixous 251). "Mothers" include established authors of the female canon (Aphra Behn, Jane Austen, Harriet Beecher
Stowe, Toni Morrison, Margaret Atwood, among others) as well as those
women who are immediately important to our professional development.
These women function as role models as well as nurturers who help us
transform ourselves from outsiders to insiders—professionals, scholars,
and writers who have acquired a public voice and who can exert power to
shape the rules within a community.

MAS: The moral support of talking with people who are inter-
            ested in the same things I am is one of the things I really
            enjoy. Equally [important] is the intellectual stimulation
            or the professionalism. It's been very nurturing to me,
            and very exciting at times, too. (1997)

In a women's writing group, the members function as mothers to each
other, reinforcing the spirit of community and collaboration. Moreover,
the gendered nature of this community is paramount. Women "need to
speak to women without the intermediary of a man, to listen more atten-
tively to women" as intellectuals both within the public sphere of print
and face to face (Felman 127). However, for burgeoning intellectuals, the
question of audience becomes even more complicated. Women who are
preparing for careers in academia (or who use academia to prepare for
other careers) know that they do not speak to completely female audiences. Felman poses a series of questions that also shaped the context of
our women's writing group:

> Whom do we write for? Whom do we wish to be read by? Whom are we afraid
> to be read by? Whom do we trust to know how to read our writing? Whom do
> we need in order to help us grasp the truth that lies in wait (for us, for others)
> in our story but that alone we do not have the strength to grasp? Who can help
> us, or enable us, to survive our story? (130)

As professionals, we write not only for ourselves or our group but also
for the market.

Margaret Atwood attests, "No woman writer wants to be overlooked and
undervalued for being a woman; but few, it seems, wish to be defined solely
by gender, or constrained by loyalties to it alone" (xii). Our writing is
commoditized when we present it for public consumption, and this public
is market driven, whether it be in the context of publishing, professional
preparation, or job hunting. Women, therefore, confront an insidious issue
as writers and as scholars—the misconception that women write for
women rather than for general audiences. This misconception places a significant limitation on the purpose, value, and power of women's writing,
creative or scholarly, to transform old rules and roles into newer, more eq-
uitable ones. "Needing to constantly prove your worth undermines
self-confidence in even the strongest women" (Aisenberg and Harrington
67). Yet this is exactly the situation many women face when they enter graduate school, even if we are not defined or limited by gender alone.

How then, to overcome the perception of gender limitation in the marketplace while still participating in the kind of women-only support structure
that theorists like Woolf, Gilbert and Gubar, and Cixous say are essential?

An ideal forum for such nurturing is a women's writing group. A women's group allows for professional, personal, and artistic development within a safe, women-only space. The group functions both theoretically and practically as a bridge between private and public, creating the necessary mother space within the larger community of the market and the mind.

> MRH: I've never in my life defined myself as feminist. I say things that people say, "Oh that sounds feminist to me." I don't think of it as a feminist thing, but as the way I look at people. Whatever kind of people: students, men, whoever. So I have difficulty separating that, what of this is being women, and what of this is that I'm with a group of people that I'm comfortable with. (1997)

Women in Academe

> TTB: I think we mentor each other. And I think it does have to do with the fact that we are all women, and women in the academy don't get a lot of credit. And here we are valued, and everybody gets a chance to talk, to share their stories, their papers, to offer their advice. (1997)

Gesa Kirsch summarizes how difficult and complex the issue of establishing oneself as an author/ity in academic discourse can be for women "because part of *having* authority entails being *perceived* as an authority" (49 italics hers). Although feminist pedagogy and scholarship has challenged traditional approaches to writing and research, women must still vest themselves in the robes of patriarchal authority and employ the genres of patriarchal discourse to be given due recognition as scholars. The disciplinary conventions of academe were established by males in the days when women were indeed outsiders to the sacred grove. This means that women are caught between two sets of norms. If a woman is patient, deferential, or soft-spoken, she seems weak and therefore not professional. If a woman behaves according to norms based on competition and aggression, she offends traditional ideals of nurturing. Yet to succeed as graduate students and as professionals, women must learn to display knowledge and argue forcefully (Aisenberg and Harrington 18). Acquiring the ability to display our knowledge in effective ways is not simply a concession to male-established rules of acting and being. It also entails our responsibility to use the power of scholarship to influence change in our communities and to use this power authentically both as women and as scholars.

Within the culture of the university our writing group provided us with a haven, a safe place to think, speak, and write. It offered the type of support that both bolstered our self-worth and validated our scholarship. It taught us to write forcefully and effectively while still providing a mother space.

TTB: Personally, for me, the idea that I have women in the acad-
            emy who are doing the same thing that I am, working to-
            ward that professionalism, is to me most important.

MAC: We're all nodding! (1997)

Our group enacted the type of "collaboration that effectively reduces alienation where no one individual constantly dominates, where all mem-bers are supported, and where individual contributions are developed upon by other members" (Gere 68). Paula Caplan recommends several types of groups that women in academia can form to succeed at and even enjoy academic life (75). For example, she recommends that women form departmental groups "designed to talk about how it feels—both the joys and the woes—[of] being a woman in academia" (87) and to share informa-tion on the unwritten rules about hiring, tenure, and workplace issues (89). We believe that writing groups for women graduate students should be added to her list.

JGB: That's definitely the place for me, being inscribed as a pro-
            fessional. I mean this has helped me reconsider my writ-
            ing process and my pedagogy, but I think the lore that gets
            thrown around is the biggie. Like we talked about comps,
            okay … being part of a community. (1997)

MAC: Not only as being inscribed but participating in a group of
            professional women. All of whom are women, interested
            in women's issues. (1997)

Blending Public and Private

MAS: The fact that the group is all women has been very impor-
            tant to me, perhaps because my earlier schooling—bache-
            lor's and master's degrees—was very male oriented. In
            other words, there weren't that many women out there to
            admire in the late 60s. (1999)

One of the primary themes that emerged from our reflections was the im-portance of blending our developing senses of ourselves as professionals with our personal lives. In *Diving Deep and Surfacing*, feminist theolo-gian Carol Christ says, "Women are hungry for stories that name our expe-riences and provide us with models of the possible" (13). Describing her depression and temporary flight from academia, when she encountered

resistance in her attempts to integrate personal experience with scholarship, Christ explains that "in telling my story, I was writing myself out of
the university" (136). Echoing the results of Belenky et al.'s famous study,
Women's Ways of Knowing, Christ claims that women need to share their
experiences with one another to name anew the great powers that give
shape and meaning to our lives (138).

While Christ's text focuses primarily on feminist scholars in religion, her
insistence on the significance of combining the personal with the academic
through story has implications for all female scholars. Women have traditionally shared only private friendships and thus have suffered from a lack
of support in their public endeavors. Males, on the other hand, have a history of friendships that provide "the enabling bond that not only supported
risk and danger but also comprehended the details of a public life and the
complexities of the pain found there" (Heilbrun 100). Male scholars also
have a lengthy tradition, visible and recorded, of academic relationships
and "stories." Women who try to fit into existing academic frameworks discover that their experiences differ from their male colleagues' journeys
through academia. Women, therefore, need a place to begin to make sense
of these differences.

> JGB: I just think [the group] would have been different with
>   men here. Not necessarily worse ... I guess just for me,
>   there aren't many spaces where there are only women, so
>   it's kind of nice to have one. (1997)
>
> MAC: I think that that's part of what the women's group means to
>   me, not because it's different with a single gender, but
>   more so because we can make assumptions about com-
>   monalties and experiences and perspectives as women
>   that don't have to be put on the table and looked at. (1997)

Conversations, storytelling, and friendships with other women who
comprehend the details of what it means, for example, to try to write a
scholarly paper with a child banging on the office door and dinner burning
in the kitchen, are not only a way to begin to construct knowledge but are
also a way to give meaning to our lives. Thus, the stories about babies and
grandbabies, husbands and significant others, daily routines, health,
classes, travel, age, and friendship that occurred in our group were rooted
in our experiences as women and were the touchstones from which we
could work toward connecting, with each other and with our emerging understanding of our various graduate and professional positions. An
all-women's writing group can provide an essential safe zone where gender
becomes a positive force in the development of women as scholars and professionals rather than an obstacle to be overcome.

A group like ours helped us to avoid the sort of schism between personal and academic that Carol Christ experienced in her work within university structures. We recognized that such a dichotomy is a false one. In our meetings we regularly articulated that belief in our openness to topics and formats, stories and methods, creating a space for the intersection of narratives, ideas, theories, and practices.

> JBH: The group was most helpful for opening up my writing to
>   other writers and other perspectives. Had I considered
>   this? Had I read this? (1999)

Our flexibility and openness to others' experiences, knowledge, and stories helped us to more accurately make sense of our individual situations. In *Composing a Life*, Mary Catherine Bateson reminds us that "we need to look at multiple lives to be able to test and shape our own" (16), and she warns us of the danger of faculty and students who are too "committed to continuity" to be able to see the inherent multiplicity in people's lives (17). And it mattered to us that we are more than students, teachers, and professionals; we are also mothers, daughters, sisters, friends. The ability to entwine the various strands of our lives within the group provided a sense of wholeness for which we yearn as women.

Such wholeness has not traditionally been valued in academe. Academia has often encouraged the split between the acquisition and making of knowledge and one's personal life (Coiner and Hume George). Success is counted by the ability to make brilliant (read rational) comments on complex (read difficult and highly theoretical) texts and situations. In these assumptions are implicit rejections of learning, speaking, and reading about personal experience, emotions, and what some scholars would deem the mundane practicalities of life—family, children, and work responsibilities outside the academy. Bringing these issues into academic experiences is, traditionally, to taint the rational with the irrational and unpredictable.

This is much like Foucault's notion of the distinction between madness and reason. Our understanding of the nature of madness is created by our understanding of reasonable, rational people—like ourselves. What is not understood is not liked, and, as different and devalued, it becomes something else entirely; it becomes irrational, it becomes "mad." Our writing group shattered many assumptions about what constitutes reason. For example, a discussion of a theoretical issue in Maryann's dissertation draft would be interwoven with the announcement that Rini's daughter had a baby. There was no sense of a rift when our personal lives entered the space of our academic lives. Rather, our dialogue interpolated our personal and public lives, which felt refreshing and supportive to us.

JGB: Our group highlighted and recognized the overlapping of cooking and babies and studying and theorizing and living as a woman and writing a paper. Well, that was important because I never wanted, as an "academic," to "forget" all the parts of myself in my attempts to be a "professional." (1999)

MAS: What Julie said about the blurring of personal and professional rings true for me as well …. I don't feel compelled to maintain a professional/public persona all the time. And if I'm preoccupied about a "personal" concern, I can mention it without feeling it detracts from me as a professional individual. (1999)

Reason and order have been defined according to the traditions of male, upper-class scholars simply because, historically, only this group was allowed to attend universities. The idea is not that women are still purposefully kept out of the academy or that we only find refuge in women's groups, but rather that certain ways of thinking, speaking, and writing are still privileged in the academy and that in our group we were able to think, speak, and write in ways with which we were more comfortable. Yet because we were aware of the larger academic context, we also pushed members toward the critical stances required in academic writing.

Being Intellectuals, Becoming Professionals

TTB: Graduate school can be a lonely mission, perhaps more particularly for commuting students and older women. I'm both. Life speeds by at an amazing rate, and it is difficult to make time for family, let alone nonacademic friends. The writing group helps fill this gap because, no matter how much we stick to the academic issues to be discussed, personal life is of interest and part of our conversations. (1999)

As Aisenberg and Harrington found in their study of academic women, "the quest for meaningful work leads eventually, after journeyings and experiments, to graduate school and to the most intense phase of the transformational process" (29). As part of this transformation, women academics, in comparison to men, relate to their scholarly work in a more personal, or even passionate, way. This is another theme repeated in our interviews—we were exhilarated by the experience of sharing our research and writing with the group. We were able to converse as intellectuals without "trying to please some man" (MAS 1997), which added to the feeling of exhilaration. Because we all treated each other as academics, we began to feel like academics, an experience replicated far too infrequently in the traditional classroom.

> MAC: It's important to me because it's a place to be okay, and still be an intellectual .... I've lived with a history of being different, being called smart or hearing, "she uses those big words." I never know how to take that because there's a personal identity side to that.
>
> TTB: Oh yeah, I think it's mostly men who are threatened by women of intelligence. I've had bosses who were intimidated by me.
>
> MRH: Most of my bosses ought to have been intimidated! (laughter)(1997)

If a woman is to produce scholarly writing, we need to add a third element to Woolf's famous caveat about money and a room of her own: she needs at least one good friend to talk with, preferably someone who is inside the academy with her. Our experiences of forming friendships within the group coincides with studies of academic collaboration among women in higher education, that "personal friendships became the base for professional work together" (Clark and Watson). When we began the group we had only a nodding acquaintance with each other, but as we came to know each other professionally we also came to know and nurture each other personally as well.

A graduate student writing group like the one we formed—with individuals at differing academic stages, in various disciplines, and with varying connections to academic people and resources—offered opportunities to practice the discourse of our fields and to make connections between the familiar and the unknown, to become insiders in academe. Deborah Brandt argues that we cannot join a discourse community unless we have "insider knowledge" about that community, at the same time that *you have to be a member first to gain insider knowledge*" (120, italics hers). This presents a dilemma that our group helped resolve. Within the group we acknowledged each others' insider status, allowing for the development of the sorts of language(s) necessary for participation in wider academic conversations.

Although male graduate students are likely to benefit from such conversations as well, the significance of our all-women group is that the relatedness necessary for women's construction of academic knowledge differs from that of our male peers. Brandt tells us that effective readers and writers see "how a text relates dynamically and immediately to people, place, time, action—even more specifically, to a me, a you, a here, and a now. *How it relates* is the real challenge in literacy learning" (100, italics hers). As women readers and writers of and within our academic con/texts, the writing group provided us a space and a place in which we could relate our graduate and public and professional experiences to our private and personal gendered lives.

ED: Interestingly, gender was not originally a concern for me. In fact, when I first sat in with the group, they told me that maintaining a women's group was important to them; I thought, "okay, whatever works for you." Only after I had been involved with the group for a number of weeks did I feel that the equal emphases on women and writing were important to me as well. The group was incredibly comfortable for me. I found it VERY easy to share intellectual and social ideas. (1999)

TTB: Although the tide is turning, and women are being made more welcome in the academy, women students and faculty still face discriminatory practices and a sexist environment …. [If a woman] has somewhere to turn, a place where people in similar situations can not only empathize but help point out the pervasiveness of such situations, to defuse it by helping depersonalize it, then she can again feel, "I am okay!" She won't be questioning her own intelligence. (1999)

Developing Scholarship

One of the most valuable aspects of a writing group is the intellectual stimulation (or nudging) that members receive from others in the group. In our group, this nudging took two forms—practical and intellectual. On a practical level, the group helped us establish and keep deadlines. When someone in the group said, "O.K., you need to have this in to the chair of your committee by the week after next. Can you bring a draft to us next week?" the invitation proffered a structure within which individuals could write. As a result, we expended the effort to compose the promised draft before the next meeting because we all needed and valued the feedback from our colleagues and because we knew that underlying their expectations was a desire to see each of us succeed. This desire can be both altruistic and focused on self. By helping others to succeed, we create more models for ourselves.

MRH: The best thing, aside from the questions, is the sense of focus, that other people are struggling with the same issues, many of the same concerns, and the reminder that regardless of how you feel about it, you've got to get it done. I found that very helpful. (1997)

The second form of nudging we experienced involved more complex interactions, in which we extended our knowledge and our thinking by serving as resonators for each other. Discussing Harold Lasswell's conception of a resonator, Karen Burke LeFevre explains:

> [A] resonator … may be someone who acts as a friendly audience or someone who lends financial or emotional support. Resonators might be groups of students or colleagues, accepting "apostles" who allow a person to investigate ideas in a safe place without the harsh evaluation that outsiders might make …. Resonance comes about when an individual act—a "vibration"—is intensified and prolonged by sympathetic vibrations. It may occur when someone acts as a facilitator to assist or extend what is regarded as primarily another's invention, or when people are mutual collaborators at work on a task. (65)

JGB: I think now what's in my head is different. There're all
            these voices that are talking while I'm writing, voices that
            weren't there before. Some of the voices are definitely
            from this group. (1997)

In reading and responding to texts and asking questions about what we saw as unclear or potentially problematic, we gained insights into how we might better illustrate an idea, describe a situation, or explain a theoretical concept. As Patti Stock maintains in *The Dialogic Curriculum*, by talking through our ideas with others, we learn from each other (passim). To use Vygotsky's terminology, we take part in a "deliberate structuring of the web of meaning" (qtd. in Emig 127). Vygotsky, as Emig explains, views writing as an expansion of inner speech, but, whereas inner speech is compact and "almost entirely predicative," written language is "maximally detailed." Writing requires us to explicitly provide subjects and topics as well as systematic connections and relationships (127).

The need to make connections and relationships explicit may appear to be self-evident, but it is, in fact, one of the areas in which working together in a group encompasses the most potential for scholarly development. By close reading and careful listening and questioning we help each other to clarify (or in some cases to establish) relationships within our thinking and to express these relationships within our texts. "Written speech," says Luria, "assumes a … repeated mediating process of analysis and synthesis, which makes it possible not only to develop the required thought, but even to revert to its earlier stages, thus transforming the sequential chain of connections in a simultaneous, self-reviewing structure" (qtd. in Emig, 128). The self-reviewing structure already inherent in writing was intensified in the exchanges that took place among our members. By submitting our texts to the group and answering our colleagues' questions about them, we engaged (or reengaged) in a self-reviewing process in ways we could not do alone.

An additional way that our group extended scholarship was by exposing us to women who were developing expertise in areas that were different from our own. Because we were all in disciplines within the humanities, we shared general areas of interest but not of expertise. As a result, the differences in our disciplinary expertise meant that we also had to teach each other and introduce discourse communities with which our peers were unfamiliar.

JGB: Even if you were doing a different comp than I was, the way that you were thinking about structuring things this way, and studying things that way, I bet I could do that for mine.

TTB: I would agree with that analysis. I think we've all learned a great deal about other topics that we've been exposed to, but there're always enough similarities going on in our own scholarship that we can make connections or can build our own knowledge that way, too. (1997)

That we were called on to explain ourselves within our own disciplinary framework helped develop us as professionals. By demonstrating knowledge of our disciplines in front of an audience, however sympathetic, we claimed those disciplines in a way that we could not have as "mere" students. It meant that we were forced to make our ideas and our writing as clear as possible, eliminating unnecessary jargon from our texts and making connections among the various materials used.

We also served as editors for the texts that we produced, dealing with aspects of writing that are often thought of as occupying a lower level than composing. However, in the process of reconstructing sentences, often through discussions that occurred in meetings, and suggesting possible changes in diction or style, we not only clarified each other's texts but also continued to extend each other's thinking.

TTB: Being open to criticism is essential in writing groups .... [It] requires trust, and trust cannot be built overnight. This issue is so entwined with the idea that we care about each other, both professionally and personally, that I am unable to separate them. (1999)

Functioning as an interested audience and providing specific questions and recommendations for our writing netted a number of benefits that we found particularly valuable to us as women graduate students. That our friends in the group sometimes did not understand what we were saying in our writing indicated that other readers would likely face the same problem. We had advance warning of areas where editors or professors were likely to take us to task. This allowed us to use time and energy more efficiently because we could make needed changes in our writing and thinking before submitting the product.

> ED: [Members] did not take arguments personally, and the
>   criticism/perspectives that they offered allowed me to re-
>   think concepts or sentences I had thought were obvious
>   or clear, when in fact these concepts may not have worked
>   at all. (1999)

Serving as an audience for each other's work is a given in a writing support group, so much so that it may seem an aspect about which no comment is necessary. However, because graduate students are expected to write in such a way as to explicitly display their knowledge of a discipline and their command of its terminology for their mentors, audience involves a particularly complex layer of expectations (Berkenkotter and Huckin). These expectations could be explored and illuminated within the context of the group. Two of the questions we most frequently asked were, "How will your audience regard this statement?" and "Will your audience already know this?" Such questions are particularly helpful in assisting the author to consciously consider what her readers (frequently professors who will be judging the final written product) will assume and what they will expect to have spelled out. Through our discussions of content, tone, diction, and sentence structure we helped each other maintain the persona appropriate to a particular text and, in the case of comprehensive exams or dissertations, the delicately nuanced ethos of a developing professional.

> ED: Being able to read, critique, and think about somebody
>   else's ideas honed my critical skills AND gave me ideas for
>   expanding, thinking about my own project. It also took
>   me outside the rather selfish, insular world of my own
>   writing, which, ironically, made my work better and
>   stirred my creativity even as I thought about what made
>   their projects tick. (1999)

Further, working in a peer-group helps preserve our self-esteem. By working within the group, we can develop our ideas and our product in the midst of friendly and caring as well as intelligent and academic peers, before submitting our writing to the scrutiny of professor-evaluators whose views can drastically affect our future lives. In his discussion of cultural consumption, Michel de Certeau concludes that the consumers of a product acquire a level of privilege greater than that accorded to the producer of the product because the consumers adapt the product to their own ends (8). Our mastery of academic products, as demonstrated within our group, helped transform us from observers of the academic to consumers of the academic in this same creative fashion.

MAC: I wanted some external "motivators" for work on my dissertation—how very functional and practical of me! How womanly of me? ... I knew you would be understanding but still give good, positive criticism. I did not expect that you would laugh at my theorizing, even when it didn't make sense. And none of you ever did .... I can laugh at myself, I couldn't have then. It felt like there was too much at stake in that final push to get finished. (1999)

Mentors and Mentoring

The process of transforming ourselves into academics also affected our interactions as peers and as mentors to each other. Sometimes we shared specific academic experiences, such as writing comprehensive examinations or writing proposals for conference papers. At other times we shared insights into the sometimes arcane administrative practices of the university or offered suggestions for dealing with particularly difficult academic situations. Such mentoring activities are not unusual in themselves; they are likely to occur in a variety of relationships where interests and goals coincide. What has been unusual in our experience is the fluid nature of the mentoring we practiced and our increasing awareness the variety of ways mentoring took place.

When we began in 1996, none of us could have planned or even recognized the variety of ways in which we would mentor each other. In fact, when we started, we didn't really understand our practices and input as mentoring at all. Jami's comment is the most specific mention of mentoring in the original interview session.

JBH: Being a first year Masters student, and many of you being at the top end of the Ph.D. thing, I think it has really helped me in the academic/professional area .... I like having a network of people, who like to do the same things, who are also women, women at the end of their program. You're all mentors to me. One day I'm going to be like all of you. At the same time. (laughter) (1997)

As the youngest member of the group, Jami might initially have been more conscious about the differences between her age (early twenties at this time) and those of us who were in our forties and fifties. However, all of us articulated ways in which the group helped us meet academic expectations, and age seemed to have little effect on the functioning of the group. In the process of reconsidering and reflecting on the value and functions of the writing group, we all became increasingly aware of the mentoring roles we took on for each other and their importance in our development as professionals. Mentoring meant learning from the experiences of others: older members in the group and those who were further along in their graduate programs. But it has also come to mean, for all of us, ways that we looked at and to each other as women and as models for assessing, reassessing, and continuing to work toward our own goals, both personal and professional.

> TTB: This group gave me basic information on subjects of great importance to graduate students: comps, proposals, defenses, and, of course, writing—dissertations, conference papers, articles for publication. Why wouldn't I be enthusiastic? (1999)

As we reconsidered the benefits and effects of the group in our recent reflections and chatroom discussions, we began to articulate and better understand the multiple ways that we were able to support each other as part of the group's process. For example, we did not have a single, "strong woman" leader. Instead, mentoring became a pervasive activity in which we engaged as part of our usual proceedings. We all offered and took insights and suggestions from each other, on occasion adding our mentoring and advisory comments almost offhandedly. In addition, this kind of advice and support occurred without the competition that is so often a factor in academic interactions, whether between students or faculty, the kind of competition that draws on traditional male-oriented ways of being and acting. For us, as found in studies of other women's groups, ideas "were articulated not by one person but instead were the products of conversations ... in which the expertise and leadership of all participants was honored" (Hayden 129).

> MRH: Something else that we had going for us was that we were not in competition with each other. Although we shared some disciplinary backgrounds, each of us was/is involved with different aspects of the disciplines, so we didn't have to worry about "turf" issues .... Groups like this work better, I think, when there is no reason for competition among the members. Challenge, yes; competition, no. (1999)
>
> ED: ... the fact that [others] are at more advanced stages of their degrees helps me see what shoals and breakers like ahead. Moreover, [we] have had interesting intense con-

> versations about all kinds of things not even related to our
> work .... We have disagreed and taken contradictory
> stands on issues, but we have (I feel) worked to see the
> other side and to find some common ground. (1999)

In part, the mentoring in our group was a result of our shared leadership and our desire to help each other succeed. In part it was a result of the discourse style we unconsciously practiced as women. Personal elements were readily incorporated into the more academic aspects of our conversations, serving not as distractions but as bases for our growing understanding of each other and of the work each of us was doing. In this way, our discourse allowed us to reframe the speech of the academy in a manner more consistent with our experience as women. Rather than limiting our use of language to the traditionally permissible discourses of the academy, we taught ourselves to conceptualize our academic lives as integrated with our whole lives, much as this article has emerged from and represents a composite of the efforts of all of the members: our ongoing, thinking, writing, and scholarship, our continuing work as educated and intelligent women.

Reconsiderations: Personal and Professional

It would be a mistake to say that we foresaw the kind of healthy interpolation that the writing group has come to represent for us or that we decided to seek out an all-women writing group. Rather, our group, and that we were all women, simply seemed to happen. Only by looking back and by reflecting, yet again, about our experiences did we begin to understand and assess the group's significance in our personal and professional lives.

Our lives have changed, as all lives must. We are all professionals, although not necessarily in ways that our efforts in the group would have predicted, and we still value the personal pieces that entwine our professional lives. Such are the commitments and conflicts that women face.

Terri Trupiano Barry, Mary Ann Sherby, and Elizabeth Demers continued to meet regularly as a group to work on their PhD's. Mary Ann completed her dissertation with support from the group in 2000, Terri in 2001, and Elizabeth will defend in 2003. Mary Ann and Terri are Visiting Assistant professors, teaching first year composition at Michigan State University. Terri and her husband recently purchased land to build their retirement home. Mary Ann Sherby and her husband have married off their two children and enjoy being grandparents to three lively boys. Elizabeth and her archaeologist husband both have jobs at the University of Nebraska at Lincoln. She is the History Acquisitions Editor for the university press.

TTB: I still think that several factors contributed to making the group, that we are all women, that we have similar scholarly interests, that we are open to criticism (because we know it is intended to improve our writing, not to display superior knowledge), and that we truly do care about each other, professionally and personally. (1999)

MAS: Not that I've necessarily felt especially put down or devalued by men .... And my husband has been very supportive of me, as have two male mentors. What's important is that in this group of women, I feel less like I have to prove myself .... If I want to voice a personal concern, I can do so without feeling it detracts from me as a professional. (1999)

ED: Other quick news: the editors of a journal are interested in an article I gave at a conference last winter, IF I can add 10 pages by September 1. Those of you who watched me cut it from 20-25 to 8-10 pages should be amused as I try to add text back. I have to thank this group, and also the woman (can't remember her name) who recommended *Women in Academe*. That meeting gave me the courage to just send the article in and not worry so much about perfection. (1999)

Julie Bevins had one child in 1996, now she has four. Busy with children and home life, Julie enjoys the learning experiences that come each new day. At this time her priorities and busy schedule have altered her perceptions of the importance of the PhD. She currently works in youth ministry in her church and finds it extremely rewarding and feels blessed to be in such enriching circumstances.

JGB: To have the time and concentration necessary [for writing], I need to get childcare, which costs money and time, commodities in short supply around here. And I have an extremely supportive co-parent in my husband, but he gets tired, too, of course. As I write this, for example, he has been banished to sleeping in the basement because our computer is in the bedroom (small house, no room of one's own here!), and it's late .... But for YOU, the amazing others, I do it. And thus the continuing value of the group .... I find it interesting that I still very much think of myself as an academic, although I have hardly cracked a book or written a word in the past year. (1999)

Jami Blaauw Hara finished her master's degree in English and began a PhD program at the University of Arizona. Finding herself uncertain as to whether she wanted a PhD or to become a "practicing academic," Jami worked with developing and editing curriculum for the University of Phoenix. She has moved back to Michigan, married and has an infant son. Currently, she is teaching writing at North Central Michigan College and online through the University of Phoenix.

JBH: When I think about where I was about two years ago when I joined the writing group, it seems so long ago and I seem now to be in such a different place .... At the time, I felt a little out of everyone's peer group, because I felt young and was not used to thinking of myself as a graduate professional. I was surprised to find that the women in the group considered me a peer, that was probably the richest part of their mentoring. I began to think of myself as a professional. (1999)

Rini Hughes finished her comprehensive exams and moved south so that her husband could take a new job. She completed her dissertation (with some long distance response from group members) in 2001. She is a list editor for H-AMSTDY on the H-Net lists. Rini's three grandsons are growing rapidly, and are waiting for a fourth sibling to join the family. Rini and her husband are moving to New York City as Bruce has taken a new position in Brooklyn.

MRH: Our group did, indeed, work from relationships, which may help explain why we were so "non-competitive." Because the people mattered to each other, the work mattered; instead of the people mattering because of the work they did. It was more focused, I believe, on whether the work itself was academically rigorous (and I don't mean "ruggedly individual," either). Would this have been different if the group was "mixed" in gender? ... I retain my concern with the possibility of too much emphasis on gender issues as such. (1999)

Maryann Crawford managed to finish her dissertation in 1997, with many thanks to the group for their support. Subsequently, she and her husband, Fred, moved so that he could take a tenure-track position and Maryann a temporary position at a regional university in the state. In the fall of 1999, Maryann switched from temporary to tenure-track. She is an Associate Professor and Director of Basic Writing/Writing Center and teaches composition and linguistics.

MAC: So what difference did gender make to me? I think it al-
            lowed me to act on assumptions of common experiences,
            a sense that we were all aware of how "vulnerable"
            women are in trying to break into, much less succeed, in a
            predominantly male academic world. The feelings I re-
            member are the fears and pressures, the questions: Could
            I finish the degree? Would I ever get a job if I did? What did
            being an academic mean to me? Ironically, that is where I
            am again. The isolation and the pressures of academe
            have felt more intense since Fred died. Writing this about
            the group, with the group, has helped—a community of
            women with whom I can share personal and professional,
            emotional and intellectual pieces of my life. (1999)

MRH: Working on this article, the process has been tremen-
            dously stimulating. It has been frustrating for the same
            reasons—I want more of this, more of the time. (1999)

JGB: We have talked about Woolf's reference to a writing
            woman's need for money and a room of her own, but I am
            certain that there is a third element necessary for a woman
            to write, and that is a discourse community which sup-
            ports that writing. (1999)

WORKS CITED

Aisenberg, Nadya, and Mona Harrington. *Women of Academe: Outsider in the Sa-
    cred Grove*. Amherst: U of Massachusetts P, 1988.
Atwood, Margaret. Introduction. *Women Writers at Work: The Paris Review Inter-
    views*. Ed. George Plimpton. New York: Viking Penguin, 1989. xi–xviii.
Bateson, Mary Catherine. *Composing a Life*. New York: Penguin Books, 1990.
Belenky, Mary Field, Blythe McVicker Clinchy, Nancy Rule Goldberger, and Jill
    Mattuck Tarule. *Women's Ways of Knowing: The Development of Self, Voice, and
    Mind*. New York: Basic Books, 1986.
Berkenkotter, Carol, and Thomas N. Huckin. *Genre Knowledge in Disciplinary
    Communication: Cognition/Culture/Power*. Hillsdale: Lawrence Erlbaum Asso-
    ciates, 1995.
Brandt, Deborah. *Literacy as Involvement: The Acts of Writers, Readers, and Texts*.
    Carbondale: Southern Illinois UP, 1990.
Brody, Miriam. *Manly Writing: Gender, Rhetoric, and the Rise of Composition*. Car-
    bondale: Southern Illinois UP, 1993.
Caplan, Paula J. *Lifting a Ton of Feathers: A Woman's Guide to Surviving in the Aca-
    demic World*. Toronto: U of Toronto P, 1994.

Christ, Carol P. *Diving Deep and Surfacing: Women Writers on Spiritual Quest*. 3rd edition. Boston: Beacon P, 1995.

Cixous, Hélène. "The Laugh of the Medusa." *New French Feminisms: An Anthology*. Eds. Elaine Marks and Isabelle de Courtivron. Amherst: U of Massachusetts P, 1980. 245–64.

Clark, Carolyn M., and Denise B. Watson. "Women's Experience of Collaboration." *New Directions for Adult and Continuing Education* 79 (1998): 63–74.

Coiner, Constance, and Diana Hume George, eds. *The Family Track: Keeping your Faculties While you Mentor, Nurture, Teach, and Serve*. Urbana: U of Illinois P, 1998.

de Certeau, Michel. *The Practice of Everyday Life*. Trans. Steven Rendall, Berkeley: U of California P, 1989.

Emig, Janet. *Web of Meaning: Essays on Writing, Teaching, Learning, and Thinking*. Upper Montclair: Heinemann-Boynton/Cook, 1983.

Felman, Shoshana. *What Does a Woman Want? Reading and Sexual Difference*. Baltimore: Johns Hopkins UP, 1993.

Gere, Anne Ruggles. *Writing Groups: History, Theory, and Implications*. Carbondale: Southern Illinois UP, 1987.

Gilbert, Sandra M., and Susan Gubar. *The Madwoman in the Attic: The Woman Writer and the Nineteenth-Century Imagination*. New Haven: Yale UP, 1979.

Hayden, Sara. "Re-Claiming Bodies of Knowledge: An Exploration of the Relationship Between Feminist Theorizing and Feminine Style in the Rhetoric of the Boston Women's Health Book Collective." *Western Journal of Communication* 61.2 (1997): 127–63.

Heilbrun, Carolyn G. *Writing a Woman's Life*. New York: Ballantine, 1988.

Kirsch, Gesa. *Women Writing the Academy: Audience, Authority, and Transformation. Studies in Writing and Rhetoric*. Carbondale: Southern Illinois UP, 1993.

LeFevre, Karen Burke. *Invention as a Social Act*. Carbondale: Southern Illinois UP, 1987.

Stock, Patricia Lambert. *The Dialogic Curriculum*. Portsmouth: Heinemann-Boynton/Cook, 1995.

Woolf, Virginia. *A Room of One's Own*. New York: Harcourt, Brace, 1929.

CHAPTER FOURTEEN

ಬಬ

Community, Collaboration, and Conflict: The Community Writing Group as Contact Zone

Evelyn Westbrook

Linda Brodkey claims that "all ethnographies begin in stories" (32). And so I will begin this ethnography of a community writing group, the South Carolina Writers Workshop (SCWW), with an anecdote.

Phyllis[1] had been reading a chapter from her historical novel about race relations in rural South Carolina at the turn of the century. Phyllis's writing is full of such powerful dialogue and poetic narration that it often humbles her writing group into silence, but this week a few members were eager to offer criticism.

Pearl piped up first: "This is great, Phyllis, but there's just *one* thing ... was the cat killed?"[2] In the scene from Phyllis's novel that troubled Pearl, the Ku Klux Klan hanged a black family's cat from a tree as a threat to blacks who continued to test their place in the South after Reconstruction. Maybel, the headstrong young black protagonist to whom the cat belonged, removed its carcass from the tree very matter-of-factly.

Not sure where Pearl's line of questioning was heading, Phyllis ventured an answer, "Yes, the cat was killed."

"Well, no one was upset about the death!" protested Pearl.

---

[1] I've changed the names of all writing group participants.

[2] Quotes during meetings are paraphrased from my observation notes. Although I tried to record the exact words participants used, the conversation sometimes went so quickly that I was only able to record the essence of members' comments. When I interviewed individuals, however, I recorded our conversations and transcribed the recordings verbatim. The quotes taken from interviews reflect, therefore, the exact word choices that participants use.

"Where *I* came from," Phyllis asserted, "black people didn't cry about cats. We cried about *important* things. It's a black thing. I write from what I'm about, from where I grew up and what was going on around me."

"I still think a little more emotion should be shown," Pearl insisted.

Phyllis gestured toward the draft in front of Pearl and said, "You can write it [your comments] down there, but I'm not going to make Maybel an emotional woman because she's not."

Eager to placate Phyllis, Dan, a white male, joked, "Well, when you're on Oprah's Book Club, be sure to remember us here [at the South Carolina Writers Workshop]."

"Oh, stop. Don't say that," Phyllis protested, "Give me some *criticism*."

"Well," said Edith, "when we give you some, you jump all over us and tell us we wouldn't understand because we're white."

The writers who belong to the SCWW,[3] a state-wide, nonprofit, noninstitutional writing group, have in common a love of writing and a desire to publish their work. In this sense, SCWW resembles hundreds of other self-reported community writing groups in the United States.[4] What distinguishes it from many other groups is not what its members *share* but how they are *different*. As Pearl told me in an interview, "You've got something in common with these people, and it gives you some place to start. But you never would have met them in your everyday, normal life." In fact, like Pearl, most SCWW members are surprised to encounter such a diverse array of people as those who frequent the writing group. Edith also commented on SCWW's surprising diversity:

> [The group is] balanced pretty much by sex. It's pretty typical of the racial makeup of Columbia and then we have varying backgrounds and socioeconomic levels and education levels and interests.

---

[3]The South Carolina Writers Workshop (SCWW) is a statewide nonprofit organization formed in 1990 "for the purpose of developing, operating, and administering programs designed to foster and improve the talents of its members. A second, but equally important, mission is to provide a creative environment in which member can regularly give readings and receive critiques by their peers" (printed in the 1991 SCWW conference brochure). Begun as the Greater Columbia Writers Workshop, the organization voted in 1990 to rename itself the South Carolina Writers Workshop. Along with this name change came financial support from the South Carolina Arts Commission, which enabled SCWW to extend its membership to the entire state. Less than a decade after its inception, SCWW now claims more than one hundred and fifty individual members and eleven chapters throughout the state.

[4]Reported in the 1984–1985 *International Directory of Writers' Groups and Associations* were 2,137 self-sponsored writing groups in the world. I can only guess that the number of writing groups has grown in the past decade as a result of the popularity of such nonacademic literacy clubs as Oprah Winfrey's Book Club. In *Writing Groups: History, Theory, and Implications*, Anne Ruggles Gere contends that writing groups are ubiquitous in most metropolitan areas, though their numbers are impossible to document.

I've tried for years to get my friend, John, to come to the group. He's a retired school-teacher, and he writes all the time. But his response is always, "Oh, what do I want to join a bunch of old ladies for?"

I tell him, "We've got marathon runners, cross-country bikers, hairdressers, and ... It's a fascinating and diverse group of people. [Everyone] is not just like me—a little old middle-aged white woman." But I can't convince him.

Edith's friend, John, articulates a common assumption that members of community writing groups are tiresomely alike. This perception probably originates from writing groups' historical roots in mutual improvement societies, where, as Anne Ruggles Gere contends, memberships formed around "natural affinit[ies]"—common occupation or status, mutual interests or concerns (51). Even today, descriptions of such specialized groups fill the pages of the *International Directory of Writers' Groups and Associations:* the American Pen Women, the Association of Hispanic Artists, the Black Writers United Club, the Writing Workshop for People over 57, and Los Escribientes. These groups' names attest to their demographics, but, of course, diversity exists even within the most homogenous groups. In the Writing Workshop for People over 57, for example, there are presumably members of different cultures, genders, sexual preferences, and classes.

Perhaps because like-minded peers have tended to populate writing groups or possibly because writing groups have historical roots in mutual aid and mutual improvement societies, much academic and popular literature on writing groups focuses on their supportive, communal nature. Donald Stewart, for instance, claims that those who find collaboration appealing are Meyers Briggs ESFJ types—extroverts who value "harmonious human contacts" above all else (76–77). Similarly, Anne Ruggles Gere contends that writing groups engender a "positive attitude" toward writing and a "warmer classroom climate" (123). Outside the power structures of the university, the nurturing and supportive nature of writing groups intensifies; here, according to Gere, writing groups operate according to what Carol Gilligan has described as an ethics of care: "Gilligan's different voice emphasizes relationships over rules, connection over isolation, caring over violence, and a web of relationships over hierarchy. Self-sponsored writing groups incorporate this cluster of caring, connection, non-rule bound, nonhierarchical characteristics" (Gere 51).

Regardless of their settings in the classroom or the community, Gere contends that writing groups have the potential to dissolve difference: "Differences of age, circumstance, and historical period disappear before this common motivation [to form communities of literacy]" (123).

Like the work of many academic theorists, including Stewart and Gere, published testimonials about writing groups tend to focus on these supportive, nurturing aspects of writing communities as well. Joan Cotich, for instance, declares that in her group "insensitive or inappropriate response undermines the very purpose of the writing group which is to nurture our writing" (12). And Julie Brooks extols the "community atmosphere" and "unconditional acceptance" of her own writing group.

Like *collaboration*, the word *community* itself, as Joseph Harris contends, is often "empty and sentimental" because it has no "positive opposing term" (20).[5] So, on the basis of their names alone, community writing groups seem to resonate doubly with connotations of acceptance, nurturing, and harmony. Yet as the anecdote that opened this chapter reveals, such groups—especially, I contend, if they are diverse— often foreground not harmony and consensus, but conflict and difference. My research and involvement with the SCWW compels me to take issue with the customary utopian metaphors used to characterize writing groups and to suggest that a more productive metaphor to describe the negotiations of difference that often take place in them is Mary Louise Pratt's contact zone. Pratt intends the idea of the contact zone, which she defines as a "social space where cultures meet, clash and grapple with each other" (34), to "contrast with the ideas of community that underlie much of the thinking about language, communication, and culture that gets done in the academy" (37). In contrast to academic models of community, which often assume a homogeneous and unified social and linguistic world, Pratt's metaphor legitimizes the role of conflict and difference in literacy communities.

What makes this SCWW community writing group a particularly interesting contact zone is that it exists outside the hierarchical power structures of the university. Although Pratt intended her metaphor to account for linguistic contexts both inside and outside of the classroom, subsequent contact zone theorists—Richard Miller, Joseph Harris, Phyllis van Slyck, and Patricia Bizzell—have considered only contact zones within the university. In classrooms, or what van Slyck calls artificial spaces, which are often more homogeneous than the communities neighboring the university, teachers must often import difference and stage conflicts through assigned multicultural readings. The problem that Joseph Harris notes

---

[5]Here Joseph Harris is borrowing from Raymond Williams's critique of "community." Almost a decade after writing "The Idea of Community in the Study of Writing," Joseph Harris still contends that we must rethink the community metaphors that we use to describe the teaching of writing. Yet he claims, in retrospect, that "Williams was wrong to say that community has no "positive opposing or distinguishing term": "the term *public* describes a form of social organization that rests not on the like-mindedness but on a more limited willingness to argue out differences, to exist in what Richard Sennett has called a 'community of strangers'" (270). To learn more about Harris's notion of a "public," refer to his afterword in *The Braddock Essays: 1975–1998*.

with this kind of "inorganic" contact zone is that it is "hard to see who (except perhaps for a teacher) would have much at stake in preserving the contact zone, since it is not a space to which anyone owes much allegiance" ("Idea" 33). The community writing group, on the other hand, is an organic contact zone to which writers demonstrate their allegiance by voluntarily returning week after week.

In short, this ethnography of the SCWW explores questions of difference suggested by Pratt's contact zone metaphor in ways that existing work on contact zones can't because it has focused on classroom contexts. Furthermore, it considers the role that conflict plays in community writing groups in ways that most work on writing groups hasn't because it has relied on nurturing ideals of community and collaboration.

Framing this ethnography within the metaphor of a contact zone, I talk about scenes that, like the one that opened this chapter, highlight how members of a diverse writing group foreground and negotiate difference. Furthermore, though my responses are contingent, I address the following questions:

- What role does conflict play in a radically diverse community writing group?
- What stakes do writers have in the negotiations of difference that take place within such groups?
- How do writers in a diverse writing group construct their identities and alliances?
- What can a nonacademic writing group teach us about "the pedagogical arts of the contact zone" (Pratt 40)?

Methodology and Focus of Study

In the tradition of Shirley Brice Heath's *Ways with Words*, this study uses ethnographic methods to account for the social and cultural contexts of literacy practices outside of the classroom. Though I was a member of the SCWW for a year prior to beginning my research, I've since attended SCWW meetings for over a year as a participant observer. During group meetings, I take detailed field notes, which allow me to explore patterns of behavior and social interaction. I follow up on these patterns through formal and informal audiotaped one-on-one interviews, which take place in my home, in other members' homes, and in public settings. To learn more about specific group interactions, I interview all key participants. These interviews not only give me access to multiple insider perspectives, but they also allow me to triangulate my findings. I turn to these multiple perspectives after I describe briefly the structure, routines, and membership of the Columbia Chapter of the SCWW.

The Columbia Chapter of the South Carolina Writers Workshop

The South Carolina Writers Workshop is what Anne Ruggles Gere calls a "self-sponsored" writing group (51); meetings are nonhierarchical, and members can join or discontinue membership at their leisure. Annual dues are fifty dollars, and these entitle writers to participate in state-wide SCWW events and contests. In addition, writers can participate in local chapter meetings even if they have not officially joined the group.

At the state-wide level, SCWW activities include biannual workshops and an annual conference. But the central activities of SCWW take place at local chapter meetings where, in the style of Peter Elbow's "teacherless" writing classrooms, members regularly read their work and receive peer critiques. This study focuses on the SCWW Columbia Chapter group meetings, which are held twice monthly at the downtown public library.

The Columbia Chapter, like all other SCWW chapters, has a facilitator whose job is primarily organizational. When, in an interview, I asked Tyson, the Columbia chapter facilitator, what his goals for the group were, he responded,

> I don't think I have an agenda for the group ... [but] one is for new people, be-
> ginners ... to make them feel warm, comfortable, and welcome. And not to be
> overwhelmed or intimidated. To provide that comfortable initial experience
> for them, and in so doing to hopefully teach them to pass that attitude along
> to other people. Also to try to keep it an environment where people can get
> feedback about their work, that we can all get exposed to discussion about dif-
> ferent things that relate to what works and what doesn't work, whether it's a
> paragraph in science fiction or a poem .... To get an eclectic experience.

Although Tyson's goals initially echo the conventional sentiments that writing groups should be warm, comfortable, safe places for writers, the more he talks, the more he emphasizes the critical role that difference and diversity play in "exposing" members to discussions about "different things" to have an "eclectic experience."

Even though there is a facilitator, SCWW meetings are democratic; time is distributed equally among group members, and writers take turns sharing their works in progress. Because group membership is open and rolling and because there is no formal commitment to the group, writers come and go as they please.[6] There is, however, a core group of regulars who attend virtually every meeting. These regulars are the members whom I interviewed and whose stories I have permission to tell. Because I refer to them simply by name in the future, I provide a sketch of their demographic characteristics in Table 14.1.[7] Although this article focuses on a few group members (Phyllis, Pearl, Edith, Modestine, and Jack), Table 14.1 includes all regular members of the Columbia Chapter of SCWW to demonstrate the racial, generational, occupational, and generic diversity of the group. I now turn to several vignettes that demonstrate how this diversity gives rise to the kind of meeting, clashing, and grappling of cultures that characterize Pratt's contact zone.

Vignettes from the SCWW Contact Zone

Let's return to the episode that opened this chapter—the debate about a character's response to the death of her cat in Phyllis's novel. Pearl suggested that it was cold, even inhumane, for Maybel not to mourn for her murdered pet, but Phyllis maintained that her character had more important things to worry about. The group's reaction to the murdered cat suggests not only how individuals in different positions within this contact zone have different interpretations of the same text but also how SCWW discussions often turn into highly charged debates over explicitly political and social issues.

Throughout the cat debate, Phyllis rooted her position in her experience as an African American: "Where *I* came from, black people didn't cry about cats. We cried about *important* things. It's a black thing. I write from what I'm about…from where I grew up and what was going on around me." By grounding her writing choices in personal experience and cultural difference, Phyllis made them difficult for a white woman to contend with. Because she could neither deny where Phyllis came from nor contest a "black thing," from which she was excluded, Pearl could only retort feebly: "I still think a little more emotion should be shown." Phyllis's rhetorical move of defending her values on the grounds that they represent a "black thing" undermined Edith and Pearl's attempts to, as Iris Marion Young would say, "parade" (166) their values as the universal norm and label Phyllis's as deviant, or in this case, inhumane.

The debate ostensibly ended here in a stalemate, with two women asserting their differences. Because Phyllis was the author, her worldview ulti-

---

[6]The "open" membership policy of the South Carolina Writers Workshop has posed several challenges to my research. At every SCWW meeting there is a different combination of members, so this study focuses on those whom I dub "regulars." Except for occasional absences, regulars attended meetings for the duration of the one and one half years of my participant-observation. (Both Rocky and Tony stopped coming to Columbia chapter meetings at the end of my first year of research, however; they began their own SCWW chapter closer to the military base where they worked.) Even more disruptive to my research than the protean membership, however, was the presence of visitors. At virtually every SCWW meeting, at least one visitor was present. This was the main reason that I decided not to record group discussions; the regulars and I had reservations about the effect that the tape recorder might have on visitors who did not know much about my research project.

[7]The information in the demographic chart is compiled from interviews and questionnaires that I distributed to group members. I did not, however, press members for more information than they volunteered; this explains why some members' profiles are less detailed than others.

TABLE 14.1
SCWW Member Demographics

Name	Race/Gender	Age	Education and Occupation	Genre
Pearl	White female	Late 30s	Two bachelor's degrees in journalism and political science; works as a victim's advocate	Novels, some short fiction
Phyllis	Black female	Early 60s	Associate's degree in accounting; retired accountant	Novels, poetry
Tyson	White male	Early 50s	Doctorate in political science; freelance writer, sports contributor to local paper, stay-at-home dad	Techno-thriller novels, short stories, essays, poems
Dan	White male	Late 30s	Master's in economics; published author	Writes humor, fiction, poetry, nonfiction
Miles	White male	Mid-20s	Earning doctorate in composition/rhetoric; teaches writing at local university	Horror novels
Edith	White female	Mid-40s	Master's degree in teaching reading plus thirty additional credit hours; fourth-grade teacher	Short fiction, poetry, essays
Deanna	Black female	Early 40s	Bachelor's degree in special education; cosmetology degree; owns hair salon and educates the community about AIDS	Autobiography
Tony	Black male	Mid-30s	Military service	Humor and short fiction
Rocky	Black female	Late 20s	Military service	Novels
Jack	White male	Over 65	Master's degree in physical education; retired college swimming coach	Memoir and creative nonfiction
Evelyn	White female	Mid-20s	Earning master's in composition and rhetoric; teaches writing at local university	Poetry and short stories
Modestine	White female	Late 50s	Bachelor's in nursing; retired registered nurse	Mystery novels

mately "won"; she "resolved" this conflict by telling Pearl, "You can write it [your comments] down there [on the draft of my chapter], but I'm not going to make Maybel an emotional woman because she's not." By encouraging Pearl to record her criticism on the text, Phyllis acknowledged the power Pearl claims as a reader at the same time that she asserted her superior authority, as a writer, to tell her story her way.

Although the debate over the cat involved primarily two participants—Pearl and Phyllis—other group members took sides along racial lines; when Phyllis justified her characters' reactions as "a black thing," Rocky and Tony, two black members, nodded their heads in agreement. And although Edith, a white member, had not yet participated in the debate, her response to Pearl's request for real criticism suggested that she sided with Pearl, another white woman: "When *we* give you some [criticism], you jump all over *us* and tell *us* we wouldn't understand because *we're* white" (my italics). Even though only one other white member took part in the debate, Edith used the collective pronoun "we" to refer to the white group members as though all had been involved.

During an interview prior to Phyllis' telling of the cat story, I asked her what it was like to read her writing, which she described as race-based, to her writing group, where white people outnumbered African Americans three to one. A transcript of our conversation follows:

Evelyn: How do you feel [sharing your writing] in our writing group if most of the group is white? When you're reading your writing and it is ...

Phyllis: And it's based on Black?

Evelyn: Yeah. Is that an issue for you?

Phyllis: Like I tell [the white people in the group] sometimes; they question me and I [say], "It's a black thing." (laughing). It's a black thing.

Evelyn: And?

Phyllis: And I watch faces.

Evelyn: Yeah?

Phyllis: Yeah, because it really is a black thing. You see, I understand a white thing; what I'm trying to get you all to do is understand a black thing. You know, because it's not going to ever be right on this earth until everybody understands everybody. It's really not going to be. And I don't know why people keep pretending they don't understand people; they do understand people.

I later asked Phyllis how she, a black woman, came to understand "a white thing." She told me, "I let different sections/segments of society read my stuff and then listen to what this group says, that group says, this group says and understands."

Getting reactions from various "sections of society," then, not only helps Phyllis to understand her readership, but it also helps her to achieve the political and social goals of her writing—to help "everybody understand everybody." For Phyllis to promote her goal of intercultural understanding, she must listen to what others have to say about her writing. In a later interview, Phyllis elaborated on this goal:

> And the only thing I want to do—I ever wanted to do—was to just spread it out there. Let it air out. Open it up. I don't care how many people point to race relations. Yeah, let people one-on-one talk. Let people realize that deep down, everybody is about the same. There's not much difference in people. It's just the outside, that's all. And that's it. That's the core of [what I have to say], and if I had been taught how to write and how to get it out when I was younger, I wouldn't have such a hard time now.

Despite group debates, such as the one about the cat, Phyllis claims that there is not much "difference between people" and that differences that do exist are mostly superficial. Yet it is difficult to reconcile this statement with her earlier insistence that some things are "black things" and others are "white things."

The way for a black person to understand "a white thing," and vice versa, Phyllis claims, is by "airing out" issues—even if this means "opening up" conflict. And, according to Phyllis, the best way to reach mutual understanding is through the kind of one-on-one talk that her story about the cat provoked. This open acknowledgment of difference allows group members to become aware of the ways that their identities are socially constructed and to realize, as Phyllis says, that their differences are not essential.

Phyllis sees conflict, not consensus or support, as central to the work that goes on in the writing group. She contends that "when people [in the group] say, 'Wow! This is good,' well, that doesn't help me very much. But when they say, 'I would use this or I would use that' or when they challenge the way I thought about [something], that's good feedback." In fact, Phyllis sees conflict as integral to arriving at understanding: "When someone questions something you do as a writer," Phyllis tells me, "they are really saying, 'Make me understand this.'"

During an interview a few weeks after the debate about the murdered cat, I asked Phyllis if, according to her criteria, she considered Pearl and Edith's comments about the cat to be "good" criticism. She responded:

> You know, I appreciated those comments, but this [pointing to the chapter of her book], this I didn't touch. When [Pearl] made the comment that

Maybel wasn't emotional enough over the cat, I made the remark—and I stand by it today—that black people don't get emotional about a cat. Not back then. They were too concerned about the children—how they were going to feed and care for them—to waste tears over a cat that could scrounge around for itself. See, I write about what I know, how I grew up. [The characters in the story] handled [the cat's death] the way I saw people handle these things many, many times. They were shocked; they really were. But they weren't weeping. Now [Maybel] *is* emotional—most black people are—but she's stoic.

When I come back from the [SCWW] meetings, I revisit all this stuff [pointing at members' comments scribbled in the margins of her drafts]. Then I look at it from a different perspective, and I say, "*this* is the reader here, and I have to listen to what she says." Yes, [Pearl and Edith] made me really think about [my writing]. But ultimately, I decided to keep it the way I had it because this *is* the character. But maybe [Pearl] has a point; maybe not everyone knows this stuff about black people.[8] According to Phyllis, then, good criticism does not have to result in changes to her writing, but it should change the way she *thinks* about her writing and her audience. Pearl's comments made Phyllis "revisit" her writing from "a different perspective," a perspective that allowed her to realize that "maybe not everyone knows this stuff about black people."

Later in the interview, Phyllis reflected on the good that came from the debate about the cat: "Now they [Pearl and Edith] kind of understand where I'm coming from. This kind of thing gives blacks a different insight into themselves and into other races. And it gives other races a look at themselves and at the black experience. You grow that way—by looking at yourself."

Not only did the debate encourage Phyllis to "look at herself," but it also compelled Edith to reflect on her values and assumptions. During an interview, Edith alluded to the debate about the cat, claiming that it had prompted the group to recognize and affirm group difference: "It's like Phyllis' story about the cat hanging from the tree and the cultural differences there. We [Pearl and I] didn't understand why the people in the story didn't get too upset about the cat being hung, and [Phyllis] said, 'But you don't understand' and explained it to us so we did .... That was definitely a cultural difference."

---

[8]Although Phyllis seems here to be comfortable speaking for *all* black people, in a later interview she expressed frustration at being called on to be the spokesperson for the African American perspective: "But I don't know what blacks want; I can't tell you what blacks want, Blacks is a people. Phyllis is a *person*. I can't tell you what blacks want, no more than I can tell you what Evelyn [referring to the interviewer] wants. People look in your face and say, "Well, what do you people want?" I've heard people say that, "What do y'all want?" I say, "My name is not y'all. My name is [Phyllis]. Do you want to ask me what [Phyllis] wants?" You know, I can tell you what [Phyllis] wants, but I can't tell you what 'y'all wants or what black people want or [what] anybody [wants]. I can't tell you that .... No one person can represent the needs and the wants and the values of a whole people. No one person can do that."

When they debated the cat incident, SCWW members formed alliances according to race. Yet, as this next vignette indicates, alliances also form along other demographic lines—most frequently gender.

Pearl had been sharing chapters from her second novel, which is about a young woman who ultimately decides to make public the sordid personal life of her father, a prominent and respected politician. When Pearl read the chapter that reveals the father's history of physically abusing his wife and sexually abusing his children, the group erupted into an impassioned discussion. Pearl, Phyllis, Modestine, and Edith agreed that despite the politician's good work in the community, they "hated" him after learning of his private abuses. After listening to their vitriol for several minutes, Jack, a sixty-six-year-old white male, objected to the way that the group members "jumped all over this man who spends 2% of his life doing bad and 98% of it doing good."

"What do you mean 2% bad?" Edith asked. "Try 98% bad and 2% good."

"I'm not saying he's *perfect*," Jack explained, "but how many politicians are? He's not a murderer or anything."

"Oh, no," said Modestine, "just a wife-beating rapist." The women continued to speak simultaneously, criticizing both Jack and the politician in the same breath. Although Jack was eyeing other male members for support, none lent him any.

Modestine silenced everyone—even the other women—when she told Jack, "Look, this may not be the time to get into this, but if you want to take this outside, I'll be happy to argue with you." Jack ignored Modestine and deferred to his opponents. Although Modestine's comments suggest that a debate over a controversial social issue is tangential to the primary purpose of the writing group—to critique members' writing—such heated arguments routinely arise in SCWW meetings.

In both arguments over the cat and the politician, men were noticeably silent. In the latter case, even though Jack initiated the debate by defending the politician on the grounds of his public service, he eventually withdrew from the conversation. In her studies of classroom writing groups, Meg Morgan found that male students are more likely to "disengage" when strong women are present. In Jack's case, however, if his identity were truly threatened by the assertive women in his group, he could have completely withdrawn; after all, group participation is voluntary. That Jack not only continued coming regularly to group meetings but also continued sharing writing and criticism indicated that this debate about the abusive politician did not pose a serious threat to Jack's identity as a white male. I assume that Jack withdrew from this particular discussion after realizing that either his stake in the issue was not as great as that of the women involved or that he was not likely to "win" the argument.

When in an interview I reminded Jack of the politician debate, he was eager to discuss it. In fact, although several months had passed, he immediately and vividly recalled the details of the incident. I asked Jack what he had meant by his 98% good and 2% bad comment, and he explained:

> I meant that [the politician] is doing some great things for the state. I mean [the people] love him. And that's how he'll be remembered. Here's this great senator in the state doing 98% good, and you're going to bust him for the 2%? But in Pearl's mind, that's not how it is. What he does to his wife and family is the 98% he's doing wrong.[9]

Then, in jest, Jack added, "And for that, I think that somebody should take the guy out back and shoot him."

Although Jack maintains that the politician cannot be widely condemned, he has come to recognize Pearl's point of view. In her mind, the terms of his equation are reversed: "what [the politician] does to his wife and family is the 98% he's doing wrong."

Although Jack expresses outrage at the politician's behavior, he still values the character's public role over his private one. This becomes even more evident when Jack describes what he imagines to be the perfect ending to Pearl's story:

> I already told [Pearl] how I think she should end the book. There should be another storm [like the one that opened the novel], and the politician goes home to retrieve his Bible [wherein he has recorded the dates on which he molested his children] and to kill his daughter because that's the only way he will save his reputation. Then, lightning should strike and hit the lawn art, and it would be one of those cupids, you know, the kid with the arrow. And the lightning will hit the lawn art, break it, and [as it tumbles to the ground], the arrow will pierce his heart. So he'll be killed by the kids he's been molesting.

Although the divine justice that Jack envisions for the politician is, he claims, "just for the pure entertainment value of the book," Jack's reasoning reveals his desire to separate public and private roles:

> You see, if this scandal goes public, the senator's mother will look bad, the family will look bad. So the politician has to die [privately] in a way that the reader will say, "That son-of-a-bitch is really getting what he deserves!" And there's no better way than the lightning. That would be a perfect ending!

---

[9]Because my recorder stopped working during this interview, I have reconstructed Jack's comments from my field notes. Jack reviewed and corrected these notes, so they accurately reflect his opinions and ideas if not his original words.

With Jack's ending, the public reputation of the senator remains un-scathed; he continues to be remembered for his service to the state, and his family is protected from scandal. Yet the politician still gets the kind of di-vine retribution that the reader demands.

In both debates about the cat and the politician, women and minori-ties—often the least vocal members in university classrooms—find in the community writing group license to argue and assert their worldviews. Phyllis and Pearl, for example, both told me during their interviews how im-portant it is for them to speak their minds in group meetings. About the need to be honest at the expense of diplomacy, Pearl told me, "I try to use tact and diplomacy, but I'm not really afraid to say what's on my mind." Like Pearl, Phyllis values honesty over tactfulness in the writing group, as she told me in an interview:

> Everyone should tell you [the truth]. You know, it's not that it [your writing] is wrong because they have this opinion of it, but if you read a lot, you know what you like, why don't you just give your honest opinion about it? You don't expect somebody to change their stuff because of your opinion, but they'll give it a second look, and they might see where they can improve it. I have had people say things about mine, and I come back and give it a second look, and I say, "Yeah, I can improve this," and I appreciate that person doing that ... That's what a writing group is there for, you know, working it out. Maybe I'll be kicked out of the writing group [for being so forthright] [(laughing)]. I hope not; I kind of like going to the writing group.

Unlike Donald Stewart, Anne Ruggles Gere, Joan Cotich, Julie Brooks, and others who suggest that a primary purpose of the writing group is to support its members, Phyllis claims that its purpose is to challenge writers to take a second, more critical look at their writing from a different perspective.

Getting other writers to take a second look at their writing often requires SCWW members to speak openly from the perspectives of the various social groups to which they belong. Yet the alliances and subject positions that SCWW writers assume change as the issues they discuss change. For exam-ple, Phyllis and Pearl, who disagreed about the cat, found themselves argu-ing the same position in the debate about the politician.

Although both the cat-hanging scene and the domestic violence episode erupted in difference that split the group down demographic lines, some debates result in more arbitrary alliances. In another chapter from Pearl's book, the same women who were unified in their diatribe against Jack dis-agreed about the way that Pearl should portray the abused wife. In this chapter, the politician brutally beats his wife and then, in an effort to recon-cile, buys her a piece of lawn art to add to her extensive collection. The wife accepts her husband's gift eagerly and seems to overlook the beating. What disturbed Edith, Modestine, and Phyllis even more than the beating was the wife's response (or lack thereof) to her husband's violence. These women did not believe that the wife would happily accept a new piece of lawn without recognizing the irony that each statue or sculpture in her garden represented a different time that she had been beaten.

On the basis of her involvement with a community organization for victims of domestic abuse, Edith claimed that the wife's willingness to forgive her husband was "totally unrealistic"; a woman might be too scared of her husband to retaliate, she explained to me later, "but after so many years of that [abuse], she would have too much built up rage to forgive him." Pearl conceded that in her experience as a victim's advocate she had seen the "kind of woman" that Edith was talking about but that she had also seen plenty of women who denied even to themselves the abuse they endured. Pearl explained that her character, who came from what she called a "white trash family," was willing to put up with the physical abuse to secure the material things she had never before had.

Edith, Phyllis, and Modestine were concerned that because the wife downplayed her abuse, a reader would not sympathize and might even blame her for it. They felt that by not voicing her abhorrence for her husband's behavior or even acknowledging the abuse, the wife was somehow complicit in what was happening to her. Despite their objections, Pearl insisted that "[the wife was] not meant to be a sympathetic figure; she stood by as her daughters got raped and didn't do anything about it."

After the debate raged for some time, Edith suggested a compromise: "Why don't you give the wife an interior monologue so that even if she doesn't outwardly show it, she can still speak out against her abuse?" Because Edith's suggestion would involve changing narrators, the group's conversation then turned to the pragmatics of shifting narrative perspectives in a text. It wasn't until the conversation turned to this relatively benign topic that men in the group reentered the discussion.

Just as the conversation about the hanged cat was really a social debate masked as a debate about characterization, this discussion, at heart, was less about the wife in Pearl's book than it was about domestic violence. Edith wanted to protect not only the wife in Pearl's novel but all victimized women from the assumption that they are partly to blame for their abuse. If the character of the wife were given a voice and if her vanity were downplayed, she could be viewed as a true victim. This, in turn, would encourage the reader to look sympathetically at other abused women.

During an interview a few weeks after this incident, I asked Pearl how she interpreted the group's feedback and how she planned to use it. She replied:

> I thought I might tone [the wife's] excitement [over the gift] down a little bit, but she's not going to be a sympathetic character. Now, whether she redeems herself at the end of the novel, I don't know. But that was something I thought

about. I thought that they made a valid point that maybe it went too far with her being overjoyed at the gift, but at the same time she's going to kind of light up [with pleasure].

That's a good example of how I stop and think about things [because of the group's criticism]. And people have certain ideas about who they … what they want your characters to be. And I think Edith, because she's been through training [to help victims of domestic violence], she had an idea. And I've seen the kind of woman she's talking about, but that's not who this character is. This character turned her back on her daughters while her husband sexually abused them, so she can't be too sympathetic. And that's why I say at the end she might have a change in her life that gives her that redeemable thing. And I keep trying to think of one redeeming quality that the father has, but I haven't thought of one yet.

Despite her peers' protestations, Pearl maintained that the wife who refused to protect her own daughters from abuse should remain an unsympathetic character. Nevertheless, she recognized that the women in her writing group had a "valid point" when they claimed that her portrayal of the wife might influence readers' perceptions of abused women in general. Although they did not convince Pearl to change her writing in any specific way, they did compel her to "stop and think about things" from an alternative perspective, which made her consider how she might redeem the wife (and even the husband) before the novel's end.

Unlike the first two vignettes, in this third anecdote SCWW members did not construct their alliances according to race or gender or any other demographic category, for that matter. Edith and Pearl, who are both white middle-aged, middle-class females, disagreed about whether or not the main character in Pearl's book (also a white middle-aged, middle-class female) should be sympathetic. These various incidents demonstrate how SCWW members do not form alliances solely along rigid racial, class, or gender lines. Rather, in a state of what Iris Marion Young calls "malleable subjectivity" (170), they constantly construct and reconstruct, assert and reassert their positions in relation to one another. Young claims that usually only privileged groups enjoy this kind of protean subject position because minority groups, are indelibly "marked with an essence" (170). What is remarkable, then, about the South Carolina Writers Workshop is that everyone's identities—even those of minorities and women—are ambiguous and shifting. Sometimes (as in the case of the cat) members position themselves according to race. Other times (as in the case of the abusive politician) they situate themselves according to gender. And occasionally (as in the discussion about the abused wife) they align themselves according to worldviews that don't fit neatly into demographic categories. In short, SCWW writers cannot easily dismiss or exclude another member as completely "other." Malleable identities open the border between the self and "other" so that writers are more willing to listen carefully to others' perspectives. For example, Phyllis may have been more willing to listen to Pearl's comments about the cat because she knew that although they represent different races, they share common experiences as women (as the discussion about the politician suggests).

Although it does not rely on essentialized notions of difference, the success of SCWW does depend on difference and conflict, which SCWW members see as positive and desirable. Tyson, the group facilitator, considers difference to be integral to what he calls the "eclectic" experience of the writing group. Additionally, Phyllis and Pearl both contend that an open acknowledgment of difference changes the way that they see their writing and makes clear the political and ethical implications of their writing. For example, hearing how white members respond to her black character's stoicism prepares Phyllis for the assumption that other readers might make about her characters—that because they don't mourn the death of the pet cat, they are inhumane or morally inferior. Recognizing this potential misunderstanding is especially important if Phyllis's goals are, as she contends, to promote intercultural understanding. Similarly, when Pearl understands that her characterization of the abused wife in her story could affect the way that readers perceive abused women in general, she can decide whether or not she wants to run such risks. In this community writing group, difference produces not hostility, exclusion, or oppression but productive workings out of social and political conflicts. And SCWW members claim to use these exchanges to rethink their writing.

The metaphor of the contact zone works to describe the ways that community writing groups foreground difference and conflict in ways that traditional metaphors of community cannot. Even though the SCWW—like any social space that foregrounds difference—places its members in often precarious and uncomfortable positions, minorities and women seem especially willing to voice their worldviews. Phyllis, for instance, feels free to articulate what she calls a "black thing." And she, Modestine, and Edith do not hesitate to voice their abhorrence of Pearl's character, the politician. Perhaps because these debates are couched within the context of fiction, or perhaps because the group exists outside of the institutional power structures of the academy, SCWW functions in many ways as the kind of "safe house" where Pratt envisions women and minorities can participate in contentious discussions of social and political issues without compromising their identities. It may be, however, that the men in this group either do not view the writing group as a safe place to speak openly about polemical issues or, more likely, see these kinds of discussions as tangential to the primary purpose of the writing group.

Even though this ethnography (unlike most other ethnographies of nonacademic literacies) focuses on a group explicitly devoted to improving members' writing, it is not easy to extrapolate pedagogical implications for writing groups in academic contact zones; the power structures in the community writing group are so different from those in the university. Nevertheless, the SCWW poses several questions to compositionists who study writing groups and contact zones within the classroom. First, the SCWW suggests an alternative vision of "safe houses." According to Pratt and Canagarajah, safe houses are "social and intellectual spaces where groups can constitute themselves as horizontal, *homogeneous*, sovereign communities with high degrees of trust, *shared understandings*, and temporary protections from legacies of oppression" (Pratt 40, my italics). Yet, the SCWW suggests that minorities and women might not need sequestered, homogeneous communities of like-minded peers to feel safe entering heated discussions of social and political issues. Perhaps minorities and women can also feel safe in places where power is equally distributed and difference is perceived as positive and desirable. Classroom structures that flatten the power hierarchy of the university might give rise to the kind of open negotiation of difference that takes place in SCWW. Networked technologies, for example, which make possible these lateral and symmetrical power relations, seem to offer such possibilities, though Lester Faigley and James Porter both note that hegemonies tend to reproduce themselves even in electronic communities.

The relationship between power and writing in the SCWW raises another pedagogical issue. At SCWW meetings, power seems to come from being a writer. When a writer shares his or her work with a group of peers, power belongs to him or her (as Phyllis's comment to Pearl, "You can write that down there, but I'm not going to make Maybel an emotional woman because she's not," makes clear). Writers have the power not only to create a story but also to assert their worldviews. And because everyone in the writing group takes turns being reader and writer, the power shifts, constantly from member to member. For instance, even though Phyllis' worldview "wins" in the cat incident, Pearl's "wins" in the domestic violence incidents (because she is the writer). But can this same kind of give-and-take of power occur in writing classrooms where readers primarily discuss assigned texts whose authors are absent?

Linda Brodkey's claim that ethnographies begin with stories opened this portrait of the SCWW. I'd like to close with the suggestion that ethnographies end with stories, too. A few of the stories that I'd like to see taking up where this one leaves off are stories about (1) the stakes that writers have in classroom writing groups; (2) the identities and alliances that writers create in various types of writing groups—academic and nonacademic, diverse and homogeneous; (3) the role that difference and conflict plays in institutional writing groups; (4) the notion of writing groups as safe houses, both inside and outside of the university; and (5) the lessons that writing groups inside and outside the university have to learn from one another. I look forward to hearing these and other stories, all of which will help us decide the roles that community, collaboration, and conflict should play in the teaching of college composition.[10]

Works Cited

Bizzell, Patricia. "'Contact Zones' and English Studies." *College English* 56.2 (1994): 163–69.

Brodkey, Linda. "Writing Ethnographic Narratives." *Written Communication* 4.1 (1987): 25–50.

Brooks, Julie. "Inside a Women's Journal Group." *Voices from the Middle* 4.4 (1997): 6–12.

Canagarajah, A. Suresh. "Safe Houses in the Contact Zone: Coping Strategies of African-American Students in the Academy." *CCC* 48.2 (1997): 173–196.

Cotich, Joan et al. "Our Writing, Ourselves: Portrait of a Writing Group." *Quarterly of the National Writing Project and the Center for the Study of Writing and Literacy* 16.2 (1994): 10–13.

Ede, Lisa, ed. *The Braddock Essays 1975–1998*. Boston: Bedford/St. Martin's, 1999.

Elbow, Peter. *Writing without Teachers*. New York: Oxford UP, 1998.

Faigley, Lester. *Fragments of Rationality: Postmodernity and the Subject of Composition*. Pittsburgh: U of Pittsburgh P, 1992.

Gere, Anne Ruggles. *Writing Groups, History, Theory, and Implications*. Carbondale: Southern Illinous UP, 1987.

Hall, John, ed. *International Directory of Writers' Groups and Associations 1984–1985*. Alexandria: Inkling Publications, 1984.

Harris, Joseph. "The Idea of Community in the Study of Writing." *CCC* 40.1 (1989): 11–22.

———. "Negotiating the Contact Zone." *Journal of Basic Writing* 14.1 (1995): 27–42.

Heath, Shirley Brice. *Ways with Words: Language, Life, and Work in Communities and Classrooms*. New York: Cambridge UP, 1983.

Miller, Richard E. "Fault Lines in the Contact Zone." *College English* 56 (1994): 389–408.

Morgan, Meg. "Women as Emergent Leaders in Student Collaborative Writing Groups." *JAC* (1993): 203–219.

Porter, James. *Rhetorical Ethics and Internetworked Writing*. Greenwich: Ablex, 1998.

Pratt, Mary Louise. "Arts of the Contact Zone." *Profession* 91 (1991): 33–40.

---

[10]I would like to thank Christy Friend and Nancy Thompson for their generous guidance on this research project. I also appreciate the thoughtful suggestions for revision that Beverly Moss, Melissa Nicolas, Nels Highberg, and Lee Bauknight offered me. Finally, I'm grateful to the members of the Columbia Chapter of the South Carolina Writers Workshop for sharing their time, stories, and thoughts.

Stewart, Donald. "Collaborative Learning and Composition: Boon or Bane?" *Rhetoric Review* 7.1 (1988): 58–83.

van Slyck, Phyllis. "Repositioning Ourselves in the Contact Zone." *College English* 59, 2 (1997): 149–170.

Young, Iris Marion. "Social Movements and the Politics of Difference." *Justice and the Politics of Difference*. Princeton: Princeton UP, 1990. 157–191.

Afterword

༄

Where Do We Go from Here?

Melissa Nicolas
Pennsylvania State University at Berks-Lehigh Valley

Beverly J. Moss
The Ohio State University

Nels P. Highberg
University of Hartford

In part, we chose our title, *Writing Groups Inside and Outside the Classroom*, because we didn't want to dissuade, by way of a label, any potential authors who would write about an interaction concerning writing and groups that may or may not necessarily be classified as a "writing group" by the academy. We expected that there were many groups of people, both inside and outside the academy, who were assembling in coffeehouses, libraries, community centers, classrooms, or other locations we couldn't even imagine, to talk about their writing. As the essays in this collection illustrate, we were right in our initial expectations.

One of our primary reasons for designing this collection was to put together a sourcebook for writing groups, a manual of sorts, for anyone interested in facilitating a writing group inside or outside the classroom. However, as the proposals started coming in, we quickly realized that our book should serve a slightly different purpose. In spite of Gere's groundbreaking study on writing groups in 1987, the scholarly discussion on writing groups has been slow to emerge; therefore, we decided that the best way to broaden this scholarly conversation was to assemble a collection that highlights the diversity of issues surrounding writing groups. This collection is an introduction to the rich possibilities that exist for research on writing groups, wherever they are located.

Because we chose essays that reflect a wide range of topics and issues with the hope that this sort of overview (always incomplete) would stimulate future conversations, we hope that readers have begun to generate their own lists of questions for further exploration. We feel that we are finishing this project with more questions than we had when we began, but because the essays in this book have pushed our thinking in different directions, the questions we leave this project with are more nuanced and complex than those we came to the work with.

The issue that strikes us with the most force is the relationship between gender and writing groups. All of the proposals we received from voluntary writing groups were from all-female or mixed-gender groups; we received no submissions from all-male, voluntary writing groups. Indeed, the only all-male writing groups discussed in this collection are the involuntary, classroom-based peer groups Rebecca Jackson used in her prison-based writing course. And, of course, we do not read first-person accounts of these inmates' experiences; rather these experiences are filtered through the eyes of their female teacher. Even in groups where there was a probable male presence—the science writing groups described by Sharon Thomas, Leonora Smith and Terri Trupiano Barry, for instance—the authors do not highlight gender as an issue.

Although statistically speaking this lack of essays about voluntary, all-male groups could be a coincidence or an anomaly, we are inclined to believe that there are social and ideological forces operating here that are worthy of future exploration. If it is true that there are fewer all-male, voluntary writing groups than female groups, why? Several of the all-female groups in this collection discuss not only the writing support they received from their group but also the affective needs that the group fulfilled. In both Trupiano Barry et al.'s academic writing group and Nowacek and Del Sol's songwriting group, there is a sense that the groups function as safe places to explore the emotional and psychosocial dimensions of writing. Do all-male writing groups serve a similar affective function?

Interestingly, some of the members of the mixed-gender Thursday Night Writer's Group discuss the way they feel about participating in the writing group, and the importance of trust and even love in long-term group interactions, but the way these issues are addressed by the male and female group members differs significantly. Carol MacDaniels, for example, writes about her experience of the group in first person, exploring the particular things she has learned about herself as a writer through her participation in the group. On the other hand, Dale Jacobs begins his exploration of the topics of love and trust in groups—potentially very personal issues—by making a third-person statement: "Writing is a social process that can only be achieved through interaction within a supportive community." Although Jacobs does move back and forth between the more "objective" third-person perspective and a more "subjective" first-person position of a group member, Jacobs does not engage in a discussion of the affective domain in the same way MacDaniels does. These subtle differences in reporting styles lead us to wonder, do men and women have different needs and expectations for group work? How is the affective domain handled in mixed-gender groups? If there are significant differences in the ways males and females work in writing groups, how should those differences be accounted for in mandated classroom writing groups?

Along with gender questions, we are left wondering about the ways race and class operate in writing groups. Both Rebecca Jackson and Evelyn Westbrook briefly comment on racial diversity and the resulting tensions of this diversity in the writing groups they studied, but we want to know more about how social markers impact the ways in which groups function or, perhaps, fail to function. The homeless writers in the Streetwise writing group, for example, bring to light some of the political and material consequences of writing and publishing. The authors of this piece ask us to revisit our ideas about the accessibility of writing. Is writing a luxury belonging only to those who can afford the time to do it? And, by extension, does participation in a writing group presuppose a certain level of economic stability? Even if, as the Streetwise group illustrates, writing and writing groups do cross social and economic lines, what are some of the key differences among groups like the Streetwise group and a group of first-year composition students in a mandated classroom group or an all-female, voluntary faculty writing group? Are there any similarities among these groups? In successful writing groups, how are issues of race, class, and gender negotiated? In unsuccessful groups, are these issues of diversity too much of a hurdle for groups to negotiate? What can teachers who use writing groups do to help students work through the inevitable tensions that arise when people from diverse backgrounds are forced to work together?

Issues of diversity, of course, do not stop with race, class, and gender. Although none of the contributors to this collections talk about sexual orientation, physical ability or the countless other differences individuals bring to the table, we believe that there is much important work to do in exploring all facets of diversity and collaboration, both in the classroom and in the community.

Also conspicuously absent from this collection is a discussion of how technology has enabled or changed the nature and function of writing groups. The Internet, e-mail, instant messaging, word processing programs, faxes, scanners, Web sites, MOOs and MUDs, and countless other technological resources currently in use or on the way have forever altered the way humans use writing to communicate. It only stands to reason that these changes in communication will (if they haven't already) affect not only the ways people write but also the ways people talk about their writing, yet we received very few submissions dealing with technology and writing groups. Since all the writing groups discussed in this collection consist of groups who have met face to face, who had real-time conversation, it may be plausible to assume that one of the fundamental elements of writing groups is this kind of physical presence, but technology promises to change this dynamic. For example, although some wired writing groups certainly consist of people who know each other in physical contexts (i.e., a group of students from the same class, graduate students from the same school who have moved to different parts of the country), technology allows for writers who have never met to form a group. It will be interesting to observe differences among groups that have a physical presence, those who know each other in person but only meet online, and those groups who have never met face to face. Will the potential anonymity of this last type of online writing group free some writers to explore their work in more depth? Are commitments in online groups the same as in face-to-face groups? How do writers who have never met each other find each other in cyberspace? How does a group of strangers negotiate the formation of a cyber community? Are there groups that start off in cyberspace and then move to face-to-face meetings? Are there real-time groups that opt to move to a virtual meeting space? How and why might these changes take place? And, most important, how do cybergroups change the nature of writing groups, if it all?

Ultimately, as we mentioned in our introduction, we all came to this project through our connection to the writing center, and, appropriately, this is where our questioning finally leads us. Several of the writing groups in this collection were started by or maintained through a writing center. In some ways, it seems natural that writing centers—loci of collaborative learning—could play a large role in aiding teachers, students, and even community members in the formation and maintenance of writing groups. Indeed, some writing centers, like the ones described by Brooke Hessler and Amy Taggart or Sharon Thomas, Leonora Smith, and Terri Trupiano Barry are already engaged in this kind of work. But is it realistic to suppose that writing centers have the resources to do this kind of work? With budgets and staff stretched to the limits, is it reasonable to ask writing centers to take on this role? Perhaps on a more fundamental level we also need to ask how incorporating writing groups into writing center missions may necessitate a redefinition of the role of the tutor since we cannot assume that facilitating writing groups is analogous to conducting a tutorial. Tutorials are usually one-on-one; writing groups (not always, but usually) involve more than two people. How would we account for these differences in both writing center theory and practice? If writing center tutors were used to facilitate writing groups, how would they negotiate their roles? Do the tutors become group members or do they position themselves as outside facilitators? How will staff be trained to assume a non-tutor-like position?

Clearly, there is much important, scholarly work to be done on writing groups. We feel this collection is an important step in the right direction because, by virtue of you reading this book, you are joining us on this exploration. To paraphrase the quotation from Maya Angelou that begins this collection, we are glad to have you, but we need to remind each other that reading about writing groups is not enough. We need to work to understand all the issues pertinent to writing groups and the role of writing centers, in particular, and composition teachers, in general, in promoting, developing and sustaining these groups. We need to write about these groups again and again.

Author Index

Note: *n* indicates footnote

A

Afanador, Lucia, 82, *93*
Aisenberg, Nadya, 210, 211, 215, *226*
Alexander, Mary, S., 32, *44*
Anderson, Benedict, 4, *10*
Angelou, Maya, 1, *10*
Anokye, Akua Duku, 28, *28*
Anson, Chris, 67*n*, 77
Aristotle, 115, *128*, 133, 135, 136, 137, 140, 144–145, *148*
Atwood, Margaret, 210, *226*
Austin, Anne, E., 118, 119, *128*

B

Bacon, Nora, 107, *110*
Bakhtin, Mikhail, 14, *28*
Baldwin, Roger, G., 118, 119, *128*
Barber, Benjamin, 113, 128
Bateson, Mary Catherine, 214, *226*
Bazerman, Charles, 83, *93*
Beale, Walter, H., 143, *148*
Belanoff, Pat, 72, 73, 74, *78*
Belenky, Mary Field, 213, *226*
Bereiter, Carl, 69, 77
Berkenkotter, Carol, 220, *226*
Bishop, Wendy, 13, *28*
Bizzell, Patricia, 67, 77, 232, *247*
Black, Laurel Johnson, 14, *28*
Bleich, David, 28, *28*
Bowe, John, 105, *110*
Bowe, Marisa, 105, *110*
Brandt, Deborah, 216, *226*

Britzman, Deborah, P., 32, *44*
Brodkey, Linda, 229, 246, *247*
Brody, Miriam, 209, *226*
Bromley, Karen D'Angelo, 126, *128*
Brooke, Robert, 14, *29*, 147, *149*
Brooks, Jeff, 49, 50, *58*
Brooks, Julie, 232, 242, *247*
Bruffee, Kenneth, A.,48, *58*, 63, 65*n*, 77, 170, *185*
Burke, Kenneth, 108, *110*

C

Canagarajah, Suresh, A., 246, *247*
Caplan, Paula J., 212, *226*
Carey, Linda, 75, *78*
Carter, Michael, 143, *149*
Chenoweth, A., 67*n*, *78*
Chin, Elaine, 171, *185*
Christ, Carol, P., 212, 213, *227*
Cixous, Hélène, 209, *227*
Clark, Carolyn, M., 216, *227*
Clark, Suzanne, 20, *29*
Clinchy, Blythe McVicker, 213, *226*
Clyde, Jean Anne, 171, *185*
Coiner, Constance, 214, *227*
Condon, Mark W. F., 171, *185*
Connors, Robert, J., 148, *149*
Corbett, Edward, P. J., 115, 117, *128*, 148, *149*
Corder, Jim, W., 125–126, *128*
Cotich, Joan, 231–232, *247*
Crowley, Sharon, 148, *149*
Cushman, Ellen, 96, 100, 110, *111*

D

Deans, Tom, 99*n*, *111*
de Certeau, Michel, 220–221, *227*
Dickens, Cynthia, Sullivan, 123, *128*
Diogenes, Marvin, 134, 137, 144, 147,
        149

E

Ede, Lisa, 4, *10*, 20, *29*, 102, 108, *111*,
        121, *128*, *185*, 232n, *247*
Elbow, Peter, 6, *10*, 33, *44*, 72, 73, 74,
        78, 110, *111*, 148, *149*,
        170–171, *185*, 234, *247*
Emig, Janet, 218, *227*
Evans, Rick, 147, *149*
Eyler, Jane, 106, 107, *111*

F

Fahnestock, Jeanne, 137, *149*
Faigley, Lester, 67*n*, *78*, 246, *247*
Faver, Catherine, A., 126, *128*
Felman, Shoshana, 210, *227*
Flower, Linda, 14, 16*n*, 20, 27, *29*, 68,
        72, 75, *78*, 95, 96, 99*n*, 100,
        101*n*, 110, *111*, *112*
Foucault, Michel, 3, *10*, 16, 20–21, 29
Fox, Mary Frank, 126, *128*
Freire, Paulo, 19, *29*

G

Geisler, Cheryl, 80, *93*
George, Diana Hume, 214, *227*
Gere, Ann Ruggles, 2, 7, *10*, 48, *58*, 65,
        65*n*, *78*, 110, *111*, 113, 117,
        118, 121, 124, *128*, 146, *149*,
        170, *186*, 212, *227*, 230*n*,
        231, 234, 242, *247*
Gergits, Julia, 25, 26, *29*
Gilbert, Sandra M., 209, *227*
Giles, Dwight, E., Jr., 106, 107, *111*
Gillespie, Paula, *49*, *58*, 71, *78*
Goffman, Erving, 22–23, 24, 25, *29*

Goldberger, Nancy Rule, 213, *226*
Goodburn, Amy, 147, *149*
Gopen, George, 82, *93*
Grimm, Nancy Maloney, 66, *78*
Gubar, Susan, 209, *227*

H

Haas, Christina, 68, 72, *78*
Hall, John, 230*n*, 231, *247*
Hall, Stewart, 31, *44*
Halloran, Michael, 116, *128*
Harrington, Mona, 210, 211, 215, *226*
Harris, Jeanette, G., 49, *58*
Harris, Joseph, 14, *29*, 232*n*, 232–233,
        247
Harris, Muriel, 71, *78*, 113, *128*
Hawhee, Debra, 148, 149
Hayden, Sara, 222, *227*
Hayes, John, R., 75, *78*
Healy, Dave, 47, *58*
Heath, Shirley Brice, 2, *10*, 108, *111*,
        233, *247*
Heilbrun, Carolyn G., 213, *227*
Heilker, Paul, 99, *111*
Herzberg, Bruce, 96, 100, 110, *111*
Hessler, Brooke, 98, *111*
Higgins, Lorraine, 95, *112*
Horton, Marjorie, S., 113, *129*
Huckin, Thomas, N., 220, *226*

I

Ina, Beth, 147, *149*
Isenberg, Joan, P., 126, *128*

J

Jalongo, Mary Renck, 126, *128*
Jarrett, Susan, C., 116, 126, *128*

K

Kelly, James, 82, *93*
Kennedy, George, A., 137, *149*
Killingsworth, M. Jimmie, 4, 5, *10*

Kingston, Maxine, Hong, 34, *44*
Kinkead, Joyce, A., 49, *58*
Kirsch, Gesa, E., 127, *129,* 211, *227*

L

Lather, Patti, 37, 38, 39, 41, *44*
LeFevre, Karen, Burke, 116, *129,* 218,
    227
Lerner, Neal, 49, *58,* 71, *78*
Leverenz, Carrie Shively, 14, *29,* 97,
    98, *111,* 141, *149*
Liddell, H. G., 116, *129*
Locker, Kitty O., 170, 171, 180, *186*
Lunsford, Andrea, 4, *10, 78,* 102, 108,
    111, 117, 121, 123, *128, 129,*
    171, *186*

M

Marcus, George, 33, *44*
McBride, James, 33, *45*
Melotto, Maeli, 82, *93*
Meyer, Emily, 71, *78*
Miller, Richard, E., 232, *247*
Mirtz, Ruth, 147, *149*
Moffett, James, 97, *111*
Morgan, Meg, 240, *247*
Murphy, Christina, 71, *78*
Myers, Greg, 89, *93*

N

Neel, Jasper, 115, 116, *129*
Newkirk, Thomas, 66, 69, 72, *78*
Noddings, Nel, 125, *129*

O

Olbrechts-Tyteca, Lucie, 122, *129,* 143,
    149
Olguin, Enrique, 108, *111*
Oravec, Christine, 137, 144, 146, *149*
Ozick, Cynthia, 66, *78*

P

Palloff, Rena, M., 107, *111*

Peck, Wayne, 95, *112*
Penfield, Elizabeth, 32, *45*
Perelman, Chaim, 122, *129,* 143, *149*
Perelman, Les, 14, *29*
Petraglia, Joseph, 97, 98, *112*
Phelps, Louise Wetherbee, 67, *78*
Porter, James, 246, *248*
Pratt, Keith, 107, *111*
Pratt, Mary Louise, 232, 233, 235, 246,
    248

R

Reamer, Frederick, G., 118, *129*
Reynolds, Nedra, 116, 126, *128*
Rogers, Priscilla, 113, *129*
Rorty, Richard, 98*n, 112*
Russell, David, 85, *93*

S

Sagaria, Mary Ann, D., 123, *128*
Sattler, William, M., 116, *129*
Scardamalia, Marlene, 69, 77
Schmitz, Betty, 108, *111*
Schramer, James, 25, 26, *29*
Schriver, Karen, 75, *78*
Schwalbe, Michael, 25, *29*
Scott, Robert, 116, *129*
Secor, Marie, 137, *149*
Sheard, Cynthia Miecznikowski, 144,
    149
Sherwood, Steve, 71, *78*
Smith, Louise, Z., 71, *78*
Smithies, Chris, 37, 38, 39, 41, *44*
Spear, Karen, 65*n,* 72, *78,* 110, *112,*
    141, 147, *149*
Spellmeyer, Kurt, 13, *29*
Spigelman, Candace, 2, *10,* 107, 112,
    186
Stevens, Ralph, 65, 65*n,* *78*
Stewart, Donald, 20, *29,* 231, 232, *248*
Stock, Patricia Lambert, 218, *227*
Stratman, James, 75, *78*
Streeter, Sabin, 105, *110*
Sullivan, Dale, 137, 140, 143, 144, *149*
Sullivan, Patricia, 64, 65, *78*
Swales, John, 82, 89, 91, *93*

Swan, Judith, 82, *93*

T

Tarule, Jill Mattuck, 213, *226*
Thomas, Jim, 22–23, *29*
Tobin, Lad, 13, *29*, 147, *149*
Trimbur, John, 98, *112*

V

Vande Kopple, William, 82, *93*
van Slyck, Phyllis, 232, *248*

Vickers, Brian, 144, 145, *149*

W

Walters, Frank, 121, *129*
Watson, Denise B., 216, *227*
Witte, Stephen, 67*n*, *78*
Woolf, Virginia, 202, 204, *205*, 207,
      209, *227*

Y

Young, Iris Marion, 237, 244, *248*

Subject Index

Note: *f* indicates figure
n indicates footnote

A

Administration, x, 52, 55, 57
Allegiance, 14, 233
Argument, 19, 32, 35, 36, 41–42, 51,
    80, 81, 83, 85, 87, 90, 91,
    104, 133, 134, 139, 142, 147,
    148, 154, 171–172, 220,
    240–241
Argumentative essays, 17
Aristotle, 115–116, 133, 135, 137, 140,
    144, 145
Assessment, 25, 27, 40–41, 54, 57, 84,
    97, 107
Audience, ix, 5, 26, 39, 42, 43, 66, 68,
    71, 72, 74–76, 82–83, 86, 97,
    98, 101*f*, 102, 103, 105, 107,
    109, 115, 121, 122, 161, 180,
    196, 198, 203, 208, 209, 210,
    218, 219–220
Authorial control, 140–142
Authority, 19, 134, 141, 143, 144,
    146–148, 171, 201, 211, 237
Authorship, 32, 33, 50, 90, 100, 106,
    107, 114, 117–118, 119,
    120–122, 140, 170, 184, 199,
    204
Autonomy, 6, 14, 90, 146
Autobiographical fiction, 34

B

Biography, 34

Boundaries, 8, 9, 21, 175, 182, 183
    classroom, 6
    crossing, 6–7, 9, 85
    disciplinary, 5, 8, 21, 80, 83, 85–86,
        93, 96, 123, 211, 219
    discursive, 16*n*
Brainstorming, 53, 60, 104

C

Coauthors, 7, 39, 85, 87, 88, 90,
    113–114, 115, 116, 140, 142,
    as epistemic, 120–122
    benefits of, 123–125
    cognitive advantages of, 120
    customs of, 118
    disagreements between, 43
    in academia, 117–118
    mentoring quality of, 126
    seniority of, 119
    studying, 114
Collaboration, x, 2, 3, 4, 9, 13, 17,
    19–20, 24, 25–28, 68, 76–77,
    93, 95, 102, 105, 108, 109,
    120, 121, 124, 125, 127, 135,
    146, 148, 169–170, 171–185,
    210, 212, 216, 231, 232, 233,
    247, 251
    in free-world classrooms, 27
    rhetoric of, 25
Collarborative writing, x, 8, 31, 41, 44,
    96, 113, 125, 171, 174, 185,
    208
Collective essay, 38
Commonality, 113, 208

Community, ix, x, 2, 4, 7, 10, 28, 48,
        65, 96, 98–101, 102, 103, 106,
        121, 126, 142–143, 146, 147,
        156, 160, 165, 175, 177, 182,
        193, 195, 202, 203, 204, 208,
        209, 211, 212, 216, 226, 231,
        240, 247
    discourse, 23, 24–25
    global, 4–5, 9
    homeless, 9
    literacy, x, 95, 101n
    literal, 21
    local, 4–5, 105
    of writers, ix, x, 3, 4, 9–10, 63, 203,
        229, 230, 231, 232, 233,
        242, 243, 245, 246, 248
    prison, 8, 16
    psychological, 21
    service, 95, 98, 99, 105
    service writing groups, 8, 95, 96,
        98–100, 101f, 105, 107,
        108, 109, 110
Community-engagement writing, 95,
        96, 98, 100, 102, 109
Confidence, 36, 84, 141–142, 201, 210
Conflict, 4, 5, 13, 14, 18, 20, 22,
        24–26, 33, 40, 44, 90, 119,
        152, 162, 167, 178, 179, 180,
        181, 183, 184, 223, 232, 233,
        237, 238–239, 245, 247
Conflict avoidance, 25
Consensus, 41, 127, 178, 184, 204,
        232, 238
    and dissensus, 142–144
Constructive communication, 98
Contact zone, 9, 26, 232, 235
    academic, 246
    inorganic, 232
    metaphor, 233, 245
    organic, 233
    theorists, 232
Content(s), 41, 53, 62, 66, 68, 69,
        72–73, 80, 87, 88, 109, 145,
        159, 167, 173, 189, 190, 191,
        209, 220
    and form, 37, 58
    domain, 82, 85
    editorial, 158, 159

    knowledge, 80, 82
    list of, 38
    strategies, 68
Contexts, 7, 13, 14, 15, 22, 23, 90, 98,
        170, 171, 189, 233
    artificial, 184
    competing, 23f
    curricular, 15
    intersecting, 26
    institutional, 184
    linguistic, 232
    physical, 252
    political, ix, 4, 119, 144, 160, 164,
        235, 238, 245, 246, 251
    rhetorical, 28
    social, 14 , 20
    traditional, 185
Creative writing, 8, 96, 134–135, 136,
        137, 144, 147, 164, 165, 175
Critical
    consciousness, 20, 99n, 100, 110
    discourse, 137
    judgement, 36, 38
    thinking, 32, 36, 38, 83, 85, 106
Criticism, 25, 27, 35, 39, 51, 55–56, 71,
        84, 121, 137, 140, 142,
        144–145, 146, 152, 164, 219,
        220, 224, 229, 230, 237, 239,
        241, 244
Cyber groups, 252

D

Deadlines, 178, 179, 180, 182, 217
Disorienting dilemma, 106, 107, 108
Diversity, ix, 18, 108–109, 230–231,
        234–246
    disciplinary, 86, 235, 249
    of perspectives, 3
    privilege, 98
    racial, 18, 251
Dynamics see Interpersonal Dynamics
        and Group Dynamics

E

Editing, 24, 39, 60, 92, 225

Epideictic models, 136–148
Episteme, 121
Ethics, 71, 115, 125, 231
Ethos, 8, 114, 115–116, 117, 118, 120,
    121, 122, 125–127, 143, 144,
    220
Exit essay, 17*n*
Expressivism, 36, 44, 48, 51, 71, 74,
    76, 84, 113, 117, 133, 137,
    140, 147, 159, 160, 161, 162,
    164, 174, 175, 195, 199, 218,
    239*n*, 241
Extracurriculum, 7, 8

F

Feature(s), 17, 68, 69, 80, 96, 114,
    136, 137, 142, 143, 147
  epideictic, 134, 135
  strategies, 68
Feedback, 24, 35, 50, 53–58, 63, 65–66,
    70, 73, 73*n*, 74, 85, 103, 106,
    107, 122, 123, 127, 134, 143,
    146, 152*n*, 193–194, 203, 217,
    234, 238, 244
Fictional autobiography, 34
First-author position, 118, 119–120
Folkways, 116
Format, 39
split-level, 39
split-text, 37
Formative attitude, 67
Free-world classrooms, 15*n*, 17, 25, 27
Fund for the Improvement of
    Post-Secondary Education
    (FIPSE) Writing in the
    Sciences Project, 79, 81, 82,
    83, 84, 89, 90, 91, 92, 93
Funding, 87, 89, 92, 101*f*, 165

G

Gender, 5, 7, 9, 114, 160, 207, 208, 209,
    210, 213, 217, 225, 226, 231,
    236*t*, 240, 244, 245, 250, 251
Genres, 34, 106, 133, 134–135, 138,
    156, 199, 201, 211

Goals, ix, 4, 5, 16*n*, 44, 50, 52, 53, 54,
    56, 57, 58, 60, 61, 63, 70, 79,
    92, 99*n*, 107, 109, 110, 135,
    140–142, 159, 164, 165, 176,
    177, 179, 199, 202, 208,
    221–222, 234238, 245
Grammar, 26–27, 49, 62, 70, 72, 75,
    83, 107, 197
Group dynamics, 164, 181, 184, 205

H

Harlem Writer's Guild, 1, 2
Heterogeneity, 97
Hierarchies, 4, 17, 19, 108, 125, 126,
    231, 246
History, x, 2, 113–114, 117, 152–153,
    158, 230*n*

I

Identity, 16*n*, 20, 21, 23, 32, 37,
    162–163, 202, 209, 216, 240,
    241
  collective, 152
  group, 2, 153, 158, 161, 165–167,
    208
  political, 160
  public, 165
  sexual, 5
Ideology, 14, 28
International Network of Street Papers
    (INSP), 151*n*, 152*n*
Interpersonal Dynamics, 102, 108,
    160, 163, 164, 167, 172, 174,
    180*n*, 184, 199, 207, 211,
    212, 213, 214, 215, 216, 217,
    222, 223–226, 250–251
Intertexts, 37–39
Interviews, 43, 80, 92, 114, 114*n*, 120,
    125, 127, 215, 229*n*, 233,
    235*n*, 242
Invention, 2, 32, 34, 218

J

Joint product, 41, 113, 114, 119, 123,
    170

Journals, (logs), 24, 26–27

K

Knowledge-making, 98, 106, 107, 121, 213, 218, 219

L

Literacy events, x, 2–5, 9, 234
Literary terminology, 34
Literate action, 95, 100, 102, 108, 110

M

Masked rejection, 24–26
Mentors, 95, 109, 126, 181, 208, 211, 220, 221–225
Mores, 116

N

Negotiating, 14, 15
    a compromise, 26–27
    between local and global dis-
        courses, 5
    discursive boundaries, 16*n*
    needs and expectations of audi-
        ence, 74
    revision, 76
    roles, 170
New Rhetoric, 122
North American Street Newspaper
    Association (NASNA), 151*n*

O

Ownership, 122–125, 134, 143, 144,
    172, 175, 176, 195, 197, 198,
    202, 204
of ideas, 43
of texts, 2, 107, 118, 171

P

Pedagogy, 2, 14, 28, 33, 58, 64, 65*n*,
    67, 71, 73*n*, 99, 100, 105,
    *106, 108, 110, 127, 148,
    152*n, 211, 212, 246
Peer
    consultants, 5
    groups in prison classroom, 13–28
    interaction, 28
    pressure, 203
    response groups, 3, 5–8, 48–51,
        55–58, 59–62, 63–64, 65,
        65*n*, 67, 69–72, 77, 83, 86,
        87, 96–98, 102, 103, 107,
        110, 122, 133–137, 141,
        144–146, 147–148, 208,
        220, 225, 230, 234, 244,
        246, 250
    review process, 35
Personal relationships, 114, 118, 125,
    216, 223–226
Physical space, 169, 172–176, 180–181,
    184
Political
    agenda, 163–164, 166, 235, 245
    identity, 160
    oratory, 135
Power, 2–4, 9, 16*n*, 20, 21, 36, 47, 49,
    90, 92, 100, 120, 121, 125,
    126, 157, 164, 169, 171, 172,
    194, 209, 210, 211, 213, 231,
    232, 237, 245, 246
Praise, 65, 67, 69, 70, 72, 133, 136,
    137, 138, 140, 144–146, 147
Pragmatics, 243
Problem solving, 18–19, 43–44, 71, 75,
    76, 77, 99*n*, 106, 119–120,
    133, 139, 145, 160, 217

R

Reader response, 74, 138–140, 148
Reciprocity, 96–98, 100, 101*f*, 103,
    104, 105, 106–110
Research, ix, 7, 8, 9, 13, 17, 20, 34, 38,
    69–70, 77–79, 80–83, 86–89,
    90, 92, 98, 99, 106, 108, 114,
    114*n*, 123, 127, 134, 136,
    156, 170, 171, 211, 215, 232,
    233, 235*n*, 249
cognitive, 68

methods, 37, 43, 123
strategies, 42
Revision(s), 2, 35, 53–55, 63, 65,
    67–68, 71, 72, 73n, 75–77,
    81, 91, 103, 123, 133–134,
    139, 139, 141, 143, 147, 148,
    171, 189, 193–195, 200–204
Rhetoric, 115, 133, 136, 137, 145
Rhetoric, 25, 28, 32, 50, 65n, 66,
    68–69, 72, 74–76, 80, 81,
    82–83, 85–86, 88, 115, 116,
    117, 133–138, 140, 141,
    142–148, 169
    classical, 8, 115, 117, 148
    deliberative, 133–136, 138–148
    epideictic, 133–148
    of dissensus, 98
Role(s)
    gender, 207, 210
    in groups, 4, 171, 174, 176–180
    mentoring, 222
    of tutors, 70–72, 251
    shifting, 180–185
    social, 14, 18n, 52, 54, 85, 139, 140,
        141, 241, 247

S

Science, 8
    and writing, 80, 87
    and graduate student writing
        groups, 79, 82, 83–84, 92,
        250
    faculty, 85, 86
    fiction, 134, 138, 143, 234
    graduate students in, 87–90
Self-disclosure, 22, 23
Self-presentation, 25
Service learning, 98, 99, 99n, 100, 106,
    107
Shorthand language, 81
Social construction, 2, 3, 4, 20, 48,
    65n, 238
Songwriting, 9
Street papers, 151n, 156, 167
Student-centered, 7, 8, 13–28, 31–44,
    47–58, 63–77, 79–93
Synergy, 36, 40, 141

T

Technology, 4, 104, 138, 251–252
Text(s), 2, 3, 4, 8, 9, 31, 32, 66, 67–69,
    72–73, 80, 81, 82, 85, 90, 91,
    92, 96, 97, 98, 99, 99n, 100,
    101t, 102, 103, 104, 105, 106,
    107, 108, 109, 114, 116, 118,
    121, 122, 123, 133, 135, 137,
    139, 140, 414, 142, 144, 145,
    146, 147, 148, 170, 171, 172,
    177, 182, 193, 194, 195, 196,
    199, 200, 201, 213, 214, 216,
    217, 218, 219, 220, 224, 235,
    237, 243, 246
    conflicting, 24–26
    cultural, 28
    features, 27, 69
    ideal, 32
    lack of, 6
    layout of, 42
    messy, 33–44
Thesis, 35, 40, 41, 45, 51, 56, 60, 61,
    68, 72, 79, 82, 84, 88
Timespace, 169, 172–173, 176–184
Trust, 23
Tutoring, 6, 8, 47–59, 64, 67, 68, 70,
    97, 252
    benefits of, 59
    hazards of, 60
    roles in group, 70–72

W

Writing Centers, ix, x, 6, 7, 8, 48, 49,
    53, 57, 64, 70, 71, 252, 253
    staffing, 8, 51, 52, 54, 60
    training, 5–6, 52, 54, 55–58, 71, 73,
        105,
Writing Groups
    academic, 3, 7, 8, 20, 48, 49, 63,
        66–67, 69, 95–99, 114,
        117–118, 121, 123, 126,
        185, 203, 208–209,
        212–217, 220–226,
        230–231, 246–247, 250
    African American, 1–2, 14
    as literacy events, 2–5, 9

as peer response groups, 3
autonomous, 6, 14, 87
ceremonial discourses of, 144
classroom, 146–148, 240, 247, 251
community service, 95–96, 98–100,
        101f, 107, 109–110
critical awareness in, 17
culture of, 15, 23, 26
dialogic nature of, 4
ethnographic study of, 7
expanding through reciprocal ex-
        pertise, 110
grammar instruction in, 26–27
history of, 117
homeless, 7, 9, 105n, 151–154, 251
implementation of, 47–48
in a prison classroom, 7–8, 13–28
interactions in, 4
non-academic, 6, 7, 97, 107, 215,
        230n, 233, 246, 247
peer, 48, 97–98, 103
prejudice in, 18

racial diversity in, 18
refusal to participate in, 15, 18–24
school mandated, 6
science, 79–93, 250
self sponsored, 230n, 231
social constructs of, 2, 4
social diversity in, 108
songwriting in, 169–185
supportive nature of, 231

voluntary, 6, 135, 250
women's, 7, 9, 37–40, 42–43, 117,
        179–205, 207–226, 231
Writing Partners program, 96, 102,
        105n, 106, 108
Writing space, 8, 9, 14, 15n, 17, 21,
        23–24, 92, 102, 109, 114,
        121–122, 125, 162, 169,
        172–173, 176–180, 184–185,
        188, 207, 209, 211–214, 21,
        232–233, 246